TITANIC

TITANIC

The Last Night of a Small Town

JOHN WELSHMAN

OXFORD
UNIVERSITY PRESS

OXFORD

UNIVERSITY PRESS

Great Clarendon Street, Oxford OX2 6DP

Oxford University Press is a department of the University of Oxford.
It furthers the University's objective of excellence in research, scholarship,
and education by publishing worldwide in

Oxford New York

Auckland Cape Town Dar es Salaam Hong Kong Karachi
Kuala Lumpur Madrid Melbourne Mexico City Nairobi
New Delhi Shanghai Taipei Toronto

With offices in

Argentina Austria Brazil Chile Czech Republic France Greece
Guatemala Hungary Italy Japan Poland Portugal Singapore
South Korea Switzerland Thailand Turkey Ukraine Vietnam

Oxford is a registered trade mark of Oxford University Press
in the UK and in certain other countries

Published in the United States
by Oxford University Press Inc., New York

© John Welshman 2012

British Library Cataloguing in Publication Data

Data available

Library of Congress Cataloging in Publication Data
Library of Congress Control number: 2011942654

Typeset by SPI Publisher Services, Pondicherry, India
Printed in Great Britain
on acid-free paper by
Clays Ltd, St Ives plc

ISBN 978–0–19–959557–0

10 9 8 7 6 5 4 3 2 1

PREFACE

Growing up as a child in Northern Ireland, in the 1960s, the sea never seemed very far away. Sunday school outings were to Newcastle, County Down, the main attractions being the amusement arcades and the boating lake, while other trips were to the Giant's Causeway and other places on the Antrim coast. Donegal was the traditional holiday destination for Ulster Protestants, particularly the beaches near Buncrana, Portsalon, and Downings. But some of my most vivid recollections are of the caravans that my parents owned, initially a small touring one, later a large moored one, which were on the Mourneview Caravan Park, near Newcastle. We went there every summer. The memories come back strongly across the years: the long trek through the sand dunes to the beach, weighed down with towels, a windbreak, buckets and spades; flying kites on the central field, and the anxiety when they inevitably crashed on other people's caravans; trying to walk along the whole of the low wooden perimeter fence, and hours spent on the swings; the evangelical groups that drew crowds of bored children on Sundays; the sweets from the shop that the Campbell family ran along with the site; the smell of fish and chips on Friday evenings, and taste of ice cream; playing in the ferns and tunnelling into the sand, imagining we were allied prisoners of war; the long walk to the toilets, the key around my neck on a string; learning to ride a bicycle, my father running alongside.

However, we were also aware of the dangers of the sea. When travelling to and from the mainland, it was the Larne to Stranraer car ferry that we used; flying was still rare and the crossing often rough. My mother had vivid memories of the tragic loss of the *Princess Victoria* Stranraer ferry in January 1953, when she was a 25-year-old teacher. Despite the heroic efforts of the *Sir Samuel Kelly*, the Donaghadee lifeboat, 135 lives had been lost, the worst maritime disaster in the waters off the British Isles. When we drove to my grandmother's house, not far from Bangor, we passed the Thomas Andrews Junior Memorial Hall, in Comber. My mother told us about its history. How, following the disaster and death of Andrews, the designer of the *Titanic*, the residents of the town and district agreed to erect a hall in his memory. It was decided that the hall would be built on the Ballygowan Road, near to both the Andrews family home at Ardara, and the linen mill they owned. The architects were Young and Mackenzie, and the builders Courtney Bros. The hall was officially opened on 29 February 1915 by Andrews's widow Helen. The ground floor held a billiard room, reading room, minor hall, committee room, kitchen, and toilets; the first-floor main hall, with stage and gallery, could seat about 700 people, and the grounds around the hall were laid out as a park. Eventually the hall was taken over by the South-Eastern Education and Library Board, and used as a primary school, called the Andrews Memorial Primary School. As the numbers of children increased, a larger school was built adjoining the hall, usually called simply 'Andrews Memorial'.

ACKNOWLEDGEMENTS

As ever, many people helped with the research and writing of this book. The staff in the Lancaster University Library have been extremely helpful, especially those involved with Interlending and Document Supply, as have been archivists in the National Archive, at Kew, London, and at the Maritime Archives & Library, Merseyside Maritime Museum, Liverpool. James Bowen sent me information about the West Midlands, and also drew my attention to the fascinating photograph of the *Titanic*'s anchor being pulled through the streets of Netherton, near Dudley, on 1 May 1911. Mick Worboys gave me information on Wallace Hartley, and on his father, John Rushton Hartley. I am grateful to Jeffrey Richards for early encouragement with the project, and for both his expertise on film, and on all matters *Titanic*. I gave a talk about the project at the Belfast Titanic Society in October 2010; I am grateful to Una Reilly for inviting me to give the paper and to Stephen Cameron for chairing the meeting. I would like to thank those who came for the helpful comments and suggestions that they made. The encyclopedia-titanica website has been a tremendous resource, especially for tracing biographical details of passengers and crew; everyone who uses it owes an enormous debt to all those *Titanic* scholars who have contributed to it.

At Oxford University Press, I would like to thank Matthew Cotton, Emma Barber, Javier Kalhat, Carrie Hickman, Suzanne Williams, Coleen Hatrick, Phil Henderson, and Andrew Hawkey. Other relatives and friends have helped in diverse ways. The Reverend John Watson read the manuscript and spent an afternoon showing my father, my son, and myself his collection of *Titanic* memorabilia, photographs, and the impressive model that he has built. Christine Oversby kindly lent me a copy of the *National Geographic* magazine, and Jonathan Derrick lent books. Anthony Feiler read through my nautical glossary and commented upon it. It was my aunt Sally Fletcher who put me in touch with Frank Harris, and it was through Frank that I first became aware of Elizabeth Leather; I am very grateful to Frank for all the material that he has sent me. I would like to thank my cousin, Marco Van Beek, for his expertise on early radio, and for the information on Marconi that he gave me. Lastly, but most importantly, I would like to thank Rose Welshman for reading through the manuscript, for the many suggestions that she made about it, for helping to choose the photographs, and for much else.

CONTENTS

Contents

LIST OF PLATES

1. Frank Goldsmith (left) and his family, 22 Hone Street, Strood, Kent (19 December 1906). © George Grantham Bain Collection/ Library of Congress.
2. Queen's Road, Belfast, with shipyard men leaving work, *Titanic* in the background (May 1911). © National Museums of Northern Ireland.
3. *Titanic*'s anchor leaving the Lloyd's British Proving House at Netherton, West Midlands (1 May 1911). © Dudley Archives and Local History Service.
4. *Titanic* propeller with shipyard workers before launch (31 May 1911). © George Grantham Bain Collection/Library of Congress.
5. White Star Line poster for the *Olympic* and *Titanic*. © Roger-Viollet/ Rex Features.
6. Benjamin, Esther, and Eva Hart shortly before sailing on the *Titanic*. Reproduced by permission of the copyright holder, Ronald C. Denney.
7. Starboard stern view of completed ship in Belfast Lough with tugs (2 April 1912). © National Museums of Northern Ireland.
8. Archibald Gracie IV. From Jack Winocour (ed), *The Story of the Titanic as Told by its Survivors* (New York: Dover Publications, 1960).

GLOSSARY

abaft	behind
aft	near or towards the stern of a vessel
after	more towards the stern
After Deck	deck towards the stern
alleyway	narrow passage, corridor
amidships	near, towards the middle of the ship lengthwise
astern	in or towards the stern, behind
ballast	heavy material used to weigh down and steady a ship
barque	small sailing ship; technically a three-masted vessel
berth	(noun) a ship's station at anchor or a wharf; a sleeping-place on a ship
Blue Riband	prize awarded to the ship which made the fastest crossing of the North Atlantic
Boat Deck	a ship's top deck, on which the small boats are carried
boatwright	maker, repairer, carpenter, joiner
Bosun	boatswain; foreman of a crew who looks after a ship's boats, rigging, and flags
Bosun's Chair	wooden seat slung from ropes
Bosun's Mate	boatswain's assistant

bow	(noun) the forepart of a ship
Bridge	(noun) platform from which the Captain of a ship gives directions
bulkhead	partition separating one part of the interior of a ship from another; protecting barrier or structure
bulwark	side of a ship projecting above the deck
'CQD'	Morse code signal call used by ships at sea in first years of wireless telegraphy
cleat	piece of wood attached to parts of a ship for fastening ropes
clinker-built	made of planks which overlap those below and fastened with clinched nails
clipper	fast sailing vessel
collapsible	lifeboat with canvas sides; the sides were collapsed for stowing and raised when in use
companionway	staircase from the deck to a cabin
Crow's-Nest	elevated shelter for a man on the lookout
cutter	small vessel with one mast
dampers	something which slows down the rate of burning of a fire
davit	crane-like arms used for hoisting and lowering, for example on a ship for a boat
deck quoits	quoits (heavy flat rings for throwing as near as possible to a hob or pin) as played on a deck
derrick	arrangement for hoisting materials, by a boom stayed from a central post
Docking Bridge	platform on the Poop Deck with instruments used to assist navigation when in port
duck canvas	kind of coarse cotton, linen; cloth for small sails, sacking

expansion joint	built-in seam in superstructure of ship that allows some flexibility in heavy seas as the hull bends upwards or downwards
falls	(noun) lowering or hoisting rope
Fantail	fan-shaped deck which overhangs the stern of a ship
field ice	large expanse of ice covering surface of ocean
fireman	stoker
flotsam	goods lost by shipwreck and found floating on the sea, as opposed to 'jetsam' which is unwanted material or goods that have been thrown overboard from a ship and washed ashore, especially material that has been discarded to lighten the vessel
Fore	the front
fore-and-aft	length-wise of a ship
Forecastle	short raised deck at the fore-end of a vessel; forepart of a ship under the maindeck; quarters of the crew
Fore Peak	contracted part of a ship's hold, close to the bow
forward	towards, in, the front part of a ship
freighter	cargo-carrying boat
gangplank	long, narrow, portable platform providing access to and from a ship
gangway	passage into, out of, or through any place, especially a ship
gasket	canvas band used to bind the sails to the yards when furled
greaser	ship's engineer
growler	small, low, flat iceberg

gunwale	wale or upper edge of a ship's side near to the bulwarks
hand	(noun) a worker in a ship
hard-a-port	see below
hard-a-starboard	in 1912 this order required the man at the wheel to turn the wheel to port, not to starboard, and the rudder and ship would turn to port. Use of these old 'helm orders' began to die out after the First World War, and were obsolete by the mid-1930s
heel	(verb) to incline, to lean on one side, as a ship
helm	steering apparatus
hold	(noun) the interior cavity of a ship used for the cargo
inboard	within the hull or interior of a ship; towards or nearer to the centre
keel	(noun) the part of a ship extending along the bottom from stem to stern, and supporting the whole frame
lash	(verb) to secure with a rope or cord
lashing	(noun) rope for making things fast
lee	the sheltered side
leeward	to or in the direction towards which the wind blows
lightship	ship serving the purpose of a lighthouse
list	(verb) to cause to heel over
log-line	line fastened to the log, and marked for finding the speed of a vessel
longitudinal	lengthwise
mail boat	boat that carried the public mail

manifest	(noun) list or invoice of the cargo of a ship to be exhibited at the custom-house
Marconi	connected with Guglielmo Marconi (1874–1937) or his system of wireless telegraphy
Master-at-Arms	ship's chief police officer
muster	(noun) an assembling or calling together for inspection, verification; assembly, register, round-up
oarlock	rowlock
Orlop Deck	lowest deck in a ship, a covering to the hold
outboard	outside of a boat or ship; towards or nearer the ship's side
pack ice	mass of large pieces of floating ice driven together by winds and currents
pay out	(verb) to cause to run out, as rope
Petty Officer	naval officer ranking with a non-commissioned officer in the army
Pilot	(noun) one who conducts ships in and out of a harbour
plates	sheet of metal or other hard material
Poop Deck	high deck at the stern
port	left side of a ship
Promenade Deck	deck on which passengers walk about
Purser	formerly a naval paymaster; officer in charge of cabins and stewards
Quartermaster	officer who deals with quarters, stores, clothing
reciprocating engine	kind of steam engine in which the piston moves to and fro in a straight line; on the

	Titanic, of the type known as four-cylinder-triple-expansion engines
rivet	bolt fastened by hammering the end
rove	metal plate or ring through which a rivet is put and clenched over
'SOS'	general distress call for use by ship's wireless operators when sending Morse code; chosen because could be sent and recognized easily; superseded 'CQD' on 1 July 1908
screw	(noun) propeller
scullion	servant
sea boat	craft considered with reference to her behaviour in bad weather
ship	(verb) to put, receive, or take on board
sounding-line	line with a plummet at the end for soundings
starboard	right-hand side of a ship
starboard beam	any distant point out at sea, at right angles to the keel, and on the right side
stateroom	private cabin
stay	(noun) a rope supporting a mast; a guy or support
steam launch	large steam-driven boat
steamer chair	reclining chair used on liners, often with a steamer rug
steerage	part of a passenger ship with the lowest fares
stem	curved timber at the prow of a ship; the forepart of a ship
stern	(noun) the hind-part of a vessel; steering-gear, helm, the steerman's place
stokehold	ship's furnace chamber

stokehole	space about the mouth of a furnace; the space allotted to the stokers
stoker	one who feeds a furnace with fuel
stow	(verb) to place, put, lodge; put away; to store; to put under hatches
superstructure	upper structure or part of a structure
tender	(noun) a small craft that attends a larger
thole	a pin in the side of a boat to keep the oar in place; a peg
tiller	handle or lever for turning a rudder
tramp steamer	cargo-boat with no fixed route
transverse	crosswise
trim	(verb) to adjust the balance of a boat
trimmer	one who trims, including (with lamps) removing what would be regarded as excess
troopship	ship for transporting troops
turbine	rotary motor in which a wheel or drum with curved vanes is driven by their reaction or impact with a fluid, typically water or steam
wash	rough water left behind by a boat
Watch	(noun) the ship's officers and crew who are on duty at the same time
Well Deck	lowered deck between the superstructure and Forecastle or Poop Decks of a ship
whaler	long, narrow boat sharp at both ends once used in pursuit of whales; similar boat carried on a large vessel as a lifeboat
Wheel-house	shelter in which a ship's steering-wheel is placed
windjammer	large sailing vessel
windward	towards or on the side the wind blows from

wireless telegraphy   signalling through space, without the use of conducting wires between transmitter and receiver, by means of electromagnetic waves generated by high-frequency alternating currents

CAST LIST

Lawrence Beesley (35) is an English science teacher. One of his pupils at Dulwich College, London, was a boy called Raymond Chandler. Beesley's wife Cissy has recently died of tuberculosis, and he has decided to visit his brother in Toronto. He is travelling Second Class.

Harold Bride (22) is the Assistant Wireless Operator. He had been born in London in 1890, and had qualified in June 1911. His sending and receiving rate of 20 words a minute had been deemed to be 'very good'.

Edith Brown (15) is travelling with her parents Elizabeth and Thomas in Second Class. She had been born in South Africa, and the family is emigrating to live in Seattle in the United States.

Frank Goldsmith (9) is travelling with his parents Emily and Frank. The family is from Strood in Kent, England, and they are travelling Third Class. Like the Browns, they are emigrating to the United States, but in their case to Detroit.

(Colonel) Archibald Gracie (53) is a wealthy American amateur military historian. He has just finished writing a book about his father, and has been on holiday in Europe. He is travelling First Class.

Elin Hakkarainen (24) is a domestic servant, originally from Helsinki in Finland, but who had been working in the United States. Her husband Pekka had also been working there, in a steel mill, in Monessen, Pennsylvania. The couple got married in Helsinki in January, and are looking forward to their new lives in the United States.

Eva Hart (7) is travelling in Second Class with her parents Benjamin and Esther. The family are from Seven Kings, east of London. They are also emigrating, but in their case to Winnipeg, in Canada. Eva is carrying a large doll that her father bought for her in Gamages Department Store in Holborn, London.

Violet Jessop (24) is a Stewardess, working in First Class. Violet was born in Bahia Blanca, Argentina, in 1887. Her best friend is another Stewardess, Elizabeth Leather.

Herbert 'Lights' Lightoller (38) is the Second Officer. He was born in Chorley, Lancashire, in 1874. The crew have been reshuffled, and he has just been demoted from First Officer to Second.

Arthur Rostron (42), is not on the *Titanic*, but is Captain of the *Carpathia* liner. He was born in Bolton in 1869, and has had a long career on various ships. On 11 April 1912, the *Carpathia* leaves New York and is heading in the opposite direction to the *Titanic*, for Fiume on the Adriatic coast.

Elizabeth Shutes (40) is a governess, travelling in First Class with the Graham family. Her charge Margaret Graham is 19, and also in the party is Margaret's mother, Edith. Elizabeth was born in 1871, in Newburgh, New York.

Hanna Touma (27) is travelling in Third Class with her children Maria and Georges. The family is from a village called Tibnin in the Lebanon and are travelling to be reunited with Hanna's husband, Darwis. He is already working in the United States, in a town called Dowagiac, Michigan.

Introduction

Most of us, at one time or another, have been passengers on an aeroplane, and have perhaps only found out (at most) the name of the person sitting next to us on arriving safely at our destination. In that respect, possibly there is a slight difference between a flight and a ship's voyage, especially a longer one. But even on a sea journey too, generally the names and individual personalities of the bulk of the passengers and crew remain hidden to us. When a flight or voyage ends in disaster, on the other hand, the lives of the passengers and crew, rich and poor, the survivors and the dead, are laid bare. That is particularly true of the *Titanic*. It was historian Walter Lord who described the sinking of the *Titanic* as 'the last night of a small town'. Lord claimed that the *Titanic* was so big, it carried so many passengers, that his task of piecing together even part of the picture had required the help of hundreds of people. Lord located sixty-three survivors. It was claimed earlier that the *Titanic* carried enough food 'for a small town'. But the small town metaphor is also helpful in conveying the sense that all aspects of society were on the ship, rich or poor, male or female, old or young, generous or selfish.

This book covers the stories of both passengers and crew, and documents individual experiences as well as broader social changes. It draws on published accounts, unpublished autobiographies, and archival materials, put into context with a range of other primary and secondary sources. The book has two main aims, which in different ways seek to both build upon and challenge Lord's *A Night to Remember* (1955). First, it seeks to re-balance the narrative, away from First Class passengers towards the experiences of those in Second and Third; away from men, towards women; away from adults, towards children; and away from the experiences of people from Britain and the United States towards those of other countries. It was Lord himself who acknowledged that the atmosphere that prevailed in Third Class has been 'a long-neglected side of the story'. But if anything it has been the Second Class passengers who have been neglected, lacking both the glamour of those in First Class, and the 'picturesque poverty' of those in Third. It is this, in part, that underlies the selection of the 12 stories. Of the eight featured passengers, two were travelling First Class; three Second; and three Third. Previous accounts have tended to emphasize the experiences of those in First Class at the expense of those in Second, and have ignored those in Third, particularly those migrants for whom English was not their first language.

Earlier accounts of the *Titanic* disaster have been dominated by men, both in terms of those who survived and those who did not. Key figures include Captain Edward Smith and Thomas Andrews. Of the 2,201 passengers and crew, 1,731 were men (12 years and older), and 470 were women and children. Of the 1,490 who were lost, 161 were women and children. A total of 373 women and children entered the lifeboats, compared with 338 men. Here six of the featured accounts are by women, and six by men. Of these, three are by people who were children at the time of the disaster. Of the featured accounts, eight are British, two American, one from the Lebanon, and one from Finland. The book employs what might be termed a 'life history' approach to uncover the lives of these people before and after the disaster.

Second, and reflecting the subtitle, the book aims not just to offer a minute-by-minute depiction of events, but also to explore key themes. These include the construction of the ship; migration, given that five of the featured passengers were migrating with their families to cities in the United States and Canada; nationality and place, since the *Titanic* was built in Belfast, sailed to Cherbourg, France, and Queenstown (now Cobh), Ireland, was heading for New York, and sank off Canada; the wider histories of radio and life jackets; the mixing of social classes in the lifeboats, and the lifeboat as a wider metaphor. Chapter 10 summarizes the findings of the Inquiries along with tracing what happened to the main characters after 1912. The final chapter, the Conclusion, returns to Lord's *A Night to Remember*, and explores the question of what caused the sinking, drawing on the availability of new forensic evidence following Robert Ballard's discovery of the wreck in 1985. It draws together the featured themes, but focuses on the key theme of social class which runs through the book, as well as assessing the relevance of the disaster to the broader social, cultural, and political history of the *Titanic*'s birthplace—Northern Ireland.

The book features the stories of both crew and passengers. The crew includes the Second Officer; a Stewardess; the young Assistant Wireless Operator who was employed by Marconi; and the Captain of a liner called the *Carpathia*. The First Class passengers comprise a wealthy American amateur military historian and an American governess. The one featured Second Class adult passenger is an English teacher, journalist, and writer. The Third Class passengers include two migrants—a woman travelling from the Lebanon with her two children; and a young Finnish woman travelling to Pennsylvania with her husband. Then there are three children—a teenage girl aged 15, originally from South Africa, and travelling to Seattle; an English girl aged 7 travelling to Winnipeg; and a 9-year-old boy from Kent migrating to Detroit. What were the earlier histories of these twelve adults and children? What were the experiences of passengers who were in Second and Third Class, and who were neither British nor American? Why, despite the emphasis on 'women and children first' were the early survivor narratives dominated by men? What happened to these people in the years after 1912? And how did their stories shape the myths that grew up around the *Titanic*?

In 1964, the future novelist Julian Barnes was waiting to go up to university, and had just got a job as a prep-school teacher. He taught for a term at a crammer half a mile from his home. The school came with a family attached, and everything was different and better than at Barnes's own home—brass taps, the banister on the stairs, genuine oil paintings, a library, old furniture. In the hall hung the blade of an oar, with the names of a college eight inscribed on its black scoop.

It was the grandfather who had founded the school, and he still lived on the premises. Now in his mid-80s, he was occasionally to be seen wandering through the house in a cream linen jacket, Gonville and Caius tie, and flat cap. He was searching for 'his class' which he never found, and talked about 'the laboratory', no more than a back kitchen with Bunsen burner and running water. On warm afternoons, he would sit outside the front door with a Roberts radio, listening to the cricket commentary. Apart from Barnes's great-grandfather, he was the oldest man the 18-year-old had met, setting off in him an adolescent anger against life and old age. The man's daughter fed him tins of baby food, and Barnes would tell him invented cricket scores. '84 for 2, Mr Beesley', he would shout as he passed him sleeping in the sun beneath the wisteria. 'West Indies 790 for 3 declared', he would insist as he delivered him his child's dinner on a tray. Barnes would 'tell him scores from matches that were not being played, scores from matches that could never have been played, fanciful scores, impossible scores'. The man would nod in reply, and Barnes would creep away, sniggering at his cruelty.

Some 52 years earlier, Lawrence Beesley had been a passenger on the *Titanic*. Among the souvenirs in his room were a blanket embroidered with the name '*Carpathia*'. The more sceptical members of the family claimed that the blanket had acquired its lettering at a much later date than 1912, and amused themselves with the speculation that their relative had escaped from the ship in women's clothing.

While it was a different passenger who escaped in women's clothing, the novelist's account of the elderly Beesley, and indeed his false cricket scores, reminds us of the dangers of trusting people and autobiographical accounts. It is necessary, therefore, to say how the twelve first-hand accounts have been used. Generally my aim has been to stay as true as possible to the original, often paraphrasing sections of them, but also deleting material that is clearly not eye-witness. It is for this reason that I have retained some of the more 'novelistic' moments of description; these are an important aspect of the recreation of the atmosphere of the story, and are in all cases a paraphrase of the sources that I am using. Factual errors, of names and events, have been corrected, and contradictions resolved, where possible. But some other changes have been necessary too. In some of the earlier accounts I have changed the point of view from the first person to the third person. I have cut the accounts and rearranged them in the process of weaving them into a broader narrative. In some, I found it necessary to modernize the style and punctuation. In another, I cut much of the contextual material, along with details of particular passengers who appear to have been included because they were mentioned in a well-known earlier account. Moreover when narrators tend to anticipate the sinking, generally I have taken these references out. On the whole, I have resisted the temptation to supply additional details in the accounts; what context there is, is in the explanatory sections. Nevertheless where it has been possible to identify characters with certainty, I have done so, as long as it seemed likely that the observer would have known their name. I return to some of these issues in the Note on Sources at the end of the book. Given the large number of nautical terms, whose origins and meanings are interesting in themselves, I have created a Glossary.

There have been many books about the *Titanic*, probably too many. One of my original premises in writing this book was the belief that in the recent emphasis on myth, the focus on individual passengers and crew members, and their stories, had been lost. It was Walter Lord who commented that the *Titanic* 'entrances the social historian. She is such an exquisite microcosm of the Edwardian world, illuminating so perfectly the class distinctions that prevailed at the time.' But the historian Stephanie Barczewski also claimed that before her account in *Titanic: A Night Remembered* (2004) none had been written by a professional historian. My aim is to adopt the 'life history' approach already mentioned, permitting a closer focus on a relatively small number of characters, and including information on their lives before, during, and after the disaster. I have deliberately avoided some of the most famous passengers and crew members. Thus there is little or nothing here about Captain Edward Smith; the 'unsinkable' Molly Brown; Wallace Hartley, the leader of the orchestra; Benjamin Guggenheim; Lady Duff Gordon, the fashion designer; J. Bruce Ismay, President of the International Mercantile

Marine (IMM) Company; or Stanley Lord, Captain of the *Californian*. Rather, my aim is to draw upon familiar and less familiar sources in order to create a more balanced narrative than that of Walter Lord. On the centenary of the sinking, it is the individual histories of twelve of the inhabitants of this small town, passengers and crew, their early experiences, family relationships, hopes, fears, and lives after the disaster that this book seeks to reconstruct. Overall, my aim has been to employ the rigorous, sceptical approach of the social historian, while at the same time retaining the vividness of the eye-witness account.

'The Biggest Anchor in the World'

The Brown family had been preparing for their voyage on the *Titanic* since Christmas 1911. Fifteen-year-old Edith Brown was born in Worcester, Western Cape Province, South Africa, on 27 October 1896. She had been a small child with slender limbs, slightly underweight, but strong and healthy. She was the first child of the marriage, and had been followed by a sister, Dorothy, born four years later, who died at the age of eight from diphtheria. Edith was devoted to her parents, and her whole upbringing was focused towards her one day becoming a young lady. She received a convent education, and was learning to play the piano. She had not been far from her parents, living in the Masonic Hotel that they ran, and as a result she had always been a great help to her mother and father.

Edith's father Thomas was born in Blackheath, London, in 1853, and had later gone to live in South Africa. He was a widower and had two sons and daughters from a previous marriage. His brother, a ship's Captain, had drowned at sea. Thomas owned both the hotel in Worcester, and the Mountain View Hotel in Cape Town, and had shares in wine and brandy companies as well as many interests in cottage properties in nearby False Bay and Muizenberg. He was a respected businessman, well liked in the community, and a prominent Freemason. Thomas was a short man of medium build with hair that was almost white and a bushy moustache. He had a round, kindly face and a pleasant disposition. He was always smartly dressed. Edith's mother Elizabeth was twenty years younger than her husband. She was related to a wealthy Afrikaner family called Louwe who owned farms and dairies around Durban. Elizabeth was of medium build and height, and was loving and devoted to those close to her. Since marrying Thomas, she had wanted for nothing, but had also made it a rule never to interfere in his business affairs.

Elizabeth always kept in contact with her sister Josephine, whose husband worked for the National Bank in Seattle, Washington State. Throughout 1910–1911, Josephine sent her sister letters full of praise of life in America. She often suggested that Elizabeth and Thomas should think about moving there and starting up their own hotel business. Over several months, Edith's parents had discussions about the prospects of starting a new venture in a foreign country. Elizabeth became more convinced, as time went by, that it would be a good move for all of them. Thomas, on the other hand, was more reluctant, perhaps because he was approaching 60. He knew that his wife was not one to try to force the issue, but he was fully aware of how excited she was at the prospect of a new life. Reflecting on the quiet life his wife and daughter were living in Cape Town, he thought that it was perhaps the right thing to do after all. Shortly after Christmas 1911, Thomas strode down Adderley Street toward the Union Castle shipping offices. He worked out that if he could arrange a passage to England within the following couple of months, he stood a good chance of booking a passage on the new liner that everyone was talking about. He had read in the *Cape Town Argus* that the *Titanic* would be sailing from Southampton on 10 April 1912 on her maiden voyage to New York. They would have to sail in February to give them some time in London for sightseeing and shopping before the next stage of their journey to America.

It was on a Thursday lunchtime on 26 February 1912 that the family arrived at the Union Castle Berth in Cape Town Docks. It was a bright, sunny day with a stiff south-westerly breeze blowing across the harbour. Two porters helped them load their luggage on board the *Saxon*. This ship was no stranger to them, as they had travelled on her before, on previous voyages to England. Once on board, the Senior Steward showed them to the First Class cabins. The only baggage they had with them was what was necessary for the voyage and hotel in London. The plan was to buy themselves new clothes there and any other items they would need for their voyage. Thomas would also purchase crockery, silverware, and linen for his planned hotel enterprise. These would be shipped out with them on the *Titanic*.

Once they were settled in their cabins, they decided to go up on deck for a stroll and to have their final look at Cape Town before leaving. By around 3.30 p.m., two tugs had arrived and positioned themselves in readiness for sailing. At 4 p.m. exactly, the ship began to move slowly away from the berth, edging her way around the rocky breakwater and finally, after releasing the tugs, heading out to the open sea. The Browns stood together on the after end of the Promenade Deck and looked back at Table Mountain. It stood out with the backdrop of a cloudless sky in all its glory in the late afternoon sunshine. Edith asked her father if he thought they might come back one day. He said that if things went as well as planned, there was every chance they would return, if only to see old friends again.

That evening and throughout the following two days, they experienced the 'Cape Rollers', a heavy swell and sea conditions well known to travellers. Many passengers were seasick, including Elizabeth. Edith and Thomas appeared to overcome the sickness and were able to go to the Dining Room for the evening meal, but Elizabeth couldn't face food and remained in her cabin for the best part of the first two days. On the third day out, sea conditions improved, and she was soon up and about and taking food again. She began to enjoy the fine weather with her husband and daughter.

As the *Saxon* continued north toward the equator, the weather improved. The swimming pool became popular with the passengers, along with a wide variety of deck games and competitions. A week after crossing the equator, they were able to see the coast of West Africa, and later passed Dakar, capital of French West Africa. Several days after that, they dropped anchor off Las Palmas in the Canary Islands, where the ship picked up mail and provisions. From a boat alongside, Thomas bought some trinkets and castanets for Edith, and a jewel box for Elizabeth. The weather over the next few days became colder. It was still winter in the northern hemisphere, and the Bay of Biscay made life on board uncomfortable for a couple of days until they entered the English Channel. The voyage was coming to an end. On their last night they could see St Catherine's Lighthouse and the lights of Weymouth and Bournemouth. The *Saxon* berthed right on schedule on a cold March morning. On disembarkation, the Browns made their way to Southampton Railway Station, where they caught a train to Waterloo. On arrival in London, they caught a hackney cab. Going over Waterloo Bridge, they passed Lancaster Place, went on to the Strand, into the Aldwych, and then along Southampton Row, finally stopping outside the Hotel Russell, where a porter came out to meet them.

Once settled into their hotel, Thomas spent the next few days booking their voyage on the *Titanic* and organizing the shipping of hotel items to be loaded on board in Southampton Docks. He managed to purchase tickets in Second Class, for £39 for the three of them. The booking clerk told him that Second on the *Titanic* was as good as First on many other transatlantic liners. After arranging all that was necessary for their voyage to America, the next plan was to get them fitted out in new clothes. They shopped in Knightsbridge, Mayfair, and Chelsea, Elizabeth and Edith purchasing wool serge, high-necked, full-length coats, along with double-breasted coats with velvet cuffs and lapels. They bought hats to match, some with feathers, some with nets, and others with wide brims. They both had a passion for the fashionable calf-length, button-up leather boots of the time. Thomas did the bulk of his shopping in Jermyn Street, in St James's. He bought several made-to-measure suits on Savile Row. With his top hat, tails, and silver-topped walking cane, he looked every bit the gentleman he was.

Unlike other hotels of similar standing, there always appeared to be a genuine friendliness with the staff at the Hotel Russell and no sign of snobbery. Thomas knew several of them from previous visits, and nothing was ever too much trouble. Elizabeth and her daughter spent much time reading the many books in the glass cabinets in one of the lounges. The rest of the time they were out sightseeing. The weather was fine for the time of year, and they had pleasant walks along Southampton Row and in Bloomsbury. The buds were breaking out on the plants and trees, and there was a feeling of spring in the air. Edith enjoyed the walks, as they gave her an opportunity to wear some of her new clothes and to look at other fashionable women. One afternoon, after a visit to the British Museum, they returned to the hotel and sat in one of the lounges, reading the newspapers.

During their last few days in London, they visited the Royal Opera House, Hampton Court, the Botanical Gardens at Kew, and the Tower of London. It was now 9 April, and on the following day they would be travelling down to Southampton. Edith's mother and father were happy, chatting and laughing as they discussed their future. Edith, at 15, was taking more of an interest in things. She wanted to know what the social life would be like on board the *Titanic*, and if there was going to be nightly entertainment. Was there an orchestra on board? If so, did they perform just for the First Class?

The Hart family was also preparing to emigrate, but in their case from Greater London to Canada. The family's life in the suburb of Seven Kings had appeared to young Eva to be a very happy one. However, during 1911 business was not so good and her father, a builder, had many long suburban roads full of 'To Let' signs and no customers for the houses. That meant substantial sums of money and capital were tied up and this became a major worry. He had come to a point in his life when he was taking a hard look into the future and could see only a continued period of uncertainty ahead. About this time, the family had a visit from a friend who had gone to Canada some years before and had come back for a holiday. He told them what a marvellous country it was, and how well he was doing with the growth of various cities and towns. In the space of one evening, which lasted well into the early hours of the next morning, Eva's father made up his mind to cut his losses in England and to emigrate in order to set up in business with his friend. They were going to build part of the city of Winnipeg, in Manitoba. At the end of the holiday, Eva's father's friend returned home, and within a few years he was extremely wealthy. Once Eva's father had taken the decision, he became very keen about going and was excited at the prospect of life for the family in Canada.

Eva had been born in Seven Kings. Both her parents were quite old when she was born as their first and only child. Her mother, Esther, had first got married when she was 18 years old. She had a very unhappy marriage and was eventually widowed in her early 30s. During the intervening years, she bore nine children, none of whom survived for more than a few months. This was due to a combination of the physical assaults she suffered at the hands of her first husband during her pregnancies, and the rare blood group she belonged to. Because of the misery she endured, Esther said she would never marry again and returned to live with her parents.

Several years later, Esther's father sought the services of a local builder in order to have a new house constructed in the nearby village of Chadwell Heath. The man who called to discuss the job was Benjamin Hart, who up to that time had remained single while building up his construction business. He went home after talking over the contract and announced to his father 'I've met the woman I'm going to marry.' So, despite her intentions, Esther married in 1900 for the second time, when she was 37 and her husband 36. Eva was born four and a half years later, in January 1905. So Eva became the tenth child her mother had carried, but the only one to survive.

Eva's parents were quite different in their looks. Esther was above average height for a woman, solidly built, with a full face. She had fair hair and green-grey eyes. Benjamin was a little shorter than his wife and was sturdily built because of the nature of his work. His outstanding feature was the black wavy hair that Eva liked to play with when he was sitting in the armchair reading the newspaper. The family lived in New Road, Seven Kings, and Benjamin became a well-known master builder in the area. Seven Kings adjoined the town of

Ilford, and was at that time a developing area on the edge of the Essex countryside. Beyond Seven Kings to the East were the expanding area of Goodmayes and the small villages of Chadwell Heath and Dagenham. The family was comfortably off. Esther had domestic servants in the house, and Benjamin owned a car at a time when they were still luxuries which only wealthy enthusiasts and businessmen could afford. The first car Eva recalled her father owning was an Argyll which unusually had a passenger door at the rear. Because it was quite a small car, he later sold it in order to buy a larger and more comfortable one. The family had this second car until Benjamin sold everything prior to their emigration on the *Titanic*.

From an early age, Eva was accustomed to being driven in a pony and trap by Esther along country lanes and over uneven roads. But she greatly enjoyed travelling by car and on one occasion went on a long journey to visit relations at Rye in Sussex. They drove into the surrounding Essex countryside to visit various friends—Hainault, Harold Hill, Loughton, and Debden were rural areas within easy reach of their home. They greatly enjoyed their trips out together and Esther made no secret of the fact that her whole life had changed for the better with her second marriage. As most of Benjamin's work was in the local area, Eva was fortunate in being able to see a great deal of him. Although he was a busy man, he always found time to play with her. She enjoyed watching him work, taking great care over some particular part of a house, such as shaping a window frame or cutting joints. It was fun playing amongst the wood shavings in his carpentry workroom.

Because of Esther's previous marriage and the fact that Eva was her only surviving child, they were a very close family. Esther loved Benjamin dearly, and Eva adored her parents. She could recall only being smacked once by her father. It was so exceptional that it stuck in her mind. It was a morning when he was taking her to feed the ducks in South Park, in Seven Kings. As they walked down the garden path, he saw a friend who greeted him with 'Do you know the King is dead?' Eva's father immediately said 'I must go in and put on a black tie.' At that time Eva started making a fuss, saying it was more important to feed the ducks. Benjamin was so angry that without more ado he smacked her. She never did see the ducks that day, but the sudden death of Edward VII on 6 May 1910, when she was only five years old, was firmly imprinted on her mind.

As soon as possible, Benjamin booked a cabin on a ship called the *Philadelphia*. It was all settled very quickly and the only person who was unhappy about the whole thing was Esther. From the very beginning she was apprehensive. This did nothing to deter her husband from taking the necessary steps for the emigration. He decided that they should travel via New York in order to visit his sister who was living there and whom he had not seen for many years. The intention was that they would continue their journey by train. He thought it would be the best route as the St Lawrence River was frozen at that time of year, and that would have meant disembarking at Halifax, Nova Scotia, and travelling across Canada by train.

The family were in the process of selling the house and getting rid of the furniture, when, with all the final arrangements in hand, their plans were thrown upside down. The combination of a serious coal and dock strike meant that the *Philadelphia* would not be sailing on its pre-arranged date. Esther was pleased when this news arrived and she felt it was a good reason not to go at all. But Benjamin was upset about the delay and started to pester the American Line shipping company responsible for arranging their journey. He constantly visited their offices and pointed out that he was not indulging in a pleasure trip but that the whole of their future life depended upon his reaching Canada by a particular date.

Because he was so bothered about the *Philadelphia* not sailing, the American Line tried to find an alternative ship that was due to sail at about the same time. Benjamin was told that they could have Second Class accommodation on the *Titanic*, which was being prepared for its maiden voyage early in April. Everybody had heard about this fabulous new liner being constructed for the White Star Line, and Benjamin told them about the comfort they could expect and what a good ship it was. He could not afford the cost of First Class accommodation. But he was prepared to pay the difference between the fare he had already paid for the *Philadelphia*, and the larger amount needed for Second Class on the new liner, knowing that the four-berth cabin would be quite comfortable and adequate for the three of them. The family's tickets cost £26 5s.

South-east of London, in Kent, the Goldsmith family were also preparing for the voyage. Nine-year-old Frank was living at that time with his family at 22 Hone Street, in Strood, across the Medway from Rochester. Frank was born on 25 December 1902, the son of Frank Goldsmith and his wife Emily. The boy had been extremely excited for many months prior to April 1912 about going aboard a ship that would one day be taking him to America. He had heard so much about the country because of letters his parents had received from his aunt, Elizabeth Emans, who was living in Detroit, Michigan. Elizabeth sent Frank the Sunday comic from their local newspaper, and described the United States as one of the most wonderful countries in the world. She kept this up until none of the family could wait any longer, and finally they were able to tell their relations in Detroit that their passage was booked. The family's Third Class tickets cost £20 10s 6d. Among the many letters that came as a result was one from a friend who asked if Frank's parents would look after a 15-year-old boy named Alfred Rush, then working as a porter. Alfred's brother, who also lived in Detroit, had arranged for Alfred to go and live with him. One of Frank's father's close friends, Thomas Theobald, a groom, had also become sold on the idea of Detroit and America, and had also booked a passage.

On each Christmas Day after they were married, Frank's parents went to the home of his paternal grandfather for a family get together. After Frank and his brother Bertie were born, they were taken there too. One of Frank's aunts, Nancy, would come down from London bringing a friend. Frank never forgot these get-togethers, but the ones that he remembered most vividly were those held after his fifth birthday. Starting that Christmas, Nancy would pressurize Frank to sing the last church hymn he had been taught in order to receive a gift from her. On Christmas Day 1910, Frank and Bertie sang a hymn that their Wesleyan Methodist Church Sunday School teacher had taught them. It was 'From Greenland's Icy Mountains'. When the two boys finished singing, Nancy gave each of them two pence, and they were very pleased and grateful. But that was the last Christmas the two brothers sang together. In December 1911, twelve months later, Bertie died of diphtheria.

Frank's mother Emily was the only one of nine children not to have emigrated. She wanted to take her Singer sewing machine with them. His father obtained a large wooden packing case about three feet high, three feet wide, and four feet long. One day, Emily lined this with their hall carpet, and his father helped her lift the sewing machine into it. A few days before, Frank's friend Arthur, who lived across the street from them, had seen him playing with his new whipping top. He liked it so much that he offered to give Frank his cap pistol if he would give him the top. Frank excitedly agreed to the swap, not realizing how firm an objection his mother had to young people possessing toy guns. Emily began putting many things into the packing case, and Frank suddenly remembered his cap pistol. He rushed into his bedroom, picked up the pistol, dashed back out into their backyard, and laid it on top of the sewing machine. Instantly Emily had cried out 'Frankie! Take this out of here and back to Arthur, right now!' Frank waited for Emily, his hand holding the toy pistol over the edge of the packing case. Inadvertently, the gun slipped out of his fingers and fell in. Frank looked and looked but could not see it. Then he ran back out onto the street before Emily reappeared, feeling that he had disobeyed her. Nothing was ever said by Emily, so he too remained silent.

Belfast had grown rapidly in the nineteenth and early twentieth centuries. The census recorded that the city's population increased from under 20,000 in 1801 to 386,947 in 1911. Its two main industries were linen and shipbuilding. In 1853, an ironmaster called Robert Hickson hired an engineer from Yorkshire called Edward James Harland, aged 23, as his yard manager. In 1858, Hickson sold Harland his share of the firm, for £5,000, most of which Harland borrowed from his friend G. C. Schwabe, a partner in the Bibby Line, of Liverpool. Schwabe's nephew Gustav Wolff joined the firm. Initially Harland and Wolff built ships for the Bibby Line, but later for the White Star Line. By 1900, Harland & Wolff was the largest shipbuilding firm in the world, employing 9,000 (largely Protestant) workers, and producing an average of 100,000 tons of shipping per year.

Harland and Wolff gradually left the firm in the hands of William James Pirrie. Pirrie was born in 1847 in Quebec, son of James Pirrie, who had emigrated to Canada in 1844 to enter the timber shipping trade. When her husband died in 1849, Pirrie's mother took her son back to Ireland to live with his grandfather. He was educated at the Royal Belfast Academical Institution, leaving in 1862 to become an apprentice at Harland & Wolff. In 1868, Pirrie was appointed Chief Draughtsman, and he became a partner in the firm in 1874. Pirrie developed contacts with several large shipping companies, and became chairman of Harland & Wolff following Harland's death in 1895.

The White Star Line, often known as the Oceanic Steam Navigation Company Ltd, was formed in 1869. From 1902 it was the constituent company of a huge international shipping combine known as the International Mercantile Marine (IMM) Company. Formed in 1902 by the American financier J. Pierpont Morgan, its aim was to gain control of the major shipping lines in the North Atlantic trade. The White Star Line became a subsidiary of the International Navigation Co. Ltd, of Liverpool, which in turn was owned by IMM. Its directors included William Pirrie and J. Bruce Ismay; from 1904, Ismay was its president. Born at Great Crosby, near Liverpool, in 1862, Ismay was the eldest son of Thomas Henry Ismay, shipowner and founder of the White Star Line. Ismay began an apprenticeship in the White Star Line in 1880, and became head of the business on his father's death in 1899. William Pirrie had realized that the survival of Harland & Wolff would depend on his skills as a business manager. Interestingly, Pirrie had distanced himself from the Unionist cause, supported Irish Home Rule, and joined the Liberal Party.

In early 1908, Harland & Wolff received an order from the White Star Line for two ships. They were intended to be the last word in luxury, and to challenge the *Lusitania* and the *Mauretania*, which had been launched by the White Star Line's main rival, Cunard. When they were launched in 1907, these were the largest, fastest, and most luxurious ships in the world. The two new ships were to be built at a cost of over £3 million. The *Titanic* was to be slightly larger and was hailed as the biggest ship in the world. The world's largest overhead gantry was erected to accommodate the massive hulls, and the world's largest floating crane was installed to lift boilers, engines, and funnels on board. The keel of the *Olympic* was laid down on 16 December 1908, and that of the *Titanic* on 31 March 1909. Between 3,000 and 4,000 of the 15,000 workers employed by Harland & Wolff were involved in the construction of the *Titanic*.

Thomas Andrews, the designer of the *Titanic*, was born on 7 February 1873 in Comber, in County Down in Ulster. His were a prominent local family, owners of a large linen mill. His father Thomas Andrews had in 1870 married Eliza Pirrie, sister of William James Pirrie. The elder Thomas Andrews was President of the Ulster Liberal Association from 1892, and a member of the Privy Council of Ireland from 1903. When he left school, in May 1889, the younger Thomas Andrews joined Harland & Wolff as an apprentice; he entered the Drawing Office in 1892, and in 1905 was subsequently promoted to be head of Harland & Wolff's design department. In 1907, Andrews was made a Managing Director of the firm. It was a powerful family. His brother James, later Sir James Andrews, was subsequently Lord Chief Justice of Northern Ireland, while his brother John was Prime Minister of Northern Ireland, 1940–1943.

Building the hull of the *Titanic*, from the laying of the hull to launch, took twenty-six months. Some items for the ship were built elsewhere. The tiles, for instance, were manufactured by J. C. Edwards, at Ruabon, Denbighshire, while the anchors and chains were forged at Messrs. Noah Hingley & Sons Ltd, Washington Street, Netherton, near Dudley in the West Midlands. The firm cast three anchors, one for the stern, and two for the bow. The stern anchor weighed 16½ tons, the bow anchors 8½ tons, while the anchor chains were of 3¼ inch diameter iron, and were each 900 feet long (10 lengths of 15 fathoms). The shanks, heads, and shackles were transported to the Lloyd's Proving House in Netherton to be assembled. Having passed the test, the anchor was taken outside and painted white. On 1 May 1911, the anchor, which was described by contemporaries as 'The Biggest Anchor in the World', was photographed as it left. The transporters were a company called Bantocks, and they arrived with a wooden ten-ton wagon and eight horses. The wagon was backed up to the anchor and it was loaded on. The horses were unhitched and replaced in the shafts by six of Hingley's own horses, massive shire horses, each weighing over a ton. In front of these horses the Bantocks horses were assembled in two single files on a long chain. They tugged the wagon up the incline from the Proving House onto the main road where the Bantocks horses fanned out either side, allowing Hingley's horses to pull the wagon across the road and to the entrance of Lee's coal yard. The wagon was then slowly turned to face up to Dudley. All the horses then took the strain and with shouts of encouragement they slowly hauled their heavy load to the railway goods yard for the next stage of the journey.

The *Titanic* was one of thirteen ships employed in the transport of passengers, mail, and cargo between Britain and the United States. The usual ports of call were Southampton, Cherbourg, Queenstown in the south of Ireland, and New York. It was a vessel of 46,328 tons (gross), length 852½ feet, breadth 92½ feet, and the height from the top of the keel to C Deck was 64 feet 9 inches. It had two sets of four-cylinder reciprocating engines, each driving a wing propeller, and a turbine driving the central propeller. Apart from the Boat Deck, the *Titanic* had Decks A to G, along with the Orlop Deck with the boilers. Steam was supplied from six groups of boilers in six watertight compartments. There were fifteen transverse bulkheads by which the ship was divided into sixteen separate compartments; those that had openings in them had watertight doors, operated directly from the Bridge. The ship was designed so that it would remain afloat in the event of two adjoining compartments being flooded. Overall, the *Titanic* was constructed so that it would comply both with the Board of Trade's regulations for a passenger certificate, and also with the American Immigration Laws. Through 1911, articles on the *Titanic* appeared in journals such as *The Engineer*, *Engineering*, and *The Shipbuilder*. The *Belfast News-Letter* commented on 1 January 1912 that 'each watertight door can be released by means of a powerful electric magnet controlled from the captain's bridge, so that, in the event of accident, the movement of a switch instantly closes each door, making the vessel unsinkable'. The fitting-out activity intensified through March, and by 2 April the *Titanic* was ready for sea. There was one day of trials in Belfast Lough, and the *Titanic* left for Southampton on the evening of 2 April, arriving there the following day.

While many passengers had made their plans months in advance, the crew of the *Titanic* were assembled much nearer the time of the maiden voyage. This included personnel who were not formally part of the crew. In March 1912, a young Marconi telegraph operator received a telegram stating that his next post was to be on the *Titanic*, and that he should report immediately to Belfast for sea trials. Born on 11 January 1890, Harold Bride was the youngest of five children. Then living in Deptford, London, the family moved shortly afterwards to Shortlands, in Bromley, Kent. After school, Bride announced that he was going to be a wireless operator. Since it was still such a new profession, and training was expensive, his parents Arthur and Mary Ann didn't discourage their son, but at the same time didn't have the money to pay for it. Harold worked in the family business between the ages of 16 and 20, and saved up. In 1910, he walked into a London Post Office to enquire about the costs of telegraphy schooling. The telegraphist on duty was called Harold Cottam. Cottam answered Bride's questions, and when the boy returned early the following week, invited him out to lunch; the two became firm friends. In the same year, Bride scandalized the neighbourhood in Bromley by building an aerial antennae in the family's garden so that he could practise his Morse code.

Harold Bride was now 22. He had attended the British School of Telegraphy, in Clapham Road in London, and the Marconi Company's Wireless Telegraphy Training School near Seaforth Sands, Liverpool. He took his operator's examination there on 28 June 1911. He had a sending and receiving rate of twenty words a minute (deemed to be 'very good'), and was awarded a Certificate in Wireless Telegraphy in July. Against his parents' wishes he went to sea soon after. He joined the Marconi Company in the summer of 1911; his first ship was the *Haverford*, but he later sailed as a radio operator on the *Beaverford, Lusitania, Lanfranc,* and the *Anselm*. About the same time as he received the telegram about his post on the *Titanic*, Bride became engaged to a girl called Mabel Ludlow; the next morning he regretted the decision, but he didn't break it off.

The *Titanic* was entered in the Liverpool customs register on 25 March 1912. By that date, some officers and crew had already begun to assemble in Belfast. Bride and his colleague John 'Jack' Phillips were already there, and were present for the ship's sea trials on 2 April. Like Bride, Phillips had received orders in March to travel to Belfast. At 25 years old, Phillips was the slightly older of the two, and also the more experienced. Born above a draper's shop in Godalming, Surrey, Phillips had gone to the local grammar school until at 15 he had finished his schooling and joined the Post Office where he trained to be a telegraphist. Phillips remained at the Godalming Post

Office until (like Bride) he left to undertake further training at the Marconi training school near Liverpool. He graduated in August 1906, and received his first post as an operator aboard the White Star liner *Teutonic*. In the years since, Phillips had served on the *Lusitania*, the *Mauretania*, a Marconi station in Clifden, in the west of Ireland, the *Adriatic*, and the *Oceanic*.

On 20 March 1912, three contented men took the midnight boat from Liverpool to Belfast, where the *Titanic* was being completed—William Murdoch, the Chief Officer; the 38-year-old Herbert Lightoller, the First Officer; and David Blair, the Second Officer. Like Bride, Lightoller had served on the *Oceanic*, as First Officer, and he had been appointed to the same position on the *Titanic*.

Lightoller, who was never known by his first name Charles but as Herbert, Bertie, or simply 'Lights', was born in Chorley, Lancashire, on 30 March 1874, and had an eventful career. In February 1888, at the age of 13, he began a four-year apprenticeship on the *Primrose Hill*, a four-masted barque of 2,500 tons. His next voyage was on the *Holt Hill*, which lost its mast in a storm in the South Atlantic, and was forced to put into Rio de Janeiro during a revolution and smallpox epidemic. After makeshift repairs, she again lost her mast in a storm in the Indian Ocean, and in November 1889 ran aground on the uninhabited island of Île Saint-Paul. The Chief Mate was killed in the shipwreck, and after eight days the survivors were rescued and taken to Adelaide.

Lightoller signed on with the clipper ship *Duke of Abercorn* for his return to England. His third voyage was again on the *Primrose Hill*, to Calcutta; on this voyage they survived a cyclone. In Calcutta, Lightoller sat for and passed his Second Mate's Certificate. While serving as Third Mate on the windjammer *Knight of St Michael*, the cargo of coal caught fire; for his efforts in fighting the fire and saving the ship Lightoller was promoted to Second Mate. In 1895, Lightoller obtained his Mate's ticket; he left the windjammers and joined the African Royal Mail Service, starting a career on steamships. He contracted malaria there, and nearly died from it.

In 1898, Lightoller left the sea and went to the Yukon in Canada to prospect for gold in the Klondike Gold Rush; unsuccessful, he had a stint as a cowboy in Alberta. In order to return home he became a hobo, riding the rails back across Canada. He worked his passage on a cattle boat, and arrived back in England, penniless, in 1899. He obtained his Master's Certificate, and in 1900 joined the White Star Line. He began as Fourth Officer on the *Medic*, later meeting Sylvia Hawley-Wilson whom he married in December 1903; the couple lived at 8 Cambridge Avenue, Crosby, Lancashire, and subsequently had five children—two daughters and three sons. Lightoller's early years on the Atlantic run were spent mainly on the *Majestic*, under the command of Captain Edward Smith. He was promoted to Third Officer on the *Oceanic*, and moved to Southampton in 1907. Lightoller then moved to the *Majestic* and the *Oceanic*, as First Officer.

Captain Smith, an experienced White Star Captain, went over to Belfast a little later on. Smith, or 'EJ', as he was affectionately known, was quite a character in the shipping world. Lightoller felt of Smith that, tall, full-whiskered, and broad, at first sight people thought to themselves 'Here's a typical Western Ocean Captain. Bluff, hearty, and I'll bet he's got a voice like a foghorn.' In fact, Smith had a pleasant, quiet voice—one he rarely raised above conversational tone—and he was invariably smiling. That was not to say he couldn't raise his voice, and Lightoller had often heard him bark an order that made a man wake up with a start. But Smith was a great favourite, and a man any officer would give his right arm to sail under. Lightoller had been with him off and on for many years on the mail boats, mainly the *Majestic,* and it was an education to see Smith captain his own ship, at full speed, up through the intricate channels entering New York. One particularly bad corner, known as the South-West Spit, used to make the crew flush with pride as Smith swung the ship round, judging his distances perfectly, the ship heeling over to the helm with only feet to spare between each end and the banks.

For some time before being appointed to the *Titanic,* Smith had been in command of the *Olympic*—in fact since she had been launched. Murdoch had also come from the *Olympic,* while Blair, like Lightoller, had been on the *Oceanic.* Lightoller was overwhelmed with the size of the *Titanic,* where he could walk miles along decks and passages, covering different ground all the time. He was familiar with nearly every type of ship afloat, from barges to battleships, but it took him a fortnight before he could with any confidence find his way from one part of the *Titanic* to another by the shortest route. For instance, there was a huge gangway door on the starboard side through which you could drive a horse and cart. Three other officers, joining later, tried for a whole day to find it. With the help of a plan it would have been fairly simple, but a sailor does not walk round with a map in his pocket; he must carry his ship in his head, and in an emergency such as fire must be able to get where he wants by sheer instinct—certainly without a chance of getting lost on the way. Commissioning a new ship was, at the best of times, a strenuous job. With the *Titanic* the work went on day and night, with Lightoller organizing, receiving stores, arranging duties, and trying and testing out the different equipment. There were the makers of a hundred and one instruments with their papers to be signed, certifying that everything was in perfect working order. All the navigation instruments were the responsibility of Lightoller, as were the fire-arms and ammunition.

The *Titanic*'s sea trials had originally been set for Monday 1 April, but they were postponed to the following day because of bad weather and high winds. The Board of Trade's representative, Francis Carruthers, was on board for the trials. Before the *Titanic* set sail, Carruthers carried out a full inspection of the ship. He and Lightoller swung out the lifeboats, and tested the anchors, bulkheads, and watertight doors. The sea trials began at 6 a.m., and lasted for just over twelve hours. The *Titanic* went from slow speed to full speed; she was put astern; her engines were put through their paces; she was put through a series of circling trials; and she was tested while her port propeller was going full astern while the starboard propeller was going full ahead. A speed run and full stop test were also carried out. The *Titanic* returned to Belfast at 7 p.m., and Carruthers completed his 'Report of Survey'. Then, at 8 p.m. on Tuesday 2 April, the *Titanic* left Belfast, and set out on the short voyage to Southampton, with 280 crew members on board, arriving there just after midnight on Thursday 4 April.

Stewardess Violet Jessop found that time flew when she was busy. Certainly the first year of her life on the *Olympic* was gone before she knew it, spent in the hectic rush which is typical of a new ship, until the novelty wore off and the passengers took their custom elsewhere. Violet and her fellow stewardesses had not had much time to get used to the *Olympic* before they were preparing to move to the *Titanic*, nor had they given their feet a chance to recover from longer hours and the long stretch of alleyways with their unfamiliar rubber decks. Violet found that once she realized change was in the air, there was a spirit of expectancy, unrest, and uncertainty, not unpleasant but bad for her nerves.

A devout Catholic who carried a rosary in her apron and believed strongly in the power of prayer, Violet was only 24, and was born in 1887, in Bahia Blanca, Argentina. Violet's father William emigrated from Dublin in the mid-1880s to try his hand at sheep farming. His fiancée, Katherine Kelly, followed him out in 1886. They were married shortly after their arrival, and their first child, Violet, was born on 2 October 1887. Violet had four younger brothers who survived childhood—William, Philip, Jack, and Patrick—and a much younger sister, Eileen, born in 1902. By then, Violet had to cope with household chores, and a succession of childhood illnesses. Many of William and Katherine's children had diphtheria, smallpox, scarlet fever, and meningitis. Violet herself suffered from tuberculosis, which disrupted her childhood and schooling. She looked after William and Philip when they had diphtheria, and also did much of the cooking, cleaning, and ironing.

After Violet's father died, the family returned to Britain, first to Liverpool and then to London, where her mother found a job as a stewardess on the Royal Mail Line. When her mother was away at sea, Violet attended a convent school, and sometimes she was left in charge of her younger sister. Then, at 21, when her mother's health deteriorated, Violet followed her mother, from October 1908, as a stewardess. 'Home', such as it was, was 71 Shirley Road, Bedford Park, in London. Violet's first ship was the *Orinoco*, a single-screw steamer built in 1886, and sailing in the West Indian service. Later, she applied for a job as a stewardess on the White Star Line. Her first ship was the *Majestic*, which she joined in September 1910, earning £2 10s a month. Violet was initially assigned to Second Class, but soon made her way into First. Her duties were to make beds, clean cabins, keep alleyways swept and dusted, bring trays for breakfast or tea, answer summonses, run errands, arrange flowers, turn down beds at night, put away clothing, and comfort the seasick. She found that most passengers in both First and Second Class were American. Subsequently she joined the *Olympic*, from June 1911. On all Violet's ships, she established a firm rapport with the ships' surgeons, following her childhood illnesses.

'Like a Big Expectant Family'

On Wednesday 10 April, Edith Brown and her parents had an early morning call at the Hotel Russell at 6 a.m. After dressing, they went down to the Dining Room for their breakfast. They ate well and, after doing their final packing, went down to the lobby to arrange for their other baggage to be carried out to a waiting cab. The cab spluttered into life amid clouds of blue smoke, and began its journey down Southampton Row. It was a beautiful Spring morning as they motored through Bloomsbury on their way to Waterloo Station. It was a time in their lives they would never forget.

On arrival at Waterloo, a porter met them, loaded their luggage onto a cart, and then walked along the platform with them to their carriage. There were groups of people standing along the length of the platform as the porter led them to their First Class compartment.

There was the occasional whiff of coal smoke and steam from the engine, just a few carriages along, as a gentle breeze swirled about the station. The porter put their luggage into the carriage compartment; the smaller items were placed in the luggage nets above the seats. After tipping the porter for his efforts, they sorted themselves out and settled down for the journey. Soon after, there was the final slamming of carriage doors, followed by a prolonged whistle from the guard and a slight jerky movement forward. They were on their way.

As they gathered speed, they began to clear Greater London, and the buildings and bridges became fewer as they headed into the countryside. Edith sat opposite Thomas and Elizabeth, and spent most of the time looking out of the window at the Surrey and Hampshire countryside. Her thoughts were on what the future might hold for her. The train continued its journey, passing Winchester. They arrived on the outskirts of Southampton and slowed down as they entered the Northam Goods Yards. The train crossed the road as it entered the docks, and headed towards Berth 44. Edith was still full of excitement as she leant out of the carriage window in an effort to catch sight of the liner. She saw several ships in the docks. Finally, looking ahead, she could see the huge, black hull of the *Titanic* rising out of the water. 'There she is!' exclaimed Edith excitedly, pointing towards the ship as the train, now moving at walking pace, drew ever closer to the passenger sheds. Edith and her parents had an excellent view. The liner looked serene lying alongside the berth, her white superstructure towering over everything on the dockside and dwarfing the cranes. Her four great, buff-coloured funnels stood proudly above everything else, smoke curling lazily from their black shiny tops. It was a breathtaking sight for those on the train, peering out of the windows and seeing the ship for the first time.

Once inside the great cargo and passenger shed, the train came to a halt, puffing, wheezing, and blowing steam and smoke everywhere around the front end of the engine. Inside, the terminal was a hive of activity with passengers and dockworkers milling about. Carts and baggage moved to and fro around the great shed and the ships' gangways. A porter helped them get their luggage to the Second Class gangway. Looking high above them, they could see rows of portholes with the morning sunshine glinting on their rims. Higher up, they could see passengers leaning on the ship's rail, shouting down now and then to friends and loved ones on the dockside. As they continued up the slight slope of the gangway to the open doors at the top, Thomas became faint and his legs began to buckle. Clutching the handrail, he tried to remain on his feet. Both women turned around and started up again, finally entering the entrance lobby.

Once on board, they immediately took in the carpeting and wood panelling. Crossing over to the Purser's Office, Thomas deposited his Gladstone bag with its gold sovereigns, bank notes, and jewellery. They were promptly assigned to a steward, who asked them to follow as he led them to their cabins on E Deck. They fell in behind him as they went along the passageway with its handrails and oak panelling. The smell of newness was everywhere. They went down two flights of stairs to arrive outside the ladies' cabin after a short walk. After opening the door for them, the steward led Thomas a bit further along the passageway to his two-berth cabin. Both women were pleased with their accommodation. The bunks, one above the other, were made up with white pillows and sheets, and counterpanes with the White Star design in the centre. The floor of the cabin was beautifully carpeted, and there were two chairs, a washstand and mirror, white towels, and water jugs and glasses. The bunks had curtains that could be drawn across, and there were also little curtains at the porthole. Thomas returned from his cabin, which was identical to theirs, to see how the women were getting on and to help with some of the luggage.

Making their way up to the open decks, Edith and her parents passed many passengers sorting out their baggage and being directed to their cabins by stewards. After going along the passageways and up several flights of stairs, they arrived on the Promenade Deck and strolled along with other groups of people. They went to the ship's rail and looked down on the dockside far below, where throngs of people milled about as cranes swung the cargo into the ship's hold. They continued their walk along the decks. While up on the Boat Deck, they noticed more smoke coming out of the funnels than they had first seen when arriving on the train. It was here that many were surprised by an ear-shattering blast from one of the ship's funnels. They all ducked at first, but on rising, they laughed, realizing that the *Titanic* was preparing for sea.

Thomas, Elizabeth, and Edith said little, but they waved along with everyone else, just enjoying the wonderful atmosphere as the ship moved away from Berth 44. Once the ship was clear, people ashore could be seen walking along the dockside to keep pace as the tugs finally helped her face seaward. Many of the passengers who had been on deck when the ship left Southampton were now seated in their respective dining saloons, enjoying lunch, their first meal of the voyage. After their lunch in the Dining Room, the Browns set off for further walks around the ship. They visited the Library, with its panelling, shelves of books, and armchairs. Standard lamps were placed around the room. Elizabeth and Edith, avid readers, were delighted.

The *Titanic*'s passenger lists recorded (with some inaccuracy) 'Tom, Eliza, and Elin Brown', ages 45, 40, and 18 respectively, travelling on ticket number 29750. The same lists also recorded 'Benjamin, Esther, and Eva Hart', ages 30, 29, and 6, travelling on ticket number 13528.

Along with many other passengers, the Hart family had joined the White Star Line Boat Train at Waterloo Station at 9.45 a.m. To avoid an early rush they had stayed overnight with Eva's uncle Harry, at his London flat. He had decided to come and see them off. As they waited for the Boat Train to start, Eva thought what a marvellous adventure it was and wondered what Canada would be like. They were on their way to Southampton where the *Titanic* was berthed, and within a few days would all be starting a new life in a foreign country. The Harts boarded at Southampton with other Second Class passengers, the ship towering out of the water above them like a large apartment block. The family's cabin was on the port side of the ship. As it was a four-berth cabin, they only lowered three of the tiered bunks and this made it much easier to move around. They had ample cupboards for all their clothes, and the cabin had its own wash-hand basin and dressing table as well as a couple of comfortable chairs. Eva's bunk was underneath the one used by her father. Much of the time it was occupied by the doll and teddy bear which she had taken to keep her company.

Among the other Second Class passengers who joined at Southampton was a young English science teacher. He went on board at 10 a.m., after staying the night in the town; his cabin was D56. As he sat that morning in the breakfast room of the Dolphin Hotel, in the High Street, the four huge funnels of the *Titanic* could be seen from the windows, towering over the roofs of the shipping offices opposite, and with a procession of stokers and stewards wending their way to the ship. Three *Titanic* passengers sat behind him in the breakfast room, discussing the coming voyage and calculating, among other things, the chances of an accident at sea. Born at

Steeple Grange, Wirksworth, Derbyshire, on 31 December 1877, Lawrence Beesley was the third of eight children. At the time of his birth, his father Henry was a clerk at Moore & Robinson's bank, and he was promoted to Manager in 1881. Beesley was educated at Derby School, and earned a scholarship to Caius College, Cambridge, where he graduated with a degree in Natural Science in 1903. In June 1901, Beesley married Cissy Macbeth at St Margaret's Church in Lancaster; they had one son, Alec, born in Cambridge in November 1903.

Following his graduation, Beesley took a teaching post as Science Master at Wirksworth Grammar School and in this period discovered a rare algae in the hills around the town; it was later named *Ulvella Beesleyi* after him. Beesley was a teacher at the Anthony Gell Grammar School from 1902 to 1904, before obtaining a post as Science Master at Dulwich College, in London. Among his pupils was a boy called Raymond Chandler. In 1905, Beesley became interested in religion, and the teachings of Mary Baker Eddy, founder of the Christian Science movement. Tragically, his wife Cissy died from tuberculosis in August 1906; she had been suffering from the disease for three years. Within a couple of years, Beesley was writing religious tracts, and instructing others from his rooms on the Marylebone Road. In 1909, his article 'The Passing Away of Human Theories', was published in the *Christian Science Journal*. In 1911, Beesley, now living alone with his son in Regent's Park, resigned his position at Dulwich College, and following two years of family trauma and upheaval, felt that he needed a holiday. He decided to visit his younger brother Frank in Toronto, made arrangements for the care of his young son, and purchased a Second Class ticket for £13 on the *Titanic*. He was planning to stay at the Cornell Club, in New York. The *Titanic*'s passenger lists recorded 'Lawrence Beesley', aged 26, travelling on ticket number 248698.

Beesley had decided to cross the Atlantic for several reasons—he thought it would be a novelty to be on board the largest ship yet launched; one of his friends who had crossed on the *Olympic* had described her as a very comfortable ship; and it had been reported that the *Titanic* had been further improved by having 1,000 tons more ballast added to steady her. Between the time of going on board and sailing, Beesley inspected the *Titanic*'s various decks, dining rooms, and libraries in the company of two friends who had come from Exeter to see him off. As Second Officer Herbert Lightoller had already found, the ship was so extensive that it was quite easy to lose one's way. Beesley and his friends wandered casually into the Gymnasium on the Boat Deck, and were exercising on bicycles when Thomas McCawley, the Gymnasium steward, came in with two companions. He insisted on their remaining there while his friends— as they thought at the time—recorded the equipment being used. It was only later that Beesley and the others discovered they were photographers from the *Illustrated London News*. More passengers came in, and the instructor ran here and there, looking the picture of robust, rosy-cheeked health and fitness in his white flannels, placing one passenger on the electric horse and another on the camel. The laughing group of onlookers watched the inexperienced riders vigorously shaken up and down as he controlled the little motor which made the machines imitate horses and camels so realistically.

Soon after noon, the whistles blew for friends to go ashore, the gangways were withdrawn, and the *Titanic* moved slowly down the dock, to the accompaniment of last messages and the shouted farewells of those on the quay. There was no cheering or hooting of steamers' whistles from the fleet of ships that lined the dock, as might have been expected on the occasion of the largest vessel in the world putting to sea on her maiden voyage. Instead the whole scene was quiet and rather ordinary, with little of the ceremony which might be thought necessary in such circumstances. But if this was lacking, two unexpected and dramatic incidents supplied a thrill of excitement and interest to the departure from the dock. The first of these occurred just before the last gangway was withdrawn—a small knot of stokers ran along the quay, with their kit slung over their shoulders in bundles, and made for the gangway with the intention of joining the ship. But a Petty Officer guarding the shore end of the gangway firmly refused to allow them on board. They argued and gesticulated, apparently attempting to explain the reasons why they were late, but he waved them away, and the gangway was dragged back amid their protests. Beesley heard later that the three brothers, Thomas, Bertram, and Alfred Slade, and another stoker called Frank Holden, had been drinking earlier in the Newcastle Hotel, and then in a pub called 'The Grapes'. They missed the boat on account of this.

The second incident occurred soon afterwards. As the *Titanic* moved majestically down the dock, a crowd of friends keeping pace with the ship along the quay, they came level with the steamer *New York* lying moored to the side of the dock along with the *Oceanic*. The crowd waved farewells to those on board as well as they could given the intervening bulk of the two ships. But as the bow of the *Titanic* came level with that of the *New York*, there came a series of reports like those of a revolver, and on the quay side of the *New York* snaky coils of thick rope were flung high in the air and fell backwards among the crowd, which retreated in alarm. Beesley and his companions hoped that no one had been struck by the ropes, but a sailor next to him was certain he saw a woman carried away to receive medical treatment. And then, to their amazement, the *New York* crept towards them, slowly and stealthily, as if drawn by some invisible force which she was powerless to resist. It reminded Beesley of an experiment he had shown many times to a class of boys learning the rudiments of physics in a laboratory, in which a small magnet was made to float on a cork in a bowl of water and small steel objects placed on neighbouring pieces of cork were drawn towards it. It reminded him, too, of seeing how, in his son Alec's bath, a large plastic floating duck would draw smaller ducks, frogs, beetles, and other animals towards itself, by capillary attraction, until the menagerie floated about as one unit.

On the *New York* there was a shouting of orders, sailors running to and fro, and the paying out of ropes and putting of mats over the side where it seemed likely they would collide. The tug which had a few moments before cast off from the bow of the *Titanic* came up around its stern and passed to the quay side of the *New York*'s stern, made fast to her, and started to haul her back with all the force her engines were capable of. However it did not seem that the tug made much impression on the *New York*. Aside from the serious nature of the accident, Beesley felt it was comical to see the huge vessel drifting down the dock with a snorting tug at its heels, like a small boy dragging a tiny puppy down the road with its teeth locked on a piece of rope, its feet splayed out, and its head and body shaking from side to side in an effort to use every ounce of its weight to the best advantage. At first it seemed inevitable that the sterns of the two vessels would collide, but from the Stern Bridge of the *Titanic* an officer directing operations stopped the ship dead, the suction ceased, and the *New York* with her tug trailing behind moved obliquely down the dock, her stern gliding along the side of the *Titanic* a few yards away. It showed very clearly the absolute helplessness of a big liner lacking engine power. But the excitement was not yet over. The *New York* turned her bow inward towards the quay, her stern swinging just clear of and passing in front of the *Titanic*, and moved slowly head on for the *Teutonic* lying moored to the side. Mats were quickly got out and they deadened the force of the collision, which (from where Beesley and his companions were) seemed to be too slight to cause

39

any damage. Another tug came up and took hold of the *New York* by the bow, and between the two of them they dragged her round the corner of the quay which came to an end at that point on the river.

The *Titanic* now moved slowly ahead and passed the *Teutonic* at a creeping pace, but notwithstanding this, the latter strained at her ropes so much that she heeled over several degrees in her efforts to follow. The crowd were shouted back and a group of gold-braided officials, probably the Harbour Master and his staff, standing on the sea side of the moored ropes, jumped back over them as they drew taut, and urged the crowd back still further. But the *Titanic* was just clear, and as they slowly turned the corner into the river, Beesley saw the *Teutonic* swing slowly back into her normal position, relieving the tension in both the ropes and the minds of all those who had witnessed the incident.

Unpleasant as this had been, it was interesting to all the passengers leaning over the rails to see how the officers and crew of the various vessels tried to avoid the collision, and to see on the *Titanic*'s Docking-Bridge at the stern an officer and seamen telephoning and ringing bells, and hauling little red and white flags up and down, as the danger of collision alternately threatened and diminished. No one was more interested than William Harbeck, an American film-maker, who, with his French mistress, Henriette Yvois, followed the whole scene with eager eyes, turning the handle of his camera with evident pleasure as he recorded the unexpected incident on film.

As they steamed down the river, the scene they had just witnessed was the topic of every conversation. Every little group of passengers drew comparisons with the collision between the *Olympic* and the cruiser *Hawke* the previous year. It seemed to be generally agreed that this confirmed the suction theory which had been so successfully advanced by the *Hawke* in the law courts, but which many people had scoffed at when the Admiralty first suggested it as the explanation of the cruiser ramming the *Olympic*. Some of the passengers and crew who were heard talking about it had clear misgivings about the incident they had just witnessed. Beesley knew that sailors were proverbially superstitious.

Frank Goldsmith's father was a toolmaker and lathe operator, and he had been given several farewell parties by family, friends, and fellow workers. At that time, when people were emigrating from England, it was the custom for a group of workmates to 'handmake' certain tools, known as 'scribing blocks'—inside and outside callipers or compasses, and others like that. Frank's family had these tools in their luggage. They also carried a bottle of Eno's Fruit Salts and a bag of Gibson's Fruit Tablets. Friends in Strood had told Frank's parents that these could prevent seasickness.

Sailing day had arrived, and the Goldsmith family had left their home, and walked down to the railway station where they joined Tom Theobald and took the train to London. There they picked up the 15-year-old porter, Alfred Rush. They headed for the Boat Train to Southampton, got off, finally got aboard with their hand baggage, and settled into their Third Class private cabin. The *Titanic* passenger lists recorded 'Frank, Emily, and Frank Goldsmith', ages 33, 31, and 9, and travelling on ticket number 363291. Interestingly, the passenger lists included a column 'Profession, Occupation, or Calling of Passengers'. This did not need to be completed for First Class passengers. But Frank's father was listed as a turner, and on the same page were a dipper, coster (seller of fruit and other wares from a barrow), ironworker, bricklayer, pugilist, farmer, general labourer, baker, gardener, fitter, butcher, painter, student, carpenter, grocer, butler, shop assistant, toolmaker, valet, blacksmith, goldsmith, and engineer.

Tom Theobald and Alfred Rush were single individual passengers, also in Third Class, but they were assigned to a male dormitory, each having paid fares of £8 1s. Frank was extremely excited, as any young person would have been. Not only was the family going to America, but on the way they were also going to another country, France, and then, as a bonus, to Ireland—two 'fairytale' places that tripled the joy in the eyes of a 9-year-old.

From their window at the Hotel Oceanic in Southampton, two other prospective passengers had been able to see the *Titanic* docked at the pier. Third Class passengers were able to board the ship between 9.30 and 11.00 a.m. The migrants and Third Class passengers had medical inspections, and were issued with green immigration cards that listed the name of the ship, port, date of departure, and their current residence. They were assigned berth numbers. Pekka and Elin Hakkarainen's cabin was situated on E Deck, on the starboard side between bulkheads O and P; their fare was £15 17s. The couple's dreams were fully realized when they boarded. It had been difficult for many to come up with their money for their passage, and the *Titanic* symbolized the prosperity they anticipated in America. Pekka, who had his job waiting for him, was excited to be returning to his work. Elin looked forward to seeing her new home.

Elin and Pekka were fleeing Finland because if they stayed, Pekka would have had to serve in the Russian Army. Elin was now 24, and had been born in Kalvola, on 20 March 1888. She was one of seven children. The Dolck family lived in Kalvola until 1899, when they moved to Hattula, a small town in the Province of Hame in the South. Elin lived in Hattula until 1907. Then, at the age of 17, she decided to leave home to go to America. Elin made her first trip in the company of four other girls, all of whom lived in or near Hattula. Through an employment agency, all five had jobs waiting for them on arrival in Boston. Most of the women who went from Finland worked as domestic servants, and Elin became a maid for a wealthy family in Quincy, Massachusetts. The staff in the home included a chauffeur, cook, butler, and two maids. The son of the family was interested in cars, and occasionally he took Elin and her four friends for a ride. The girls tried to get together and socialize on their days off. Although Elin was generally happy in her new adopted homeland, she was also homesick, and in July 1911 decided to return to Finland for a visit.

Pekka Hakkarainen had been born on 1 January 1884, in the town of Kuopio, in the Central Province. He was the youngest of three children. Pekka had moved from Kuopio to Paattinen in Turku, in 1902. It was not long before he, too, boarded a ship and sailed to America. Soon after he had emigrated, Pekka had settled in Monessen, a small town located 30 miles south of Pittsburgh, along the Monongahela River. He lived in a Finnish boarding house and was a foreman at the American Sheet and Tin Plate Company, earning $5 a day. Many men that came from Finland worked there; although they worked long, hard hours, they earned good wages. However, in August 1911, Pekka became homesick and he returned for a visit to Finland. Elin's sister Aurora also lived in Monessen and knew Pekka from the Finnish Temperance Hall, a social place where people went to play games, square dance, sing folk songs, and socialize with others. Aurora asked Pekka to look up her sister, Elin.

Upon arriving back in Finland, the 27-year-old Pekka met the 23-year-old Elin, and fell in love. They were married in Helsinki in January 1912. The Hakkarainens were very happy and excited to be going back to America to begin their new life together. Their original plan was to return on the *Mauretania* shortly after their wedding, but after hearing about the *Titanic*'s maiden voyage in April, they decided to wait and take it instead. The young couple had begun their trip in April 1912, as had some of the other Finnish passengers who were sailing on the *Titanic*. They travelled to Hanko, in southern Finland. From there, they left for Hull, where they boarded the passenger steamer *Polaris* at the Albert Dock, bound for Southampton. The steamer had arrived in Southampton the previous day. On the list of 'alien' passengers embarked at Southampton, the two were listed as 'Pekka and Elin Hakkevainen', aged 28 and 27, Finns who had arrived in the United Kingdom in Hull, and who were travelling on ticket number 3101/9.

As the experience of the Hakkarainens demonstrated, emigration was on the rise in Finland, and it has been estimated that between 1883 and 1914, 282,943 Finns left their country. Finland had been under Russian domination since 1809, and for years many Finnish men were forced to serve in the Russian army. As the autonomous Grand Duchy of Finland, men were drafted, not to defend Finland, but to fill the ranks of the armies of Tsar Nicholas II. While the political situation remained unstable, many chose to leave for America instead of fighting with the Russians. Other reasons were related to the economic, agricultural, and industrial conditions at that time. Hanko in Finland was a major launching point for migrants to the United States, Canada, and Australia. The *Polaris* on which the Hakkarainens travelled was owned by the Finland Steamship Company. The line had been founded in Helsinki in 1883, and was Finland's oldest shipping company. Between 1896 and 1900, the company had bought ten new ships, among them the sister ships, *Arcturus* and *Polaris*. The export of butter from Finland was growing rapidly, and the two ships were put on the Hanko–Hull route; the emigrants travelled on the butter ships.

Elin Hakkarainen, Edith Brown, Eva Hart, and Frank Goldsmith were migrating with their families to cities in the United States and Canada, and indeed this was the reason why they were on the *Titanic* in the first place. En route, the ship was scheduled to stop at Queenstown in Ireland, which had become famous as a port of emigration. One of the best natural harbours in the world, from the 1820s ships called there to pick up Irish migrants. At that time called Cove, it had been renamed Queenstown shortly after a visit by Queen Victoria in 1849. Shipping lines began to call at Queenstown, and the first White Star Line ship to call there had been the *Oceanic* in 1871. Between 1855 and 1912, 4.8 million people emigrated from Ireland, half of them from Queenstown, and in 1912 nearly 30,000 Irish emigrated, two-thirds going to the United States, and another 6,000 to Canada. By 1912, there were twenty emigrant lodging houses in Queenstown, another fourteen boarding houses, and one or two hotels.

In the decade after the American Revolution, about 5,000 people emigrated to the United States every year. By the early 1900s, that many were arriving at the Immigration Station on New York's Ellis Island every day, with a record of 11,747 being set on 17 April 1907. Altogether, some 12 million migrants went through Ellis Island. The Immigration Station opened in January 1892, but five years later the wooden structure, along with many immigration records, burned down. A new, fireproof, French Renaissance-style building opened in December 1900, welcoming 2,251 arrivals that day. Whereas First and Second Class passengers were processed on board ship, ferries and barges brought those from Third out to Ellis Island from steamships. Doctors watched as migrants entered the building and climbed the stairs; a limp, laboured breathing, or other suspected problems led to a medical examination. Inspectors questioned each individual, and among the twenty-nine categories were name, home town, occupation, destination, and amount of money carried. Those allowed to pass continued downstairs, exchanged money, bought provisions, and perhaps rail tickets. A third stayed in New York City; the rest headed elsewhere.

Medicine was an important instrument employed to assimilate migrants into American society in a way that would preserve the established order's cultural preferences and priorities. On the one hand, migrants were perceived as the bearers of diseases harmful to the native-born population; on the other, ethnic prejudices and public hysteria often created false linkages between illness and specific migrant groups. The fear of rejection loomed uppermost therefore in the minds of many migrants as they travelled towards the United States, and the medical examination forged memories that would last forever. Nevertheless relatively few migrants were turned back. The United States Public Health Service inspected more than 25 million arriving migrants between 1891 and 1930, but it issued only 700,000 medical certificates for disease or defect. The Immigration Service denied entry to roughly 79,000 of those medically certified. On average, 4.4 per cent of migrants were certified annually between 1909 and 1930, and disease was never the most important reason for migrant rejections from the United States.

The historian Amy Fairchild has argued, in *Science at the Borders* (2003), that 'the exam, which literally touched millions of immigrants, served a much more complex social function than simple exclusion on the basis of disease, class, or race'. Instead, the migrant medical inspection became part of an effort to discipline the labour force. The procedure that migrants endured at Ellis Island was part of a process of inclusion. Only when groups of migrants failed to conform to social expectations about the fit industrial worker did the migrant medical examination exclude those groups at the nation's borders. In

Fairchild's view, the medical examination served two purposes—to discipline the industrial working class, and to exclude migrant groups that did not make a positive contribution to the industrial workforce. Officials placed little emphasis on racial distinctions between people, with the goal of exclusion; rather the impulse was to absorb migrants into the labouring body. A good industrial citizen was one that would remain healthy, be a useful worker, and not become dependent on charity. Fairchild reiterates that 'the immigrant medical inspection represented a new technique for discipline in the new social and economic order, signalling a transformation in the nature of discipline and power, from corrective to preventive, from violent to normative'. In the United States, migrant medical inspections were gradually abandoned, or accomplished as part of the quarantine exam. Ellis Island closed completely in 1954; its buildings deteriorated until their restoration in the 1980s and the opening of the magnificent immigration museum there in 1990.

There were important contrasts between the experience of the passengers in Third Class, many of them migrants, and those in First that Violet Jessop was looking after. Tickets for the *Titanic* had a tear-off counterpart section on which booking details were duplicated. Third Class passengers gave up the counterpart to emigration officials during inspection procedures before boarding. In return, they were provided with individual inspection cards, and these also served as boarding passes. Cabin passengers in First and Second Class had counterparts, but these didn't need to be given up until after they had boarded. It was the responsibility of the ship's master or owner to pass these slips of paper on to the emigration officials. First and Second Class passengers thus needed a separate boarding pass.

When Violet joined the *Titanic* at Southampton, everything about the ship struck her and her companions as wonderful. The ship was familiar in many respects because of the *Olympic*, but grander and improved in every way. The crew felt proud of the *Titanic* because, in small ways, they were responsible for many changes and improvements that would make their life aboard less arduous and the ship more of a home. It was unusual for members of the crew to be consulted about changes. So when Thomas Andrews had asked for their opinions, they thought it a great privilege, and their esteem for him, already high, knew no bounds.

It was therefore like a big expectant family that Violet and her colleagues joined the *Titanic*, each looking to see whether his or her suggestion had been acted upon. The stewards, composed of men from the *Olympic* and other ships of the White Star Line—all picked crew—were delighted to find that their welfare in terms of their quarters (the 'glory holes') had not been overlooked. Violet said that no place could usually be so utterly devoid of glory, of comfort and privacy and so wretched a human habitation, as their quarters; they were foul places, nearly always infested with bugs. But this time, the crew found that they had been listened to. So they responded with a spontaneous vote of thanks and personal gift to Andrews. Rather diffidently, they asked him to honour them with a visit, which he did to receive their thanks. His gentle face lit up with genuine pleasure, for he alone understood how deeply these men must have felt in order to show any sentiment at all. He knew only too well their usual uncouth acceptance of most things, good or bad.

Life aboard the *Titanic* started off smoothly. Even Jenny, the ship's cat, immediately picked herself a comfortable corner; she varied her usual routine on previous ships by presenting the ship with a litter of kittens in April rather than at Christmas. Jenny had her kittens near Jim, the scullion whose approval she always sought on these occasions and who was devoted to her. This big, patient, overworked man, whose good humour was contagious, always seemed to need something to be kind to. But Jim was quieter than usual and somewhat distracted on the trip. He had left his wife behind, generally as cheerful as himself but on this occasion anxious that he should not join the new ship's crew because their baby was due. Jim wanted to give in to his wife's wish for she demanded so little of him, but there was the one-roomed home to keep going, so Jim had sailed, with a promise to bring beautiful clothes for the baby from New York.

Eagerly Violet and her companions joined the new ship—hundreds of curious eyes, each looking for what interested them most. Violet found that her bunk was placed the way she had suggested for privacy, and that there were the separate, though small, wardrobes for her and her companion, essential when two people of completely different tastes had to live together in a confined space. No longer would there be anxiety as to whether a colleague's clothes revealed her devotion to whisky and smoke. Violet's fellow stewardess, Elizabeth Leather, was the last person in the world Violet would have accused of drinking to excess. Elizabeth was staid, placid, restful, and with a dry wit that didn't bear a trace of malice. Born in Liverpool in June 1861, Elizabeth's father, Edward Edwards, had been a journalist on the *Liverpool Mercury*. She was one of ten children, and was nicknamed by her older brothers 'Sissie' (sister). She married a veterinary surgeon called Arthur Leather, but he was a drinker and died young; the couple had no children. After his death, Elizabeth went to sea as a stewardess with the White Star Line in order to support herself, giving her address as 28 Park Road, Port Sunlight. Now aged 50, Elizabeth had also served on the *Olympic* as a stewardess; on the *Titanic* she received monthly wages of £3 10s.

Violet and Elizabeth went aboard with plenty of time to spare. They enthused over the then-quite-novel idea of small private decks for the best suites, and the superb lace bedspreads they each had in their sections. They marvelled at the masterpieces of woodcarver's art from Ireland and Holland. There seemed to be nothing missing to satisfy the long list of distinguished names on the First Class passenger list, names well-known both in Europe and America. Violet and her colleagues felt the familiar thrill when they scanned the passenger list and found famous names. They speculated whether the owners of the suites would match the staff's conceptions of them, but what concerned them even more was what their idiosyncrasies might be. No doubt the stewardesses would find the passengers all very different to how they pictured them, for people nearly always were. Violet had found that the romance she could not help weaving around certain personalities, due mostly to the press, was often shattered on first meeting them. So it was not surprising when John Jacob Astor brought his bride Madeleine of about seven months, about whom there had been so much publicity, on board. Instead of the radiant woman of Violet's imagination, who had succeeded in overcoming much opposition and marrying the man she wanted, she saw a quiet, pale, sad-faced, and dull young woman arrive listlessly on the arm of her husband, apparently indifferent to everything around her. It struck Violet for the first time that all the wealth in the world did not make people happy.

Violet's daydreaming ended with the further arrival of passengers. Her heart sank as Mrs Klapton, clutching her pet Pekinese, bore down towards her section followed by a maid. Mrs Klapton invariably reduced each successive maid to submission before she boarded the ship. Their spirits would finally be broken by a combination of their mistress and the rough sea voyages. When she looked at that maid, Violet reflected that, although in many ways her job was not that prestigious, she could consider herself lucky. Two affable and well-groomed men passed by. Professional gamblers like that seemed to be travelling on every busy trip. With their suave manners and cold eyes, they would go to the Smoking Room. Violet felt sure that if one could but look through Purser Hugh McElroy's photograph album—his hobby and kept safely under lock and key—those faces would stare coldly from the pages of his rogues' gallery. Next appeared a delightful older couple—old in years and young in character—whom they were always happy to see. Isidor and Ida Straus had grown old together gracefully, and they were, as usual, charmed to see the stewardesses and with all the arrangements made for their comfort. They gave each of them an individual word of greeting as they made their way to the deck above to wave farewell to friends.

Suddenly, like the meteoric person she was, Miss Marcia Spatz arrived, all packages, hat boxes, and flowers galore—never-ending boxes of flowers from innumerable sources. She came with her usual determined look. On these occasions, Violet knew before the day was over she would need all her reserves of patience. She went forward to greet her. Miss Spatz appeared surprised to see the stewardess, registering both pleasure and annoyance, pleased because she would have someone who understood her many needs, and yet regretting it was not a stranger she could bully to her heart's content. In the distance Violet could see old Miss Townsend arriving. She had been blacklisted by another famous shipping line because of her unreasonable behaviour and her demoralizing effect on other passengers. She began by demanding mirrors everywhere and that the furniture in her stateroom be changed at once. Probably her happiest moments were spent watching the agonized struggles of a couple of perspiring stewards tackling the job.

Their red faces, however, were not all due to their exertions on her behalf. They had taken the precaution, when detailed for Miss Townsend's cabin, to step down to the pantry bar and refresh themselves with a couple of quick doubles, which whipped up their flagging spirits and sent them back determined to tell her off. But one glance at those chilly eyes only redoubled their efforts with the furniture. The one hope uppermost in their minds was getting her settled as soon as possible. Some uncanny instinct attracted William Hughes, the Second Steward, to them, drawing him from a crowd vainly sorting baggage that had no labels. He whispered a warning about the further use of whisky, which was received with an innocent look of surprise. The mere sight of Hughes always had the effect of sobering them as if by magic—although they never admitted it—for he was the object of respect, wonder, and fear all round. He had the power to detect the many transgressors among the crew. Violet had known him to be down on E Deck, busily engaged in an absorbing job, when suddenly and without reason he would dart up to B Deck and walk straight into the cubby hole where one of the Bedroom stewards was secretly enjoying a surreptitious cigarette—an offence regarded as a most heinous crime in passengers' accommodation—prior to taking his place in the pantry to carve at dinner time. On this particular day, Hughes looked satisfied, for things so far had gone well. The baggage, the bane of his life, had been satisfactorily distributed in spite of some passengers' eccentricities about labelling.

Gently, the *Titanic* disengaged herself from the side of the dock and they were off. Slipping gracefully away, full of high hope, over the din of send-off—goodbyes, fluttering flags, and waving handkerchiefs. The ship was proudly escorted by the tugs, tooting their farewells, while from the dock the sounds grew fainter. Few members of staff had the time or opportunity to witness the departure. Violet had often wished she could see the ship from some other vantage point, to know just how she moved on her way. She would have liked to have been a watcher instead of a worker. But however beautiful she pictured their new ship, she realized only too well it had to remain a wish, until a day when bills for rent, coal, and footwear did not loom so startlingly on her horizon.

Getting acquainted either with people or a ship was not an easy matter in bad weather; both showed to the worst advantage under unflattering conditions. But in this case, the sky was blue and the sea calm as far as the eye could see. Contentment and restfulness, following the recent strain of departure, spread over the *Titanic* as she cut her way proudly across the Channel. Even the two stewards had their beer in peace. William Hughes was taking things easy after his feverish activities in the last few weeks in Belfast. In fact, the well-known eccentrics among the passengers appeared to have become a little more human. Violet and her colleagues took full advantage of this lull in their demands to get settled, hard to do on any ship but infinitely more difficult on a new one.

Violet and Elizabeth started on their cabin, putting in place all the knick-knacks from their former cabin, like the family pictures and the calendars of restful country scenes, given to them at New Year in anticipation of the new ship. Also, the 'tidies', the receptacles for odd scraps, made by well-meaning friends, had to be placed to the best advantage under some extra light fittings. These had been obtained, with much ingenuity and tact, without Chief Electrician Peter Sloane's knowledge, and fixed up on the quiet by willing juniors. All these things had to be done in spare moments; the constant tap-tapping of busy hammers came from many a staff cabin. The work was helped along by the jests of curious colleagues who had dropped in on the pretext of offering help, but in reality for a drink and smoke in the privacy of the cabin.

For Violet, to have a breather during duty hours to pay social calls seemed too good to be true. She took the opportunity to run up to the Second Class Bar for a friendly call on Jack Stevens, to hear all about his new home, his recent wedding and, most importantly, his bride. Violet and Jack had been friends for a long time, the kind of friends that didn't mind giving each other a bit of frank opinion when the occasion arose, without fear of destroying the friendship. They had always got much enjoyment from exchanging experiences, for Jack had a strong tendency to see the ridiculous in sea life. In addition, they could always use each other's company as a shield and safeguard against social dangers, trusting each other as people do who know exactly the footing on which their friendship is based.

It was not strange, therefore, that Violet should seek Jack out to exchange opinions about the new ship; he alone knew that Violet did not like big ships, and that she was secretly afraid. However, they drank a toast to his happiness and to the *Titanic*. Then he proudly showed Violet all the improvements he had made to make his bar work easier. One night after dinner, Violet ran down to hear Matthews, the Chief Pantryman, tell of his experiences in Belfast while the *Titanic* was being built, beaming proudly. He strutted about like a benevolent Father Christmas, dispensing hospitality in the shape of double helpings of Christmas pudding to 'the boys', stewards from the age of 14 to 60. On their round of visits they did not forget William O'Loughlin, the Surgeon, whose door was always open and a temptation to bandy words with one who regarded life with a twinkle in his eye. To peep into his magnificently appointed cabin and hear his sometimes extravagant description of how he spent his holidays was always a joy. They teasingly asked him how anyone so charming and kind had remained a bachelor, and counselled him to take a good wife, to which he replied: 'Sure, haven't I worn all the knees out of me pants proposing to ladies and sure they won't have anything to do with me at all.' Meanwhile the eyes of Violet and her companions wandered round his room adorned with silver-framed photographs of beautiful and talented women.

Often during their rounds they came upon Thomas Andrews going around unobtrusively with a tired face but a satisfied air. He never failed to stop for a cheerful word, his only regret that they were getting further from home. They all knew the love he had for Ulster, and suspected that he longed to get back to the peace of its atmosphere for a much needed rest and to forget ship designing for a while.

After the sea trials in Belfast Lough, on Tuesday 2 April, the crew had finally taken over from the shipbuilders and proceeded to Southampton. It was clear to everybody on board that they had a ship that was going to create the greatest stir British shipping circles had ever known. For one thing, the *Titanic* was the first ship to be fitted with a third propeller, driven by a low-powered turbine. For manoeuvring, the two wing propellers alone were used, but once clear of the land, steam from low-pressure cylinders was turned into this turbine, and it gave the ship a wonderful turn of speed. While in Southampton, there was a reshuffle among the senior officers. Because the *Olympic* was laid up, the directors of the White Star Line thought it would be a good idea to send Henry Wilde, its Chief Officer, just for the one voyage, as Chief Officer of the *Titanic*. The thinking was that his experience of the sister ship would be useful. This decision threw Herbert Lightoller and William Murdoch out of their stride, and, apart from the disappointment of being demoted, caused some confusion. Murdoch, having been Chief Officer, took over Lightoller's duties as First Officer, while Lightoller stepped into Blair's shoes, as Second Officer, and picked up the many threads of his job, and Blair was left behind. The other officers remained as before, and a couple of days in Southampton saw Murdoch and Lightoller settled in their new positions and familiar with their duties.

Lightoller felt that the Board of Trade inspections on Tuesday 9 April were carried out to everyone's satisfaction. The lifeboats and lifesaving equipment were tested, exercised, and passed, and the 'fireworks' (distress rockets, distress signals, blue lights, and so on) examined, tried, and approved. All these, and the many other details linked to an Atlantic liner preparing for sea, were gone through. Lightoller claimed that since the *Titanic* was a new ship, even more care was taken than usual, compared to a ship on her settled run. The Board of Trade surveyor, Captain Maurice Clark, lived up to his reputation of being the best in the South of England at that time. Many small details, that another surveyor would have taken in his stride, accepting the statement of the officer concerned, were not good enough for Clark. He had to see everything, and check every item on the survey for himself. He would not accept anyone's word as sufficient—and got cursed by the crew as a result. He did his job, and did it thoroughly. Finally, the day for sailing arrived, and from end to end the ship, which for days had been like a nest of bees, resembled a hive about to swarm. As 'zero' hour drew near, order could be seen arising out of chaos. On the stroke of the hour, the gangway was lowered, the whistle blown, ropes let go, and the tugs took the strain. The *Titanic* was on its way.

Like Lawrence Beesley, Lightoller found that before the *Titanic* cleared the dock, they had a striking example of the power that lay in her engines and propellers. The *Oceanic* and *New York* were lying moored to the wharf alongside each other. They happened to be in a position where the *Titanic* had to make a slight turn, which required coming astern on her port engine. The terrific suction set up in that shallow water simply dragged both liners away from the wharf. The *New York* broke away altogether, and the *Oceanic* was dragged off until a 60-foot gangway dropped from the wharf into the water. It looked as if nothing could stop the *New York* crashing into the

Titanic's stern, and in fact it was only Captain Smith's experience and resourcefulness that saved her. The *Titanic* dwarfed these two ships, and made them look like cross-Channel ferries, and the wash from her propellers was similarly large. Just as a collision seemed inevitable, Captain Smith gave the *Titanic* a touch ahead on her port engine, which simply washed the *New York* away, and kept her clear until a couple of tugs, to everyone's enormous relief, got hold, and took her back alongside the wharf. Lightoller felt that to the casual observer the whole incident would have been just a thrill—perhaps not much more even though there had been a collision. For the crew, who were habitually suspicious, it would have meant something much deeper.

The greatest care had to be taken while threading their way down the comparatively shallow channel of Southampton Water and eventually out to Spithead. There was a general feeling of relief when at last they got the ship into deep water. They then went across the Channel to Cherbourg—a short run which barely warmed the ship up.

'A Wonderful Passage
Up To Now'

At 3.40 p.m. on Wednesday 10 April, passengers arriving at the Gare Maritime in Cherbourg on the *Train Transatlantique* from Paris were told that the *Titanic* was running late because of the near collision with the *New York* at Southampton. At 6.30 p.m., the *Titanic* dropped anchor, and 22 passengers disembarked. The tenders *Nomadic* and *Traffic* had been specially constructed at Harland & Wolff for use in Cherbourg because the Olympic Class liners were too large to fit in the small port. The *Nomadic* ferried 172 First and Second Class passengers out to the ship, *Traffic* the remaining 102 Third Class passengers and the mail. By 8 p.m., all the passengers were aboard and the tenders returned to the shore.

Among the Third Class passengers who boarded were a mother and her two children. The tickets bought by the family had cost £15

4s 11d, and they had been waiting in the French port for six days, in a hotel with other migrants. While the *Titanic* was undergoing its sea trials in Belfast Lough, Hanna Touma and her two children had been travelling to Beirut, in the Lebanon, thousands of miles to the East. Hanna was born in a tiny village called Tibnin, in the Lebanon. It was a tradition that the siblings of the family acquired their father's first name as their last name. Hanna's father's name was Youssef Razi. Therefore her maiden name was Hanna Youssef Razi. In those days, no one in the Lebanon had birth certificates. Age was calculated by the 'seasons' of the year. Hanna was born fifteen seasons before the turn of the century, on 10 April 1885, and her future husband Darwis Touma thirty seasons before the turn of the century, or 1870. They had got married in 1899. Hanna had been 14, Darwis 29. The couple had two children, Maria and Georges. Maria was born in October 1902, and Georges in February 1904.

Working in the onion fields, Darwis Touma had saved a little money to pay for a passage to America. His brother, Abraham, had gone with him. They settled in the small town of Dowagiac, in Michigan. Their plan, like that of most migrants, was to earn enough to send for their families to join them. Darwis had little success in this, and seven years passed. He could not save as he had been sending Hanna a little money from time to time. Abraham, on the other hand, had saved enough since he had no dependants to support. He knew his brother was unhappy, and how much he missed his family, so he decided he would use some of his money for Hanna's passage. Abraham sent his sister-in-law enough money for the trip, along with a piece of paper which said 'Dowagiac, Michigan'. His intention was to surprise his brother. Hanna treasured this piece of paper. Even though she had no idea where this place was, it was where her husband lived, and that was where she was going. From some time after Darwis had left for America, and until she died, Darwis's aunt lived with Hanna and the children. Hanna worked the farm after Darwis left, and saved what she could. Darwis's aunt had some money which was left to her when her husband died. So when Hanna received the letter from Abraham with the money for her and the children to go to America she wasted no time selling her personal items and the hut that she lived in.

Hanna and the children travelled from Tibnin to Beirut by camel caravan. The days were long and exhausting, the nights short, and they did not have enough sleep or rest. The caravan company supplied the tents that they slept in, and the food which they ate—yoghurt, cheese, and olives stuffed in pitta bread, spiced with onions and garlic. While this was a typical Arab meal, washed down with homemade wine, Hanna was a Christian. About a dozen other families from Tibnin accompanied the Touma family. Since the villagers brought their own musical instruments with them, the evenings were enjoyable. They had homemade flutes made from hollow pipes, and small hand drums covered with goat skins. Everyone danced in a circle with the men spinning their handkerchiefs high in the air. Even Maria and Georges enjoyed dancing as, along with a few other children, they tried to keep up with the adults.

When Hanna and the children reached Beirut, they left the camel caravan behind, and followed those going to America on a freighter to France. On the voyage, the food was poor and the cabin cramped. It took five days. The migrants boarded a train in France, and on the three-day journey to Cherbourg the children ran through all the carriages to see if there were any other children on the train besides the ones travelling with the villagers. Maria and Georges found that the other children spoke differently, and they could not understand them, but they found ways to amuse themselves.

Earlier the same day the *Titanic* had sailed down Spithead, past the Isle of Wight which looked beautiful in spring foliage, exchanged salutes with a White Star tug lying-to waiting for one of the inward bound liners, and the passengers saw in the distance several warships with attendant black destroyers guarding the entrance from the sea. In the calmest weather the ship got to Cherbourg at dusk and left again, after taking passengers and mail on board, at about 8.30 p.m. The ship reached Queenstown on the Irish coast at about noon on Thursday 11 April, after an enjoyable voyage across the Channel, although the wind was almost too cold in the morning to allow people to sit out on deck.

The coast of Ireland looked beautiful as the *Titanic* approached Queenstown Harbour, the brilliant morning sun showing up the green hillsides and picking out the groups of houses dotted here and there above the rugged grey cliffs that fringed the coast. The ship took the Pilot on board, ran slowly towards the harbour with the sounding-line dropping all the time, and came to a stop well out to sea, with the propellers churning up the bottom and turning the sea brown with sand. It seemed to schoolteacher Lawrence Beesley as if the ship had stopped rather suddenly, that perhaps the harbour entrance was too shallow. Passengers and mail were put on board from the tenders *America* and *Ireland*, and nothing gave a better sense of the enormous length and bulk of the *Titanic* than to stand as far astern as possible and look over the side from the top deck, forwards and downwards, to where the tenders rolled at her bow, tiny beside the majestic vessel that rose deck after deck above them. There was something very graceful in the movement of the *Titanic* as she rode up and down on the slight swell in the harbour, a slow, stately dip and recover, only noticeable by watching her bow in comparison with some landmark on the nearby coast. The two little tenders tossing up and down like corks beside her illustrated vividly the advances that had been made in comfort aboard the modern liners.

Another incident occurred at Queenstown which some passengers saw as an omen. As one of the tenders neared the *Titanic*, some of those on board gazed up at the liner towering above them, and saw a stoker's head, black from his work in the hold below, peering out at them from the top of one of the enormous funnels—a dummy one for ventilation—that rose many feet above the highest deck. He had climbed up inside for a joke, but for some of those who saw him there the sight seemed ominous. Shortly afterwards, the work of transfer was ended, the tenders cast off, and at 1.30 p.m., with the propellers churning up the sea bottom again, the *Titanic* turned slowly through a quarter-circle until her nose pointed down along the Irish coast, and then steamed rapidly away from Queenstown, a little house to the left of the town gleaming white on the hillside for many miles astern. In the ship's wake, hundreds of gulls had soared and screamed, quarrelling and fighting over the remnants of the lunch that had poured out of the waste pipes as the *Titanic* lay-to in the harbour entrance. Now they followed expecting more. Beesley watched them for a long time and was astonished at the ease with which they soared and kept up with the ship with hardly a motion of their wings.

Picking out a particular gull, Beesley watched it for minutes at a time and saw no movement of its wings upwards or downwards. The bird would tilt to one side or another as the gusts of wind caught it, rigidly unbendable, as an aeroplane tilts sideways in a puff of wind. And yet with graceful ease it kept pace with the *Titanic* forging through the water at 20 knots. As the wind met the gull it would rise upwards and obliquely forwards, and come down slantingly again, its wings curved in a beautiful arch and its tail feathers outspread as a fan. Beesley realized the bird knew a secret than Man was only just beginning to learn—that of utilizing air currents up and down on which it could glide at will with the expenditure of the minimum amount of energy, or of using them as a ship does when it sails within one or two points of a head wind. Airmen, of course, were beginning to imitate the gull, and Beesley thought that soon perhaps an aeroplane or glider might be seen dipping gracefully up and down in the face of an opposing wind and all the time forging ahead across the Atlantic. The gulls were still behind the ship when night fell, and still they screamed and dipped down into the broad wake of foam which the *Titanic* left behind. However in the morning they were gone; perhaps they had seen a steamer in the night bound for their Queenstown home and had escorted her back.

All afternoon, the ship steamed along the coast of Ireland, with grey cliffs guarding the shores, and the hills rising behind gaunt and barren. As dusk fell, the coast rounded away to the North West, and the last they saw of Europe was the Irish mountains dim and faint in the dropping darkness. With the thought that they had seen the last of land until they set foot on the shores of America, Beesley retired to the Library to write letters. From the time of leaving Queenstown on the Thursday to the Sunday morning the sea was calm—so calm, indeed, that very few people were absent from meals—the wind westerly and south-westerly ('fresh' as the daily chart described it), but often rather cold, generally too cold to sit out on deck to read or write. Many of the passengers spent much of the time in the Library, reading and writing letters. Beesley wrote a large number, and posted them each day in the box outside the Library door.

Each morning, the sun rose behind the ship in a sky of circular clouds, stretching round the horizon in long, narrow streaks and rising tier upon tier above the skyline, red and pink and fading from pink to white, as the sun rose higher in the sky. For someone like Beesley who had not crossed the Atlantic before (or even been out of sight of the shores of England), it was beautiful to stand on the top deck and watch the swell of the sea extending outwards from the ship in an unbroken circle until it met the skyline with its hint of infinity. Behind, the wake of the vessel was white with foam where the propeller blades had cut up the long Atlantic rollers and with them made a level white road bounded on either side by banks of green, blue, and blue-green waves. These soon swept away the white road, though for the time being it stretched back to the horizon and dipped over the edge of the world back to Ireland and the gulls. Along it, the morning sun glittered and sparkled. And each night the sun sank right in their eyes along the sea, making an undulating glittering pathway, a golden track charted on the surface of the ocean which the ship followed unswervingly until the sun dipped below the edge of the horizon, and the pathway ran ahead faster than they could steam, and slipped over the edge of the skyline. It was as if the sun had been a golden ball and had wound up its thread of gold too quickly for Beesley and the other passengers to follow.

From noon on the Thursday to noon on the Friday the ship travelled 386 miles; from Friday to Saturday 519; and from Saturday to Sunday 546. Purser Hugh McElroy said that the second day's run was a disappointment, and they would not now dock until the morning of Wednesday 17 April instead of Tuesday night. However on the Sunday they were glad to see a longer run had been made, and it was thought they would make New York on the Tuesday night after all. The Purser remarked 'They are not pushing her this trip and do not intend to make any fast running: I don't suppose we shall do more than 546 now; it is not a bad day's run for the first trip.' This was at lunch, and the conversation then turned to the speed and build of Atlantic liners. All those who had crossed many times were unanimous that the *Titanic* was the most comfortable ship they had been on, and they preferred the speed they were making to that of the faster ones. First, there was less vibration. Second, the faster ships bore through the waves with a twisted, screw-like motion instead of the straight up-and-down swing of the *Titanic*. Beesley called the attention of his table to the way the ship listed to port, and they all watched the skyline through the portholes as they sat. It was clear that she did list, for the skyline and the sea on the port side were visible most of the time, whereas on the starboard side there was only sky. The Purser remarked that probably coal had been used mainly from the starboard side.

It was interesting to stand on the Boat Deck, as Beesley frequently did, in the angle between Lifeboats 13 and 15 on the starboard side, and watch the general motion of the ship through the waves resolve itself into two movements—one seen by contrasting the Docking-Bridge, from which the log-line trailed away behind in the foaming wake, with the horizon, and observing the long, slow heave as they rode up and down. Beesley timed the average for one up-and-down vibration. The second movement was a side-to-side roll, and could be calculated by watching the port rail and contrasting it with the horizon. It seemed likely that this double motion was due to the angle at which their direction to New York cut the general set of the Gulf Stream sweeping from the Gulf of Mexico across to Europe. The almost clock-like regularity of the two vibratory movements was what attracted Beesley's attention: it was while watching the side roll that he first became aware of the list to port.

Looking down astern from the Boat Deck or from B Deck to the Third Class quarters, Beesley noticed how the passengers were enjoying every minute of the voyage; a skipping game of the mixed-double type was the favourite, while an Irish migrant went around playing the *uilleann* or elbow pipes; he had played 'Erin's Lament' on leaving Queenstown. Standing aloof from all of them, generally on the raised Stern Deck above, was a man of about 20 to 24 years of age, well-dressed, always with gloves and nicely groomed, and obviously quite out of place among his fellow passengers—he never looked happy. Beesley watched him, and guessed he was a man who had been a failure in some way at home and had received the proverbial shilling plus Third Class fare to America. He did not look resolute or happy enough to be working out his own problem. Nils Johansson, from Svaneryd, in Sweden, on the other hand, was working in the United States, and was bringing home his fiancée, Olga Lundin. They were going to his uncle's home in Chicago. Johansson was travelling in Third Class, but had placed Olga in Second; they originally had both had Third Class tickets but Olga had moved to get a better cabin. Johansson would climb the stairs leading to the Second Deck and talk affectionately with Olga across the low gate which separated them.

Like Lawrence Beesley, but from Third Class, Frank and Emily Goldsmith stood close to the centre of the ship's stern rail watching Ireland slowly disappear from view. With a thumping heart Frank cried 'Mummy! At last we are on the Atlantic.' The next few days were exciting. Like any 9-year-old boy, Frank had searched for all the other boys so that they could get together and wring every drop of pleasure from their environment. Soon they had built up a small gang of about eight, and had been having lots of fun together, prior to reaching Queenstown. After leaving Ireland, one of the first things they tried was climbing onto a baggage crane. The aim was to grasp the cable under the crane's arm and from a hanging position move hand over hand to the end of the arm, then drop to the deck. Frank was the first boy to try this prank, but he was also the last. Unknown to the boys, the deck maintenance crewmen had just treated the cable with grease to protect it from corrosion. When Frank felt the slippery cable, he hung onto it with all his strength. He heard loud laughter that started just a few seconds later. Afterwards, it took several vigorous washings before Emily could clean his hands.

Frank and the other boys spent a lot of time peering down into the ship's boiler rooms, watching the stokers and firemen at work. The men were singing, and often, while the boys looked down, they rattled their shovels on the grates of the burners, keeping time. The days passed, and on the Sunday morning Emily took Frank to Sunday school and the church service. When it ended, she took him to the Purser's Office. There was usually a list of the names of the passengers the Purser wished to see on the window, and on it she saw 'Alfred Rush' listed. They went upstairs to the open deck near the stern of the ship. Looking around, Emily saw Alfred and called to him. He came over, and she told him that he should go down to learn why the Purser wanted him. Shortly afterwards he came running back upstairs, dashed over to them, and thrust his hand out, crying 'Look, Mrs Goldsmith! I've got a birthday present!' In his hand there was a sixpenny piece. It was a refund of an overpayment of his baggage charges. Frank said 'Alfie, a birthday present?' Alfred said 'Why yes, Frankie. I am 16 years old today. Look, I am wearing my long trousers.'

On the morning of Friday 12 April, Edith Brown had been awake for some time in her cabin in Second Class, thinking about what her new life would be like in Seattle and wondering what it would be like not knowing anyone. Lying there quietly, she could hear the distant, regular throb of the engines from deep down in the ship. In the passageway outside their cabin, there was a clink now and then of crockery from the morning tea being served. She finally sat up, pulled her blankets to one side and, turning, climbed down the little bunk ladder to the cabin floor. At the same time her mother, in the lower berth, pulled her curtains open and greeted her daughter, who was now crossing the cabin floor to look out of the porthole. Both women had slept well; they decided it was the sea air. Looking out of the porthole, Edith could see that it was the start of another nice day, with a calm sea and the sun trying to break through the grey early morning cloud. Both women decided to dress before Thomas arrived to take them up on deck for a morning stroll before breakfast.

During his walk around the Boat Deck, Captain Edward Smith stopped at the Browns, who were sitting in deckchairs. The Captain asked them all if they were enjoying the voyage. Thomas answered for them, saying that sailing on the *Titanic* had been a most enjoyable experience, especially on her maiden voyage. Captain Smith then turned his attention to Edith. Smiling, he asked 'And how about you, young lady?' Edith, first looking at her mother and then back to the Captain, said 'It's the best ship we've ever been on.' Captain Smith, laughing at that, said he was glad to hear it. Edith then asked if there were dogs on board the ship. The Captain said the ship did have dogs on board, and that the Chief Butcher usually looked after them. They could be exercised on one of the upper decks, known by the crew as the 'Dog Deck', and situated up by one of the funnels. Edith asked the Captain if he had a dog. He said he did. 'But not on board ship, I hasten to add. He's back home, where he should be. When I get back to Southampton after this voyage, I shall have more time to spend with him.'

Sunday 14 April started much the same as the previous few days for Elizabeth and her daughter, with Elizabeth on that occasion being first out of bed and peering out of the porthole. On returning to her bunk, she noticed Edith stirring and apologized if she had woken her. She went on to mention that the sea remained calm and the weather fine. A short time later, Thomas tapped on their door as usual, to let them know that he was up and about and would be waiting for them to join him up on deck for their early morning walk. They enjoyed their regular walks about the decks before break-fast in order to get some sea air and an appetite before going down to the Dining Saloon. Once up on deck, they soon realized that, despite the calm weather, it was much cooler outside; certainly the coldest day of the voyage so far. After a brisk walk around the Boat Deck, they decided they should go below.

In the Dining Room, several other passengers commented on the drop in temperature. Others spoke again about the vibration being felt in some cabins during the night. Some were under the impres-sion that the ship gathered speed at night, when everyone was asleep, and returned to the normal cruising speed at daybreak. Before din-ner that evening, the Browns decided to brave the cold and went up on deck to witness a calm, almost glass-like sea and a beautiful sun-set. Once again it was too cold to remain up there for long and, after taking in the splendour of the setting sun, they went below to take their seats in the Dining Room. During the meal, the conversation came round to the noticeable drop in temperature during the day. At 10 p.m., Elizabeth and Edith decided to retire to their cabin for the night, leaving Thomas to return to the Smoking Room after escort-ing his wife and daughter below.

Archibald Gracie IV found that, towards evening on the Sunday, it was reported that wireless messages from passing steamers had been received advising the officers of the *Titanic* of the presence of icebergs and ice floes. The increasing cold and need to be more warmly dressed when out on deck appeared to confirm these warnings. But despite them, the ship did not slow down, and the engines kept up their steady running. On his various trips across the Atlantic, it had been Gracie's habit, whenever the weather permitted, to take as much exercise as he could. However on board the *Titanic*, during the first days of the voyage, from Wednesday to Saturday, he had spent his time talking to other passengers and reading books from the ship's well-stocked Library. He enjoyed himself, in part because there was nothing to indicate or suggest they were on the stormy Atlantic. The motion of the ship and noise of its engines were barely noticeable on deck or in the saloons, day or night. But when Sunday morning came, Gracie felt it was time to take some exercise, and he decided to use the squash court, gymnasium, and swimming pool for the rest of the voyage. He was up early before breakfast and met Frederick Wright, the Racquet Court Attendant, for a half hour warm-up, before a swim in the six-foot deep tank of salt water. Wright reminded Gracie of hundreds of young Englishmen he had seen and with whom he had played cricket.

Gracie was an amateur military historian and member of the wealthy family of New York State. He had boarded at Southampton, having paid a First Class fare of £28 10s; he occupied Cabin C51. Gracie had been born on 17 January 1859, in Mobile, Alabama. His father, General Gracie, had been educated in Heidelberg and at West Point Military Academy. He had resigned from the Army in 1856 to go into the cotton-brokerage business. At the outbreak of the American Civil War, he broke with his Unionist father and served with the Confederate forces as Militia Captain of the Washington Light Infantry. In 1862, he had been promoted to Brigadier General and fought through the Battle of Chickamauga, one of the bloodiest battles of the Civil War. General Gracie had been killed in December 1864 while observing Union Army movements at the siege of Petersburg,

Virginia. Respected by his troops, he had been eulogized in the poem 'Gracie, of Alabama'.

His son Archibald was a graduate of St Paul's Academy in Concord, New Hampshire, and also of West Point; he later became a Colonel in the Seventh Regiment, United States Army. Gracie was independently wealthy, and active in the real estate business; his home was on 16th Street in Washington. Now aged 53, Gracie was married with four daughters. Gracie was only five years old when his father died, and later he spent seven years writing a book *The Truth About Chickamauga* (1911). In 1912, following its publication, he decided he needed to relax, and took a trip to Europe on the *Oceanic*. He took return passage on the *Titanic*. Its passenger lists had recorded him as an 'alien' passenger embarked at Southampton, 'Col Archibald Gracie', travelling on ticket number 113780.

One of the best-known characters on the ship was Thomas McCawley, the Gymnasium steward whom Lawrence Beesley had met soon after he went on board, a sturdy man in white flannels. With tireless enthusiasm he had showed Gracie and other passengers the various mechanical devices under his charge, and urged them to use them, demonstrating bicycle racing, rowing, boxing, and camel and horseback riding. The exercise and swim gave Gracie an appetite for a hearty breakfast. Then a church service in the Dining Saloon had followed. He was impressed with the 'Prayer for Those at Sea' and the words of the hymn 'O God Our Help in Ages Past'. He had finished Mary Johnston's book *The Old Dominion* (1906), and returned it to the ship's Library.

During the day, Gracie saw much of Isidor and Ida Straus. In fact, from the very beginning of the trip the three had been together several times each day. He had been with them on the deck the day they left Southampton and witnessed the accident to the American liner, *New York*, lying at her pier, when the displacement of water by the

Titanic had pulled the smaller ship from her moorings and nearly caused a collision. At the time, Straus was telling Gracie that it seemed only a few years earlier that he had been a passenger on the *New York*, on her maiden trip, and when she was thought of as the last word in shipbuilding. He had drawn attention to the progress that had been made since, by comparing the two ships lying side by side. During their daily talks, Straus had told Gracie much about his remarkable career, beginning with his early life in Georgia when, with the Confederate Government Commissioners, he had run the blockade of Europe as an agent for the purchase of supplies; his friendship with President Cleveland; and also the honours he had received. On the Sunday, Straus had finished Gracie's own *The Truth About Chickamauga*. About midday, the couple were particularly happy, anticipating sending a telegraph to their son and daughter-in-law who were on their way to Europe on board the *Amerika*. Some time before 6 p.m., contented, they told Gracie of the message they had received in reply.

After dinner, as usual, Gracie adjourned to the Palm Room with his companions James Clinch Smith, a lawyer originally from New York, and Edward Kent, an architect from Buffalo, New York, to have coffee and to listen to the music of the *Titanic*'s band. From the Palm Room, the men always went to the Smoking Room, and almost every evening joined in conversation. Major Archibald Butt, President Taft's Military Aide, discussed politics, while Clarence Moore, a businessman from Washington, told the story of his trip some years earlier through the West Virginia woods and mountains, when he had helped a newspaper reporter obtain an interview with the outlaw, Captain Anse Hatfield. Francis D. Millet, the painter, sculptor, and writer, and Director of the American Academy in Rome, was planning a journey west. Arthur Ryerson, originally from Cooperstown, New York, had boarded at Cherbourg with his wife Emily, their children Suzette (21), Emily (18), and John (13), and the family's maid. The family were returning home because of the death of their son Arthur. During these evenings, Gracie talked to John B. Thayer, Second Vice-President of the Pennsylvania Railroad, and George D. Widener, son of the Philadelphia streetcar magnate. For the first time on the voyage, Gracie's stay in the Smoking Room on this particular evening was short, and he retired early at around 9 p.m. Charles Cullen, his Bedroom steward, promised to waken him the next morning for another game of racquets, work in the gymnasium, and a swim before breakfast.

Eva Hart found that, during the voyage, the pattern of their lives was that her mother slept all day, and her father looked after her. She had most of her meals with him and then, when the time came for Eva to get ready for bed, Esther got up. She bathed Eva, put her to bed, and then dressed before going up to dinner. Esther spent the evenings with Benjamin and the other passengers; then, when everyone else went to bed, she sat fully dressed with her sewing or her reading. She did this every night they were at sea. Other people in Second Class learnt about this and became accustomed to seeing her only at breakfast and dinner. She never appeared for lunch. When they saw her at breakfast they sometimes laughed and said 'What have you heard during the night?' and 'Are you taking care of us?' They did not take her foreboding seriously, and thought she was worrying needlessly.

Eva had a marvellous time being looked after by her father. Benjamin was much less strict than Esther, and Eva, in her turn, adored him and was delighted to have so much of his time. He played with her, took her to the nursery, bought her toys, and together they explored as much of the ship as they could. In the course of their explorations, Eva made friends with a small dog and spent a great deal of time playing with it. She loved it so much that she hurried through her breakfast each morning and then rushed off to find it, as by then she hadn't seen it for more than twelve hours. At the age of 7, that length of time seemed an eternity. Benjamin saw how fond she had become of this small, flat-faced, endearing dog and promised to buy her one when they got to Canada. When Eva wasn't playing with the dog or sightseeing around the ship, her special playmate was another girl of about her own age. Nina Harper was particularly fond of the large teddy bear which Benjamin had bought from the Christmas display at Gamages Department Store in Holborn in London. Nina was on her way to the United States, and she was travelling with her father John, minister of the Walworth Road Baptist Church in London, and her aunt Jessie Leitch. The two girls made quite a spectacle as they dragged this teddy with them all over the ship.

On the Saturday night, Esther had stayed up as usual and heard an odd sound which she did not associate with the normal life of the ship. Because of this she roused her husband and persuaded him to go on deck to find out what it was. When he came back he was rather annoyed and said 'Oh, don't ask me to do that again. I felt so foolish when I bumped into one of the officers and he wanted to know what I was doing up there. All I could say was that my wife had heard something odd.' The following morning, when they were at breakfast together, they noticed that the temperature was much colder. And during the meal, several people came over to their table and asked Esther if she had heard the noise during the night. After they had eaten and were leaving the Dining Room, Esther saw a notice pinned on the green baize board inside the door informing passengers of a church service later in the morning. So instead of going to bed, as she had done on other mornings, she stayed up and attended the 11 a.m. service.

As it was near lunchtime when the service finished, Esther decided that on this occasion she would stay up and join them for lunch. Because of this, Eva's father made quite an occasion of it. The meal included Chicken Maryland, salmon, ox tongue, and a wide range of cheeses. Afterwards, Eva and her parents went to the Library to rest for a short time before Esther left them to go to bed. She took the opportunity to write a letter to her family back in Chadwell Heath. On notepaper embossed with the White Star Line flag and headed 'On board RMS Titanic', she wrote:

My Dear ones all,

As you see it is Sunday afternoon and we are resting in the library after luncheon. I was very bad all day yesterday could not eat or drink, and sick all the while, but today I have got over it. This morning Eva and I went to church and she was so pleased they sang 'O God Our Help in Ages Past', that is her hymn she sang so nicely. So she sang out loudly she is very bonny. She has a nice ball and a box of toffee and a photo of this ship bought her today. Everybody takes notice of her through the Teddy Bear. There is to be a concert on board tomorrow night in aid of the Sailors' Home and she is going to sing so am I. Well, the sailors say we have had a wonderful passage up to now. There has been no tempest, but God knows what it must be like when there is one. This mighty expanse of water, no land in sight and the ship rolling from side to side is being wonderful. Tho they say this Ship does not roll on account of its size. Any how it rolls enough for me, I shall never forget it. It is very nice weather but awfully windy and cold. They say we *may* get into New York Tuesday night but we are really due early on Wednesday morning, shall write as soon as we get there. This letter won't leave the ship but will remain and come back to England where she is due again on the 26th. When you see the letter all of a screw is where she rolls and shakes my arm. I am sending you on a menu to show how we live. I shall be looking forward to a line from somebody to cheer me up a bit. I am always shutting my eyes and I see everything as I left it. I hope you are all quite well. Let this be an all round letter as I can't write properly to all 'till I can set my foot on shore again. We have met some nice people on board, *Lucy*, and so it has been nice so far. But oh the long, long days and nights. It's the longest break I ever spent in my life. I must close now with all our fondest love to all of you. From your loving Ess. Heaps of love and kisses to all from Eva.

Following her normal routine, Esther got up again on Sunday in order to join her husband for dinner. By this time Eva was already asleep in her bunk cuddling her doll. After dinner, Benjamin became annoyed. He and his wife had gone for their usual short after-dinner stroll around the Promenade Deck, and everywhere they went there was gambling of some kind going on. He had an aversion to betting of any sort because his own father had been a compulsive gambler. As a result, he had seen what a detrimental effect it could have. During that walk around the ship, he saw sweepstakes being run and all sorts of books being made on the progress of the *Titanic*. Although there was no possibility of capturing the Blue Riband, the ship had gone more than 500 miles in one day. As a result, the passengers were wagering on almost everything—how far they had gone in a day, how near land they were, and what time they would dock.

This all annoyed him, so that he said 'I can't stand all this gambling. I'm reading an interesting book so I shall go to bed early and read.' So, with Eva already tucked up and asleep in bed and Benjamin lying in his bunk reading, Esther continued her lonely, self-imposed vigil, reading in the chair by the side of Eva's bunk and all the time waiting and listening.

Like the Hart family, Lawrence Beesley found on the Sunday that a service was held in the Saloon by the Purser in the morning. Going on deck after lunch, he and the other passengers noted such a change in the temperature that not many cared to remain to face the bitter wind. Beesley felt there was no wind blowing at the time, for he had noticed the same force of wind approaching Queenstown, to find that it had died away as soon as they stopped, only to rise again as they steamed away from the harbour.

Returning to the Library, he stopped for a moment to read again the day's run and observe their position on the chart. The Reverend Ernest Carter, a Church of England clergyman, was similarly engaged, and the two renewed a conversation they had enjoyed for some days. It had begun with a discussion of the relative merits of Carter's university (Oxford) with Beesley's (Cambridge) as worldwide educational agencies, the opportunities at each for the formation of 'character', and had led on to the lack of sufficiently qualified men to take up the work of the Church of England, and from that on to Carter's work as a vicar. He told Beesley some of his problems in his parish, St Jude, Commercial Street, in Whitechapel in London, and spoke of the impossibility of doing half his work in his Church without the help of his wife Lily. Daughter of Thomas Hughes, author of *Tom Brown's School Days* (1857), Beesley knew her only slightly, but meeting her later in the day realized something of what Carter had meant in attributing a large part of his success to her. Carter next mentioned the absence of a service in the evening and asked if Beesley knew Purser Hugh McElroy well enough to request the use of the Saloon. The Purser agreed at once, and Carter made preparations during the afternoon by asking everyone he knew—and many he did not—to come to the Saloon at 8.30 p.m.

The Library was crowded that afternoon, owing to the cold on deck. However through the windows they could see a clear sky with brilliant sunlight that seemed to augur a fine night and clear day. The prospect of landing in two days, with calm weather all the way to

New York, meant that everyone was content. Beesley could later recall every detail of the Library that afternoon—the beautifully furnished room, with armchairs, and small writing- or card-tables scattered about, writing-bureaus round the walls of the room, and the glass-cased shelves flanking one side—the whole finished in mahogany relieved with the white-fluted wooden columns that supported the deck above. Through the windows there was the covered corridor, reserved by general agreement as the children's playground. Here were playing two boys, Loto and Louis Hoffman, with their devoted father never far away from them; it was said that the boys' mother was dead. In the corridor were Arthur West and his wife Ada with their two children, Constance and Barbara; he was usually carrying one of them. Originally from Truro in Cornwall, Arthur had previously worked in a department store and the family were now emigrating to Florida, where he planned to work in the fruit business. They were all young and happy; Arthur was always dressed in a grey 'knickerbocker' suit, with a camera slung over his shoulder.

Close to Beesley, so near that he could not avoid hearing scraps of their conversation, were two American women, both dressed in white—young, and probably friends. One had been to India and was returning by way of England, the other was a school teacher in America, a graceful woman with a distinguished air heightened by a pair of pince-nez perched on the end of her nose. A man was talking to them, a well-known resident of Cambridge, Massachusetts, genial, polished, and courteous towards the two women, whom he had known only for a few hours. From time to time, a child broke in on their conversation and insisted that they take notice of a large doll clasped in her arms. In the opposite corner were William Harbeck and Henriette Yvois, the American film-maker and his French mistress, very fond of playing Patience, which she was doing now, while her lover sat back in his chair watching the game and interrupting from time to time with suggestions. In the middle of the room were two Catholic priests, one quietly reading. Father Thomas Byles was originally from Leeds, and was travelling to New York to officiate at his brother's wedding in Brooklyn. The other was a dark, bearded man, with a broad-brimmed hat, talking earnestly to a friend in German and evidently explaining some verse in the open Bible before him. Father Josef Peruschitz was a Benedictine monk, born in Straßlach-Dingharting in Bavaria, and travelling to Minnesota, to teach at the Swiss Congregation's Benedictine School. Near them was a young engineer, also Catholic, on his way to Mexico.

Looking over this room, with his back to the library shelves, was Thomas Kelland, the Library steward, thin, stooping, sad-faced, and generally with nothing to do but loan out books. However this afternoon he was busier than Beesley had ever seen him, giving out baggage-declaration forms for passengers to fill in. Beesley had filled in his that afternoon and slipped it into his wallet instead of returning it to the Steward. The property deposited in Beesley's case was money, placed in an envelope, sealed, with his name written across the flap, and handed in to the Purser; a small piece of cardboard was his receipt. After dinner, the Reverend Carter invited everyone to the Saloon, and with the assistance at the piano of a man who had sat at the Purser's table opposite Beesley, he started about 100 passengers singing hymns. The pianist was Douglas Norman, an electrical engineer from Glasgow, who was going out to join his brother fruit-farming at the foot of the Rockies. They were asked to choose whichever hymn they wished, and with so many to choose from, it was impossible for him to have more than the favourites sung. As he announced the hymns, it was clear that he was very knowledgeable about their history; he gave a short sketch of the author of each one and in some cases talked about the circumstances in which they had been composed. Beesley thought everyone was impressed with

Carter's knowledge of the hymns and his eagerness to tell them all he knew about them. Many chose hymns dealing with dangers at sea, and Beesley noticed the hushed tone with which all sang 'Eternal Father, Strong to Save'.

The singing went on until after 10 p.m., when, seeing the stewards standing about waiting to serve biscuits and coffee before going off duty, Carter brought the evening to a close with a few words of thanks to the Purser for the use of the Saloon, a short account of the happiness and safety of the voyage so far, the great confidence all felt on board this great liner with her steadiness and size, and the happy prospect of landing in a few hours in New York at the close of a delightful voyage. After the meeting had broken up, Beesley talked with the Carters over a cup of coffee, said goodnight to them, and retired to his cabin at about 10.45 p.m.

Beesley recalled when he had first seen the ship from his hotel window in Southampton. Being on the *Titanic* was a new adventure. Everything was shiny and new and he could still smell the fresh paint. The White Star Line had gone all out to provide very adequately for all classes including Third. Beesley had been fortunate enough to secure a two-berth cabin to himself—D56—quite close to the Saloon and convenient for getting about the ship. On a big ship like the *Titanic* it was a consideration to be on D Deck, only three decks below the top or Boat Deck. Below D were cabins on E and F Decks, and to walk from a cabin on F up to the top deck, climbing five flights of stairs on the way, was a considerable task for those who did not take much exercise. Older people, in cabins on F Deck, would have hardly ever got to the top deck during the whole voyage had they not been able to ring for the lift-boy. Nothing gave a greater impression of the size of the ship than to take the lift from the top and drop slowly down past the different floors, discharging and taking in passengers just as in a large hotel. The lift-boy was quite young—not more than 16—a bright-eyed boy, with a love of the sea, the games on deck, and the view over the ocean. One day, as he let Beesley out of his lift and saw through the vestibule windows a game of deck quoits in progress, he said, in a wistful tone, 'My! I wish I could go out there sometimes!' Beesley wished he could, too, and offered to take charge of his lift for an hour while he went out to watch the game. Smilingly the boy shook his head and went down in answer to the ring of the bell from below.

The United States Immigration Service's rule to keep the Third Class passengers segregated was built into the structure of the *Titanic*. However, the accommodation for Third Class was quite good on the *Titanic*, compared to earlier vessels. The areas were located on the lowest passenger deck; passengers here were barred from the areas reserved for First and Second. The *Titanic*'s Third Class accommodation included both open-berth and cabin space, which could hold two, four, and even six passengers. The more people that took one cabin, the cheaper the individual rate was. Most sleeping accommodation was arranged in rows of bunk beds. Married couples' cabins were located far astern. Despite the claims, Elin Hakkarainen found that the Dining, General, and Smoking Rooms were very plain. The walls were coated with white enamel paint, and pine and oak panelling. The furniture was made from teak. The seats in the General Room were arranged in pew-like fashion with an open floor space for dancing and games. This room was open for all the men, women, and children to use. The General Room also had a piano. The Smoking Room had individual chairs and tables for playing cards and games. The White Star Line did not provide musicians for Third Class dancing and entertainment. Instead, music was provided by the passengers themselves. A long passageway (known as the 'working alley'), connecting the fore and aft areas of the ship, was located on E Deck. This made it possible for passengers to cross the entire length of the ship without going through the First or Second Class areas. Two Dining Rooms, located in the centre of the ship, could seat 473. This made it very convenient for the passengers to enter from both ends of the ship. Each passenger was issued with a table ticket, which indicated which sitting they would have. The times of the various sittings were posted at the door to the dining area.

On the Sunday, Elin and her husband Pekka were tired from the many activities that were available on board the ship. They attended the church service after breakfast, strolled on the decks, watched the sea, and enjoyed a sumptuous lunch and dinner. During the evening, they stayed in the General Room playing games, dancing, and socializing with friends from Finland. They could hardly believe that in two more days they would be landing in America. Elin was the focus of attention in her group, because she had been to America before, and knew what the procedure would be on arriving and what could be expected once they passed through Ellis Island. At 11.20 p.m., they left the General Room to watch the sea from the Well Deck. Not being able to see very clearly from this point, they climbed the stairs to the Poop Deck and watched the wake of the ship from the Fantail. The air was cold and crisp, and the sea smooth. Although the moon was not visible, the sky was bright and Elin had never seen so many stars. After a few minutes they were chilled to the bone, so they returned to their cabin which was located directly below the Smoking Room on E Deck. By the time they reached it, the time was 11.35 p.m. They were so cold from the walk on the deck that they went to bed immediately.

Herbert Lightoller, the Second Officer, found that, each day, as the voyage went on, everybody's admiration of the ship increased, for the way she behaved, the absence of vibration, and the steadiness even with the ever-increasing speed. As the days went by, the officers and men settled down, until the Watches went by without pause or hitch. All during Sunday 14 April the sea was calm—unusual for that time of year—not that it caused any great anxiety. However while the sea immediately around the *Titanic* was free of ice, there had been an extremely mild winter in the Arctic, hundreds of miles away, and as a result ice and glaciers had broken away in phenomenal quantities, so that never before had there been such quantities of icebergs, growlers, field ice, and float ice, stretching down with the Labrador Current. In his fifteen years' experience in the Atlantic, Lightoller had never seen anything like it—not even in the South Atlantic, when in the old days of sailing ships he used to sometimes go down to 65 degrees south of the equator.

Wireless reports of ice having been sighted in different positions were coming in through the day from various ships. That was not unusual at that time of the year, and none of the reports indicated the extent of the ice seen. The reports read 'Iceberg (or icebergs) sighted in such and such a latitude and longitude'. Later on in the day, they got reports of ice sighted in larger quantities, and also two reports of field ice, but in Lightoller's opinion they were in positions that did not affect the *Titanic*.

For the last hour of Lightoller's Watch, he had taken up a stationary position on the Bridge, where he had an unobstructed view right ahead, and perhaps a couple of points on either bow. With 10 p.m. came the change of the officers' Watches. On the Bridge, after checking over such things as position and speed, the officers coming on deck usually had a few minutes' chat with their opposite number, before officially taking over. The Senior Officer, coming on Watch, looked for his man in the pitch darkness, and just talked for a few minutes, while adjusting his eyesight after having been in the light. When he could see all right he let the other man know, and officially 'took over'. Lightoller and William Murdoch, the First Officer, were old friends, and for a few minutes—as they usually did—they stood there looking ahead, and talking over times and incidents past and present. They both remarked on the ship's steadiness, the absence of vibration, and how comfortably she was slipping along. Then they passed on to more serious subjects, such as the chances of sighting ice, reports of ice, and the positions. They also commented on the lack of definition between the horizon and the sky. The ship was then making an easy 22 knots. It was pitch dark and deadly cold. There was not a cloud in the sky, and the sea was like glass.

Murdoch took over from Lightoller in the ordinary way. Lightoller passed on the 'items of interest'—course, speed, weather conditions, and ice reports—wished him joy on his Watch, and went below. But first of all Lightoller had to do the rounds, and in a ship of that size it meant a mile or more of deck, not including a few hundred feet of ladders and staircases. Being a new ship it was all the more necessary to see that everyone was alert. Lightoller had been right fore-and-aft several decks, along a passage known as 'Park Lane', leading through the bowels of the ship on one side, and bringing him out by a shortcut to the After-Deck. Here he had to look round to see that the Quartermaster and others were at their Stations, and then went back to his cabin. The temperature on deck felt somewhere around zero, and Lightoller quickly rolled under his blankets. There he lay, thinking, waiting until he could warm up, and get to sleep.

Stewardess Violet Jessop was also finding that the voyage was happy and peaceful. On the fourth day out, when the sun failed to shine so brightly, and when a cold nip crept into the air as evening set in, it only served to emphasize the warmth and luxuriousness of the ship. On the Sunday evening, the music was at its liveliest, led by John 'Jock' Hume, the First Violin; when Violet ran into him during the interval, he laughingly called out to her in his rich Scottish accent, that he was about to give them 'a real tune, a Scots tune, to finish up with'. Jock was always eager and full of life. Greyish skies replaced sunshine but the calm sea continued, a calmness that only the ocean knew: perfect serenity for miles, broken by the rhythm of the water lazily lapping against the ship's side, as her great hulk moved through it. It was a little colder, the grey sky deepening into haziness as evening fell, making the water look like molten silver. The soothing peace and ever increasing chill drove everyone indoors, an excuse for bed and a good book.

Violet slipped out on deck for a few moments alone with her thoughts, her nightly custom before retiring. It was quiet, but had become penetratingly cold. Little wisps of mist wafted gently inboard from the sea and left her face clammy. Violet shivered. It was a night for bed, warmth, and thoughts of home and fireside. She thought of the man in the Crow's Nest as she came indoors, an unenviable job on such a night. The alleyways were mostly deserted except for a few stewards on the Late Watch, yawning with one eye on the clock. There were a few people here and there, some returning from the Smoking Room to finish their conversation over a last drink with friends in their staterooms. Others were just slipping up for air before turning in. Violet passed a honeymoon couple. George and Dorothy Harder, from New York, had embarked at Cherbourg. They averaged one big quarrel per day which, though nobody witnessed it, was easily recognizable by the tense, determined expression on both young faces.

Later, there would be radiant smiles. It looked as if they had been arguing again; the woman sat alone, a picture of affronted dignity.

It was good to be in her own bunk at last, devouring the batch of English illustrated newspapers and magazines which Thomas Kelland, the Library steward, had thoughtfully dropped in to the cabin as he passed. *The Tatler* and *Sketch* could catch Violet's imagination quickly and transport her to other scenes with all the latest gossip and the newest clothes. She was back in England for a few minutes. But suddenly she remembered that she had an extraordinary prayer on a piece of paper, reputedly found near the tomb of Jesus and composed by an unknown author, and translated from the original Hebrew. An old Irish woman had given it to Violet with strict instructions to study its strange wording and say it daily for protection against fire and water. Every day Violet had meant to look it over, but something else always claimed her attention. So it had been left unread in her prayer book, a prized memory of old convent days. Her conscience pricked her; the trip was half over and her promise to the woman remained unfulfilled. Violet made up her mind there and then to read it. She peeped over at Elizabeth Leather in her bottom bunk and warned her that she had better share the safeguard of this prayer, passing it down as she spoke. Elizabeth returned it after she had read it, saying it was indeed a beautiful prayer but a strangely worded one. Violet then composed herself to read it properly rather than as a piece of quaint writing. She pushed her magazines to one side, in order to relax and concentrate. At the end, her book closed, she lay lazily reflecting on many things, comfortably drowsy.

The *Titanic*'s Marconi telegraph equipment had a daytime range of 250–400 miles, and much longer ranges could be achieved at night, on occasions more than 2,000 miles. On the night of Sunday 14 April, Harold Bride was not sending messages, but was asleep. The Assistant Wireless Operator had boarded the *Titanic* at Belfast with his friend Jack Phillips, and had signed on at Southampton, giving his address as Bannister's Hotel, London. As a Marconi employee, Bride was not formally part of the crew; he received monthly wages of £2 2s 6d. In the early part of the voyage he hadn't had much to do. Bride and Phillips shared the shifts; Phillips 8 a.m. to 2 p.m., and 8 p.m. to 2 a.m.; and Bride 2 a.m. to 8 a.m. and 2 p.m. to 8 p.m. There were three rooms in the Wireless Cabin—for sleeping, for the dynamo that provided the power, and for operating the equipment.

On the Sunday, Bride and Phillips in the Wireless Cabin had received the warnings of ice and icebergs throughout the morning and afternoon that Lightoller had dismissed as unimportant. At 9 a.m., a message had been received from the *Caronia* of the Cunard Line: 'west bound steamers report bergs growlers and field-ice in 42N from 49 to 51 West April 12.' The *Titanic*'s position at that time had been latitude 43° 35' N., longitude 43° 50' W, and Captain Smith had acknowledged receipt of the message. Then at 1.40 p.m., a message had come from the *Baltic* that included the passage: 'Greek Steamer *Athenai* reports passing Icebergs & large quantity of Field Ice today in Lat 41.51n Long 49.52w.' At that time, the *Titanic*'s own position had been 42° 35' N., 45° 50' W, and again Captain Smith had acknowledged receipt of the message, saying 'thanks for your message and good wishes Had fine weather since leaving'. At 1.45 p.m., the German steamer *Amerika* had sent a message to the Hydrographic Office in Washington that was picked up by the *Titanic*: 'Amerika passed two large icebergs in 41.27 N 50.8W on the 14th April.' This message had been put aside by Jack Phillips.

Then, at 7.30 p.m., the *Titanic* had picked up a message from the Leyland liner the *Californian* to the *Antillian* that included the phrase 'three large Bergs five miles to southward of us'. At 9.40 p.m., the steamship *Mesaba* of the Atlantic Transport Line had reported 'in Lat 42N to 41.25 Long 49W to Long 50.30W saw much heavy pack ice and great number of large icebergs also field ice'. Finally, at around 10.40 p.m., the *Californian* had signalled that 'we are stopped and surrounded by ice'. Jack Phillips had been busy and had responded with the message 'Keep out! Shut up, shut up! I am busy, I am working Cape Race.'

What Phillips meant by this was that he was in contact with Cape Race, the Marconi station on Newfoundland. Bride had gone to bed next to the Wireless Cabin at around 8 p.m., and was due to be up and to relieve Phillips earlier than usual. The wireless had broken down, but had done so early enough for Bride and Phillips to be able to fix it. They had noticed earlier in the day that something was wrong, and Bride and Phillips had worked for seven hours to find the fault. They finally found that a secondary circuit had burnt out, and had repaired it. As he took the night shift, Phillips said to Bride, 'You turn in, boy, and get some sleep, and go up as soon as you can and give me a chance. I'm all done for this work of making repairs.' Bride had undressed and had gone to sleep. Later he was conscious of waking and hearing Phillips sending the messages to Cape Race. Bride read what he was sending, and found it was traffic matter. Bride then remembered how tired Phillips was, and, still in his nightclothes, went to take over from him.

Wireless communication was still in its infancy. Born in Bologna, Italy, in April 1874, Guglielmo Marconi had been educated by private tutors owing to his poor health. At Livorno in 1891 he attended physics lectures given by Professor Giotto Bizzarini and took private instruction in physics from Professor Vincenzo Rosa; he learnt Morse code and the techniques of transmission. Marconi's understanding of physics was improved by reading technical articles about electricity. In 1894, in Beillese, Marconi used improved oscillators (as transmitters) and resonators (as receivers), and devised every part of a practical system of telegraphy without wires. Marconi moved to England in 1896, and filed a patent for his wireless in June of that year. In July 1897, Marconi set up the Wireless Signal and Telegraph Company, later becoming the Marconi Wireless Telegraph Company, and carried out several successful transmissions, with the first successful transatlantic transmission in 1901. Later developments included the establishing of the first radio factory at Chelmsford, in 1898, and the Wireless Telegraph Training College, in 1901. In 1900 the company spawned a subsidiary, the Marconi International Marine Communications Company. Over the following years, Marconi overcame the initial deficiencies of his system and developed the technology necessary for its practical use. Many shipping companies subscribed to the service, in part because it was not necessary to purchase the apparatus; Marconi leased the equipment along with trained operators. A conference held in Berlin in 1906 had stated that each ship had to have a three-letter call signature for easy identification. In the case of the *Titanic*, this was 'MGY'. 'CQD' was the preferred option for the official distress call.

The *Republic* was a steam-powered ocean liner of some 15,400 tons that had been built in 1903 by Harland & Wolff. Built for the IMM Company's Dominion Line, and originally named the *Columbus*, after two voyages with Dominion she was sold to the White Star Line and renamed the *Republic*. In the early morning of 23 January 1909, while sailing from New York to Gibraltar and other Mediterranean ports with 742 passengers and crew, and with Captain Inman Sealby in command, the *Republic* entered a thick fog off the island of

Nantucket, Massachusetts. The steamer reduced speed and regularly signalled its presence by whistle. But at 5.47 a.m., another whistle was heard, the *Republic*'s engines were ordered to full reverse, and the helm put 'hard-a-port'. Out of the fog, the Lloyd Italiano liner the *Florida* appeared and hit the *Republic* amidships. Two passengers asleep in their cabins on the *Republic* were killed, and on the *Florida* three crewmen were killed in the bow. The Engine and Boiler Rooms on the *Republic* began to flood, and the ship listed.

Captain Sealby led the crew in organizing the passengers on deck for evacuation. The *Republic* was equipped with the new Marconi telegraph system, and became the first ship in history to issue the 'CQD' distress signal. Wireless Operator Jack Binns stayed at his post for eighteen hours. The *Florida* came to the rescue, as did the United States Coastguard's cutter *Gresham*. Passengers were distributed between the two ships, but with 900 migrants already on the *Florida* this left the ship dangerously overloaded. The White Star liner *Baltic* also responded to the distress call, but due to the fog it was not until the evening that it located the drifting *Republic*. Once on the scene, the rescued passengers were transferred from the *Gresham* and the *Florida* to the *Baltic*. Captain Sealby and a skeleton crew remained on the *Republic*, and tried to save her, but she sank the following day. At 15,378 tons, she was the largest ship to have sunk at that time.

Jack Binns was born in Brigg, in Lincolnshire, in September 1884. He was raised by his grandmother and uncle in Peterborough, where his uncle was a tailor. On leaving school in 1898, he went to work aged 14 for the Great Eastern Railway. However that year he had a serious accident to his legs. Binns spent a year in bed, much of it reading, and on return to work was employed as a Junior Telegraph Operator. By 1901, he was Senior Operator, Second-in-Command, of the Colchester Telegraph Office, in Essex, and then worked in the racing town of Newmarket. In 1904, Binns attended the Marconi School near Seaforth Sands, Liverpool, and then worked on German ships, starting with the *Kaiser Wilhelm der Grosse*, of the Hamburg Amerika Line. Harold Bride was not first choice as Assistant Wireless Operator on the *Titanic*. It had been Binns who had been due to be assigned to the *Olympic* and the *Titanic*. However his appointment was vetoed by the Chairman of the White Star Line, J. Bruce Ismay, who thought it would be unlucky. Instead Binns was assigned to the *Caronia*, and then to the *Minnewaska*.

'Ice, Flat Like a Pocket Watch'

Lookout Frederick Fleet, from Liverpool, had worked for the White Star Line for seven years. He took watch in the Crow's Nest with Reginald Lee at 10 p.m., relieving George Symons and Archie Jewel. Just after seven bells, at about 11.40 p.m., Fleet saw a black object ahead, high above the water. He struck three blows on the gong, the accepted warning for something ahead, and immediately afterwards telephoned the Bridge saying 'Iceberg right ahead'. They replied 'Thank you'. Almost immediately, First Officer William Murdoch gave the order 'Hard-a-starboard' and telegraphed down to the Engine Room 'Stop. Full speed astern'. The helm was already hard over, and the ship's head had fallen two points to port, when the ship collided with an iceberg well forward on the starboard side. Murdoch at the same time pulled the lever which closed the water-tight doors in the Engine and Boiler Rooms. The Captain rushed out on to the Bridge and asked Murdoch what the ship had struck. He replied 'An iceberg, Sir. I hard-a-starboarded and reversed the engines, and I was going to hard-a-port round it but she was too close. I could not do any more. I have closed the watertight doors.'

Down in No. 6 Boiler Room, stoker Frederick Barrett, also from Liverpool, was talking to Second Engineer James Hesketh when he heard a bell and noticed a red light come on, signalling that the engines should be stopped. Barrett was the man in charge of the Watch and he called out 'Shut all dampers.' But before they were all shut off there was a crash and on the starboard side, at the after end of the Boiler Room, water came pouring in, like a fire hose, through the side of the ship, about two feet above the floor plates. As the watertight door closed, Barrett and Hesketh jumped into the next section, No. 5 Coal Bunker. But there too, water was pouring in at the same height, two feet above the plates. Hesketh shouted out 'All hands stand by your stations'. Because the watertight doors had been closed, Barrett and Jonathan Shepherd, the Junior Assistant Second Engineer, went up the Escape of No. 5 and down the Escape of No. 6. They tried to get back to No. 6 Boiler Room, but there was about eight feet of water when they got there, ten minutes later. Water was coming into No. 5, but not so fast as to flood it. They rang through from the Engine Room to send all the stokers up, and for Barrett to remain there. The electric lights went out, and Barrett sent two stokers to get lamps from the Engine Room. The fires were drawn, but then Shepherd fell and broke his leg. Barrett and Herbert Harvey, one of the engineers, carried him into the Pump Room. Then water came with a rush through a gap between the boilers.

After undressing and climbing into the top berth, Lawrence Beesley had read for about twenty-five minutes. During this time he noticed the increased vibration of the ship, and assumed that they were going at a faster speed than at any time since they had left Queenstown. Earlier, when he sat on the sofa undressing, with his bare feet on the floor, the jar of the vibration had come up from the engines below very noticeably. As he sat up in the berth reading, the spring mattress supporting him was vibrating more rapidly than usual—the cradle-like motion was always noticeable as he lay in bed, but that night there was a marked increase. The vibration must have come up almost directly from below.

As Beesley read, the quietness of the night was broken only by the muffled sound that came to him through the ventilators, of stewards talking and moving along the corridors. Nearly all the passengers were in their cabins, some asleep in bed, others undressing, and others only just down from the Smoking Room and still discussing many things. Then there came what seemed to him nothing more than an extra heave of the engines and a more than usually obvious dancing motion of the mattress on which he sat. Nothing more than that—no sound of a crash or of anything else—no sense of shock or jar that felt like one large object meeting another. And soon the same thing was repeated with about the same intensity. The thought came to Beesley that they must have still increased the speed further.

And so, with no thought of anything serious having happened to the ship, he continued his reading. Still the murmur from the stewards and adjoining cabins, and no other sound—no cry in the night, no alarm given, and no one anxious—there was nothing to make the most timid person afraid. But in a few minutes Beesley felt the engines slow and stop. The dancing motion and vibration ceased suddenly after being part of the passengers' lives for four days, and that was the first hint that anything out of the ordinary had happened. We have all heard a clock suddenly stop ticking in a quiet room, and then have noticed the clock and the ticking, of which we had previously been unaware. So in the same way the fact was suddenly brought home to all in the ship that the engines had stopped dead. But the stopping of the engines gave them no information—they had to make their own assessments as to why they had stopped. Like a flash it came to Beesley: 'We have dropped a propeller blade: when this happens the engines always race away until they are controlled, and this accounts for the extra heave they gave.' It was not a very logical conclusion, for the engines would have continued to heave until they stopped, but it was at the time a plausible hypothesis.

Beesley jumped out of bed, slipped a dressing-gown over his pyjamas, put on his shoes, and went out of his cabin into the hall near the Saloon. Here a steward was leaning against the staircase, waiting until those in the Smoking Room above had gone to bed and he could put out the lights. Beesley said 'Why have we stopped?' 'I don't know, sir,' he replied, 'but I don't suppose it is anything much.' 'Well,' Beesley said, 'I am going on deck to see what it is', and started towards the stairs. The steward smiled indulgently at Beesley as he passed, and said 'All right, sir, but it is mighty cold up there.' Beesley did feel rather absurd for not remaining in the cabin. But it was his first trip across the Atlantic, he had enjoyed every minute of it and was eager to note every new experience, and to stop in the middle of the sea with a propeller dropped seemed sufficient reason to go on deck. And yet the steward, with his fatherly smile, and the fact that no one else was about the passages or going upstairs, made Beesley feel guilty in an inexplicable way.

Beesley climbed the three flights of stairs, opened the vestibule door leading to the top deck, and stepped out into an atmosphere that cut him, dressed as he was, like a knife. Walking to the starboard side, he peered over and saw the sea calm and black many feet below. Forward, the deserted deck stretched away to the First Class quarters and the Captain's Bridge, and behind, to Third Class and the Stern Bridge. There was nothing more as far as they could see in the darkness—no iceberg on either side or astern. There were two or three men on deck, and with one—Douglas Norman, the electrical engineer from Glasgow who had played hymns in the Saloon—Beesley compared notes. Norman had just begun to undress when the engines had stopped and he had come up at once. Neither of them could see anything, and all being quiet and still, the two went down to the next deck. Through the windows of the Smoking Room they enquired if any of the passengers knew more. They had felt rather more of the heaving motion, but none of them had gone out on deck, even when one of them had seen, through the windows, an iceberg go by towering above the decks. He had called their attention to it, and they had all watched it disappear, but then at once resumed their card game. Beesley and Norman asked them the height of the iceberg. Some said 100 feet, others 60. One of the onlookers was an engineer from Leicester called Denzil Jarvis who was travelling to America with a model carburettor, part of an internal combustion engine. He had filled in his declaration form near Beesley in the afternoon, and had questioned the Library steward how he should declare his patent. Jarvis said of the iceberg, 'Well, I am accustomed to estimating distances and I put it at between 80 and 90 feet.' They made guesses as to what had happened to the *Titanic*. The general impression was that they had just scraped the iceberg with a glancing blow on the starboard side, and had stopped as a precaution, to examine the ship thoroughly all over. 'I expect the iceberg has scratched off some of her new paint,' said one, 'and the Captain doesn't like to go on until she is painted up again', Beesley and the other passengers laughed.

One of the card players, pointing to his glass of whisky sitting at his elbow, and turning to an onlooker, said 'Just run along the deck and see if any ice has come aboard: I would like some for this.' Amid the general laughter, and seeing that no more information was forthcoming, Beesley left the Smoking Room and went down to his cabin, where he sat for some time reading again. Shortly afterwards, hearing people walking along the corridors, he looked out and saw several standing in the hall talking to a steward—most of them women in dressing-gowns. Other people were going upstairs, and Beesley decided to go on deck again, but as it was too cold to go in a dressing-gown, he put on his Norfolk jacket and trousers. There were now more people looking over the side and walking about, asking each other why they had stopped. Beesley stayed on deck for a few minutes, walking about vigorously to keep warm and occasionally looking downwards to the sea as if something there would indicate the reason for the delay. The ship had now resumed her course, moving very slowly through the water with a little white line of foam on each side. The passengers were all glad to see this—it seemed better than standing still. Beesley soon decided to go down again, and as he crossed from the starboard side to the port to go down by the vestibule door, he saw an officer climb on Lifeboat 16 on the port side and begin to throw off the cover.

No one paid any particular attention to him. Certainly no one thought they were preparing to man the lifeboats and leave the ship. All this time there was no apprehension of any danger in the minds of the passengers, and no one was in any condition of panic or hysteria; it would have been strange if they had been, given that there was no definite evidence of danger. As Beesley passed to the door to go down, he looked forward again and saw to his surprise an undoubted tilt downwards from the stern to the bow—only a slight slope, which no one had noticed—at any rate, they had not remarked on it. As he went downstairs a confirmation of this tilting forward came in something unusual about the stairs, a curious sense of something out of balance and of not being able to put his feet down in the right place. Naturally, being tilted forward, the stairs sloped downwards at an angle and tended to throw him forward. Beesley could not see any visible slope—it was perceptible only by his sense of balance.

On D Deck, there were three women standing in the passage near the cabin. 'Oh! Why have we stopped?', they said. 'We did stop,' Beesley replied, 'but we are now going on again.' 'Oh, no,' one replied, 'I cannot feel the engines as I usually do, or hear them. Listen!' They listened, and there was no throb audible. Having noticed that the vibration of the engines was most noticeable lying in the bath, where the throb came straight from the floor through its metal sides, he took them along the corridor to a bathroom and made them put their hands on the side. They were much reassured to feel the engines throbbing down below, and to know they were making some headway. Beesley left them and on the way to his cabin passed some stewards standing unconcernedly against the walls of the Saloon. One of them, Thomas Kelland, the Library steward, was leaning over a table, writing. They had neither any knowledge of the accident nor any feeling of alarm that they had stopped and had not yet gone on ahead full speed—their attitude expressed complete confidence in the ship and its officers.

Turning into his gangway, Beesley saw a man standing at the other end fastening his tie. 'Anything fresh?' he asked. 'Not much,' Beesley replied, 'we are going ahead slowly and she is down a little at the bows, but I don't think it is anything serious.' 'Come in and look at this man,' he laughed, 'he won't get up.' Beesley looked in, and on the top bunk lay a man with his back to him, closely wrapped in his bedclothes with only the back of his head visible. 'Why won't he get up? Is he asleep?' Beesley asked. 'No,' laughed the man, dressing, 'he says…'. But before he could finish the sentence the man above grunted 'You don't catch me leaving a warm bed to go up on that cold deck at midnight. I know better than that.' They both told him laughingly why he had better get up, but he was certain he was just as safe there and all this dressing was quite unnecessary, so Beesley left him and went back to his cabin. He sat on the sofa, and read for ten minutes, when he heard through the open door, above, the noise of people passing up and down, and a loud shout from above: 'All passengers on deck with lifebelts on.'

Beesley stuffed the two books he was reading in the pockets of his Norfolk jacket, picked up his life jacket (funnily enough, he had taken it down for the first time that night from the wardrobe when he first retired to his cabin) and his dressing-gown, and walked upstairs tying it on. As he came out of his cabin, he saw Purser Reginald Barker, with his foot on the stairs, whisper to a steward and jerk his head significantly behind him.

Archibald Gracie's cabin was an outside one on the starboard side, behind the middle of the ship. He was enjoying a good night's rest when he was roused by a sudden shock and noise forward on the starboard side, which he claimed he immediately knew had been caused by a collision, possibly with another ship. Gracie jumped from his bed, turned on the light, and glanced at his watch on the dresser. He opened the door of his cabin and looked out into the corridor, but could not see or hear anyone—there was no commotion whatsoever. However immediately following the collision came a great noise of escaping steam. He listened intently, but could not hear the engines. Taking off his nightclothes, Gracie dressed quickly in underwear, socks and shoes, trousers, and a Norfolk jacket. It was a short distance from his cabin to the stairway through the corridor, and he went up to the Boat

99

Deck above. He found only a young boy there. From First Class, forward on the port side, Gracie and the boy strained their eyes to discover what had struck the ship. Gracie looked from various vantage points where the view was not obstructed by the lifeboats on the deck, but while he swept the horizon near and far he discovered nothing.

It was a beautiful night, cloudless, and with the stars shining brightly. The atmosphere was quite cold, but no ice or iceberg was in sight. If another ship had struck the *Titanic* there was no trace of it. Not satisfied with a partial investigation, Gracie made a complete tour of the deck, looking in every direction. Going towards the stern, he vaulted over the iron gate and fence that divided First and Second Class. He disregarded the 'Not Allowed' sign, and looked around towards the Officers' Quarters expecting that he would be challenged. Given the collision he had expected to see some of the ship's officers on the Boat Deck, but there was no sign of an officer anywhere. Making his tour of the Boat Deck, the only other people he saw were a middle-aged couple from Second Class promenading unconcernedly, arm in arm, against the wind, forward on the starboard side, the man in a grey overcoat and cap.

Having learnt nothing, Gracie went down to the glass-enclosed A Deck, on the port side, and looked over the rail to see whether the ship was on an even keel. He could still see nothing wrong. Entering the companionway, he passed J. Bruce Ismay, President of the IMM Company, hurrying up the stairway with a member of the crew. He wore a suit, and, as usual, had no hat. Ismay seemed too preoccupied to notice anyone so Gracie did not speak to him, but looked very closely at his face, to try to learn how serious the accident might be. It occurred to Gracie that Ismay was putting on as brave a face as possible in order not to cause any alarm among the passengers.

At the foot of the stairway were several male passengers, and Gracie discovered that others were roused as well as himself, among them his friend, James Clinch Smith. Smith had paid a fare of £30 13s 11d, and occupied cabin A7. He had grown up in Smithtown, New York, worked as a lawyer, and had been living in Paris with his wife Bertha. Gracie learned from Smith that the ship had struck an iceberg. He opened his hand and showed Gracie some ice, flat like a pocket watch, coolly suggesting that he might take it home for a souvenir. He had a dry sense of humour. While they stood there, they heard (like Lawrence Beesley) the story of the collision—how someone in the Smoking Room, when the ship struck, had rushed out to see what it was, and returning, told his companions that he had a glimpse of an iceberg towering 50 feet above the deck. Gracie learnt that the Mail Room was flooded and that the postal clerks were at their positions, in two feet of water. They were engaged in transferring to the Upper Deck, from the ship's Post Office, the 200 bags of registered mail that contained 400,000 letters.

Now Gracie and Smith noticed from the door of the companionway that the ship was listing. They kept quiet about it, not wanting to frighten anyone or cause unnecessary alarm, especially among the women, who had just appeared on the scene. Although they realized how serious the incident was, they did not feel they should offer their opinions. The two men resolved to stick together, and lend a helping hand to each other whenever it was needed. Gracie had in his mind's eye everything that he had read and heard about shipwrecks, and he pictured Smith and himself clinging to an overloaded raft in an open sea without enough food and water. They agreed to go back to their cabins and join each other later. Gracie quickly packed all his possessions into three large travelling bags, so that his luggage would be ready in the event of a transfer to another ship.

He put on the Newmarket overcoat that reached below his knees, and as he passed from the corridor into the companionway his worst fears were confirmed. Men and women were putting on life jackets, the stewards assisting in adjusting them. Steward Charles Cullen insisted on Gracie returning to his cabin for his. He did this and Cullen fastened it. Gracie brought out the other one so that someone else could use it.

Many men and women had already assembled out on A Deck, on the port side, towards the stern. Gracie looked for and found three sisters whom he had met when they boarded the ship at Southampton: Charlotte Appleton, from New York and wife of his friend Edward from school; Malvina Cornell, also from New York; and Caroline Brown, from Belmont in Massachusetts, all of whom were old friends of Gracie's wife. The three were returning home from the funeral of a fourth sister, Lady Drummond. Gracie had read accounts in the London newspapers about her death, and the sisters had also told him all about it. Accompanying them was their friend, Edith Evans. Isidor and Ida Straus, the Astors, and others were among those congregated on the port side of A Deck, including, besides Smith, two of Gracie's group of after-dinner companions, Hugh Woolner, a businessman, and Mauritz Björnström-Steffansson, a student and military attaché at the Swedish Embassy in Washington.

The band began to play, and continued while the lifeboats were being lowered. Gracie did not recognize any of the tunes, but they were cheerful. The hopes of the passengers were buoyed with the information, given by the ship's officers, that there had been an exchange of wireless messages with passing ships, one of which was coming to the rescue. To reassure the women, Gracie showed them the bright white light of a ship about five miles away. John Jacob Astor asked Gracie to point the light out to him. In doing this they both had to lean over the rail of the ship and look close in towards the bow, avoiding a lifeboat that was being made ready with its gunwale lowered to the level of the floor of the Boat Deck above. However instead of growing brighter, the light grew dim and less and less distinct, and then disappeared completely.

When Gracie and the others realized that the ship whose lights they had seen was not coming towards them, their hopes of rescue were dampened, but the men's advice to keep calm prevailed, and to reassure the women they repeated that the *Titanic* was 'unsinkable'. Edith Evans told Gracie a story that years ago in London she had been told by a fortune teller to beware of water, and now she knew she would be drowned. Gracie's efforts to persuade her otherwise were futile. Though she told her story, she did not seem afraid. Ida Straus promptly and emphatically exclaimed: 'No! I will not be separated from my husband; as we have lived, so will we die together.' Isidor Straus too, declined Gracie's urging that, because of his age and condition, an exception should be made and he be allowed to accompany his wife in the lifeboat. 'No!' he said, 'I do not wish any distinction in my favour which is not granted to others.' They said they were fully prepared to die, and they calmly sat down in steamer chairs on A Deck, prepared to meet their fate. Further attempts to make them change their minds were of no avail. They moved to the Boat Deck above, but their maid, on the other hand, did get into a lifeboat.

Hanna Touma was standing in the doorway of the family's cabin, talking to one of the migrants from her village, when the collision occurred. It was just a jolt, but it made the door slam shut, cutting Hanna's index finger. Two of the men were sent to find out what had happened while Hanna went to the Infirmary to get her hand bandaged. Everyone she passed was wondering what had caused the jolt, and why the engines had stopped. The people looked worried, but Hanna could not understand what they said. The men returned and said the ship had struck an iceberg. They were instructed to stay calm in their cabins and pray.

'They want me to pray,' said Hanna, 'that I will do but I better find out what I have to pray about.' Half an hour later, she took Georges by the hand and headed for the top deck. They were helped up from deck to deck by the crew. When they reached the top where the lifeboats were, Hanna saw people dressed in furs and beautiful clothes. Men were in evening dress, and music was being played. No one seemed to take it seriously, but when Hanna saw these people complaining and getting into the lifeboats, she knew that was the thing to do. She instructed Georges to stay put. She had to return for Maria, and the precious piece of paper that stated where her husband lived.

Hanna arrived back at the cabin in time to see Maria come out of the one next door where she had been sleeping. 'Maria,' she shouted, 'quick, get dressed. Georges is right up on the top deck; we must run as fast as we can because he is all alone up there.' She quickly helped Maria into her coat, grabbed her money and the precious slip of paper, and raced down the passageway that led out of Third Class. They climbed up from deck to deck, stopping only to grab three life jackets, and they found Georges just where Hanna had left him. He related in tears how some of the people wanted to put him in a lifeboat, but he would not go without his mother.

Down on E Deck, Edith and Elizabeth Brown had been woken by a shudder and several bumps. Edith, occupying the upper berth, switched on her light, parted the surrounding curtains, and peered down at her mother lying in the bunk below. Elizabeth had also heard the noises and, on turning on her own light, stared up at her daughter in bewilderment. Edith quickly threw back her bed covers, swung her feet out, and climbed down the ladder to the floor. She crossed the cabin to the porthole, pulled the curtains back, opened the port glass, stuck her head out, and stared into the blackness. At first she could see nothing, but as her eyes became accustomed to the darkness gradually began to make out the ship's lights reflecting on the water far below.

It was flat calm with no wind and, looking up, she could see a mass of stars in the moonless night sky. Looking down once more and towards the stern of the ship, she noticed a great deal of turbulence and foam as the ship's propellers churned up the water. The *Titanic* was going full astern, and this was causing a great deal of vibration. Glasses clinked in the washstand, their door handle rattled, and the wood panelling and other fittings around their cabin creaked and squeaked. Edith, somewhat mystified by what she was seeing and hearing, pulled her head back in order for Elizabeth to see that the ship was stopping. Elizabeth crossed the cabin. With her head outside the porthole, she quickly took in the scene. She again crossed the cabin to sit on the edge of the bunk. With a worried look on her face, she said to Edith, 'I wonder what that is all about, then?'

The excessive vibration felt earlier had now stopped, and the only sound was the faint whine of an electric motor somewhere far inside the ship. The night air from the open porthole made the cabin feel colder, and Elizabeth asked Edith to close it. As Edith went again to the porthole, she took another look. She found that the water was now quite still around the ship, and all was quiet. On closing the porthole, Edith crossed the cabin to sit beside Elizabeth. She said 'Everything seems so quiet.' Before Elizabeth could answer, Thomas, still in evening dress, rapped on their door, stood in the doorway of their cabin, and said to them both, 'There's talk that the ship has struck an iceberg.' He advised them to put on warm clothing and life jackets and to follow him back up on deck. Elizabeth looked at him in disbelief. Thomas, on the other hand, was not to be deterred. On entering the cabin, he reached up to the top of their wardrobe and pulled down the two life jackets stowed there. Elizabeth had always been a nervous person, and this wasn't helping. Edith, on the other hand, wasn't worried at this stage and obediently did as she was told.

Both women put on jumpers and topcoats before Thomas began to help them on with their life jackets. Elizabeth remained speechless as her husband busied himself, adjusting the bulky life jacket and tying the tapes in front with a large bow. The life jackets were cumbersome, made up of square chunks of cork held together with stitched duck canvas. When placed over the head, they hung from the shoulders and tied at the waist. With their heavy clothing, both women looked twice their size. This caused Edith to forget the seriousness of the situation, and giggle for a moment. Before leaving their cabin, Edith spotted her diary on her bunk. As she never went anywhere without it, she quickly put it in her pocket as they went out. She left behind the beautiful gold-and-coral necklace Thomas had bought her in London. As they walked along the passageway toward the first flight of stairs, Elizabeth wanted to know why her husband wasn't wearing his life jacket. His reply was that they shouldn't worry; he would find one later. The important thing was to get up to the Boat Deck.

They continued up more flights of stairs. As they went, they met many passengers on their way down, muttering and claiming it was too cold to remain up there for long. Many were in evening dress, and some were wearing coats over night attire. Several were wearing life jackets. In the passageways, stewards could be seen rapping on doors and calling out 'Everyone up with life jackets on please!' There was little response. The whole scene was quite relaxed, with the odd quip from some about having a good night's sleep disturbed. Others just closed their doors again.

106

On arrival at the final flight of stairs, they stepped out onto the Boat Deck, joining a group of people already gathering around Lifeboat 14. (While in their cabin, Thomas had seen a small notice behind the door saying that passengers should assemble at Lifeboat Station 14 during any emergency.) They could hear music coming up from the decks below. Elizabeth nervously said to Thomas that some people didn't seem too worried about the situation; perhaps things weren't as bad as they were being made out to be. Thomas's firm reply left her in no doubt that as far as he was concerned they were doing the right thing. It was better to be prepared in case things got out of hand and they had to get into the lifeboats. People remained in small groups around Lifeboat 14, indulging in light-hearted conversation as they watched seamen take the covers off and prepare them for lowering.

Edith felt tired after being woken from a deep sleep. She thought how good it would be if the whole thing was called off, and she could get back into her comfortable bunk. With puffs of vapour from her breath visible as she spoke, Edith asked Thomas how long he thought this was going to last. He told her to be patient; he would be tucking them both in for the night once the emergency had been called off. However, Thomas wasn't too convinced by his own reassurance. And he knew he would have to calm Elizabeth, who was becoming increasingly distressed as she saw more boats being lowered and people being ordered into them. Thomas did his best to calm her down by saying that she shouldn't upset herself, as he would be look-ing for another boat once he knew they were settled in Lifeboat 14 and away from the ship. He knew she didn't believe him, but what more could he say? Edith held tightly onto her father as she stood alongside him, stamping first one foot and then the other in order to maintain some circulation.

Lifeboat 14 had Fifth Officer Harold Lowe in command. He was a Welshman in his late twenties, and was in the process of ordering people into the lifeboat in no uncertain terms. His voice had authority and could be heard on several occasions shouting at some of the crew to get a move on. As people were being helped into the lifeboats, there was a sudden ear-shattering roar. This only made matters worse. All communication between officers, crew, and passengers had to be carried out by shouting through cupped hands. People were beginning to show real fear, as many thought the ship would explode. They couldn't understand why the steam was being blasted off with such force. Women carrying small children made attempts to cover the children's ears with their hands or shawls. Other families clung to each other, fearing the worst. The poor lighting on the ship increased the problems the crew faced. After some twenty minutes or so, as the roar of steam slowly abated, the orchestra could be heard once again. The preparation and lowering of lifeboats meant that the boat's crew needed plenty of room to prepare the boats, and passengers had to be kept clear.

High up on the Boat Deck, Edith, pointing to the horizon, said excitedly 'Look, father! There's a light over there. Perhaps they will come over to help us.' Thomas and Elizabeth both looked and could also make out a light flickering on the horizon. Several other passengers had their attention drawn to the light. Elizabeth had stopped crying, but Thomas continued to hold her close. He had his arm around her waist as they watched the boats being cleared away along the Boat Deck. Edith watched the women and children being helped by their husbands and fathers as they stepped across into Lifeboat 14, awkwardly standing on the cross benches before sitting down.

Edith tried her best to remain calm, but her mother's state didn't help. She, too, dreaded the moment when they would have to get into their lifeboat and leave Edith's father behind. Lifeboat 7 was one of the first away, but it was only half full. Other boats were in the process of being lowered, some swinging about clumsily as the boat's crew tried to steady them by pushing their oars against the ship's side. There were shouts from the lifeboats being lowered to loved ones left back on the deck. The crews shouted to the passengers in the lifeboats to sit down and keep still. It was a precarious situation, for many still hung from their davits. There was a dog barking somewhere up by the funnel deck, a continuous hissing from the waste pipes at the top of the funnels, and the strains of music were still heard. The foremost funnel had become silent. The time the Browns were all dreading had finally arrived. Edith and Elizabeth were helped into Lifeboat 14, leaving Thomas behind. It went down the ship's side in jolts and jerks before finally hitting the water, causing many to fall about. As a result, it took in a great deal of water.

The *Titanic* carried 3,560 life jackets, of the latest overhead pattern approved by the Board of Trade, which had been distributed throughout the sleeping accommodation. Early life jackets were probably inflated bladders and animal skins, or hollow, sealed gourds, and were used for crossing deep streams or rivers. In the eighteenth century, life jackets for seaman were discouraged, as press-ganged sailors might have used them to swim for freedom. It was only later that safety devices made of wood and cork were used by Norwegian seamen. The first life jacket was invented by Captain Ward, a Royal National Lifeboat Institution (RNLI) inspector, in 1854, a cork vest for weather protection and buoyancy. Called lifebelts in 1912, the cork 'overhead' life jackets had a canvas covering. Cork was subsequently replaced with kapok, and later foam. It was Peter Markus who developed an inflatable life jacket for hunters and fishermen in his home state of Minnesota. He patented an 'inflatable life preserver' in 1928, with further patents for improvements in 1931 and 1932. It saved the lives of 98 of 100 men when the US Navy dirigible *Macon* crashed in the Pacific in 1935. The term 'Mae West' for the inflatable life jacket, named after the Hollywood actress, only became common later, after the outbreak of the Second World War. Markus's patent was later challenged by the Californian inventor Andrew Toti. He claimed he had developed a life vest after he had acquired a boat at 16, and his mother would not let him use it because he could not swim. But records prove that the Markus 1928 claim is the earliest American patent for an inflatable life vest like the one commonly called the Mae West; Toti would then have been only 11 years old.

Violet Jessop had earlier heard a crash, and then a low, rending, crunching, ripping sound, as the *Titanic* shivered a little and the sound of her engines gently ceased. There was dead silence for a minute. Then doors opened and voices could be heard in gentle enquiry. Violet lay still. She could not express what was in her mind at that moment, not even to herself. She must not show the fear that she had successfully suppressed so far. She had been aboard the *Olympic* when it had collided with the *Hawke*, the previous year, but only once, in an unguarded moment during a storm, had that fear betrayed her. Afterwards she had felt humiliated by the jests and jeers of other people. Violet waited for Elizabeth Leather to speak, for she knew she was awake. She looked over the side of her bunk, and Elizabeth returned Violet's look, saying, in her calm way, 'Sounds as if something has happened.' Suddenly, there was movement. Men were returning to duties they had but recently left. Violet realized that she too must hasten on duty, for she had quite a number of women in her section. The two stewardesses started to dress rapidly and in silence. Violet's teeth chattered a little and she found she was all fingers and thumbs.

Stanley, one of the Bedroom stewards, came knocking at Violet's door, his face paler than usual as he remarked casually, 'I'm calling all our people, sister.' He always addressed Violet as sister when they were alone. 'Anything you'd like me to do for you on my way? You know the ship is sinking?' Sinking? The word repeated itself as Violet finished putting on her uniform and quickly followed Stanley to their section. Of course the *Titanic* couldn't be sinking! She was so perfect, so new—yet now she was so still, so inanimate; not a sound after that awful grinding crash. Automatically, Violet untied and readjusted a child's life jacket, much to the little one's interest and sleepy bewilderment. Violet continued through her section trying to reassure people, answering questions to which there seemed no answer. Everywhere she found extraordinary calm. People who had been asleep were dressing, fumbling sleepy-eyed with buttons. They were unemotional, probably thinking like she did that it was unbelievable. Those who had not yet retired for the night were standing in groups, chatting quietly. Suddenly orders came down, striking a deeper chill. 'Everybody to the lifeboats!' They continued to adjust life jackets, reminding people to put on warm clothing, and to take blankets and valuables. They repeated as they went from room to room that this was just a precautionary measure. Reluctantly, people started up the companionways, still inclined to chat, some joking and taking their time about it. From above, officers' anxious faces peered down, loath to create undue alarm but wishing people would hurry. To those few who showed concern, a reassuring answer was forthcoming: 'There are plenty of boats in the vicinity; they'll be with us any moment now.'

All Violet's passengers were upstairs at last, and she looked around. There was no sound, the *Titanic* was as steady as a rock; she might have been in dock and all the crew gone home. Violet returned to her cabin and found Elizabeth. What should she do next? Absentmindedly, Violet began tidying up, folding her night-gown, putting things in their place, when she saw Stanley at the door again, watching her. Then he almost shouted as he seized her arm: 'My God, don't you realise that this ship will sink, that she has struck an iceberg, that you have to follow the rest upstairs as quickly as possible?' Without replying—there suddenly seemed nothing to say—Violet started fumbling in her wardrobe, then remembered she had no warm coat with her. It had been spring a few days before. Stanley made to grab what he saw on a hanger, while Elizabeth laboriously got into a mackintosh. 'No, Stan, that won't do,' Violet said, as he brought forth her new spring outfit. 'That's no rig for a shipwreck, all fussed up and gay.' Suddenly she was trying to be witty, afraid that if she wasn't she might cry. 'What about a hat?' said Stanley, opening Violet's hat box. 'What, that thing with Sweet Peas all around it? No, Stan, you would not wish me to go up in that, even for precautionary measures.' Violet joked with him as she tied on a borrowed scarf, locked their door, and called out 'So long, Stan, come up yourself, won't you?' as she went in front of Elizabeth up to the Boat Deck. Halfway up, she looked down and waved to Stanley. He was standing in the corner where he usually kept his evening watch with his arms clasped behind him. He suddenly looked very tired.

Second Officer Herbert Lightoller had been about to drop off to sleep when he felt a sudden vibrating jar run through the ship. Up to this moment the *Titanic* had been steaming with such a pronounced lack of vibration that this sudden break in the steady running was all the more noticeable. Not that it was by any means a violent collision, but just a distinct and unpleasant break in the monotony of her motion. Lightoller instantly leapt out of his bunk in his pyjamas and ran out on deck. He peered over the port side, but could see nothing there; he ran across to the starboard side, but there was nothing there either. As the cold cut him like a knife, he returned to his cabin and hopped back into his bunk.

It was about ten minutes later that Fourth Officer Joseph Boxhall opened Lightoller's door and, seeing him awake, quietly said 'We've hit an iceberg.' Lightoller replied 'I know you've hit something.' Boxhall then said 'The water's up to F Deck in the Mail Room.' That was enough. Not another word was spoken. Boxhall went out, closing the door, while Lightoller slipped into some clothes as quickly as possible. The ship had been running under a big head of steam, so the instant the engines were stopped the steam started roaring off at all eight exhausts, kicking up a huge sound that would have dwarfed that of 1,000 railway engines thundering through a tunnel. All the seamen came tumbling up on the Boat Deck in response to the order 'All hands on deck'. They were just following the instinct that told them that it was there they would be required. Up to this time the crew had had no opportunity for boat drill, beyond just lowering some of the lifeboats in Southampton. Lightoller found it was utterly impossible to convey an order by word of mouth; speech was useless, but a tap on the shoulder and an indication with the hand, dark though it was, was sufficient to set the men about the different jobs, clearing away the boat covers, hauling tight the falls, and coiling them down on deck, clear and ready for lowering.

The passengers by this time were beginning to flock up on the Boat Deck, with anxious faces, the appalling din only adding to their anxiety. All Lightoller could do was to give them a smile of encouragement, and hope that the infernal roar would stop. His lifeboats were all along the port side, and by the time he had got his Watch well employed, stripping the covers and coiling the ropes, it was clear the ship was settling. So far she had remained perfectly upright, which was apt to give a false sense of security. Soon the Bosun's Mate came to Lightoller and indicated with a wave of his hand that the job Lightoller had set him of clearing away was pretty well completed. The Second Officer nodded, and indicated with a motion of his hand for him to swing the lifeboats out.

The *Titanic* was fitted with a type of davit called the 'Welin'. In operation it was merely a matter of shipping and manning the handles of the davits and the lifeboats were quickly swung out. It was clear to Lightoller that the ship was seriously damaged and taking in a lot of water. By the time all the lifeboats had been swung out, the ship was well down forward, and the water was practically level with the main deck. Even so, Lightoller did not think that the ship was actually going to sink. There had been no opportunity or time to make enquiries, but he figured out in his own mind that she had probably struck the iceberg a glancing blow with her bow and opened up one or perhaps two of the forward compartments, which were filling and putting her down by the head. He thought she would go so far, until she regained her buoyancy, and there she would remain. The bulkheads were new and sound and should be able to withstand the pressure, and there was no reason to suppose they would not be equal to the task. All the watertight doors had been closed automatically from the Bridge, at the time of the collision— all except one place where there was no door.

Having got the lifeboats swung out, Lightoller made for the Captain, and met him nearby on the Boat Deck. Drawing him into a corner, and cupping his hands over his mouth and the Captain's ear, Lightoller yelled at the top of his voice, 'Hadn't we better get the women and children into the boats, sir?' The Captain heard him, and nodded in reply. One of Lightoller's reasons for suggesting getting the lifeboats afloat was that he could see a steamer's lights a couple of miles away on the port bow. If he could get the women and children into the lifeboats, they would be perfectly safe in the smooth sea until this ship picked them up, if that became necessary. His idea was that he would lower the lifeboats with a few people in each and when safely in the water fill them up from the gangway doors on the lower decks, and transfer them to the other ship. However, having got Captain Smith's permission, he indicated to the Bosun's Mate, and they lowered down the first lifeboat level with Boat Deck. Just at that moment, fortunately, the din of escaping steam suddenly stopped, and there was a death-like silence. It was startling to hear his own voice after the appalling din of the last half hour or so.

Lightoller got forty people into Lifeboat 4, and gave the orders to 'lower away', and for the lifeboat to go to the gangway door with the idea of filling each boat, to its full capacity, as it floated. At the same time he told the Bosun's Mate to take six hands and open the port lower-deck gangway door, which was abreast of No. 2 Hatch. He took his men and proceeded to carry out the order. Lightoller still hoped that they could save the ship. Passing along to load and lower Lifeboat 6, he could hear the band playing cheerful music. He didn't like jazz music as a rule, but he was glad to hear it. It helped them all.

Passengers naturally kept coming up and asking whether Lightoller considered the situation serious. In all cases he tried to cheer them up, by telling them 'No', and that it was a precaution to get the lifeboats in the water, ready for any emergency. In any case they were perfectly safe as there was a ship only a few miles away. He pointed out the lights of another ship on the port bow which they could see as well as he. At this time they were firing rocket distress signals, which exploded with a loud report a couple of hundred feet in the air. Every minute or two one of these went up, bursting overhead with a cascade of stars. 'Why were we firing these signals, if there was no danger?' was the question, to which Lightoller replied that they were trying to call the attention of the ship nearby, as they could not reach her on the wireless.

About 11.40 p.m., Esther Hart felt a bump to the ship. It was so slight that it felt like a train jerking, and if she hadn't been wide awake it certainly wouldn't have wakened her. It was not even enough to cause her glass of orange juice to slop over. It didn't wake Eva either, and didn't disturb Benjamin. Despite the minor nature of the jerk and the false alarm of the previous night, Esther immediately woke them both and asked Benjamin to go and find out what had happened. He wasn't pleased at being woken from a deep sleep. While he voiced his objections, Esther got Eva awake and out of her bunk. She started to dress Eva while she, too, protested loudly. Eventually, Benjamin pulled his trousers on over his pyjamas and put on a sheepskin coat. Then he went out to try to find out what had caused the collision. He returned quickly, and came back into the cabin with a pale face. He was a changed person, not the man Eva knew as her father, and she was so frightened she started to scream. He didn't need to say anything to Esther; she knew what had happened. Without more ado, he took off his coat, saying to her 'You'd better put this thick coat on, you'll want it', and then changed into an ordinary overcoat for himself. During this time, Esther's face had undergone a transformation; she too was pale, her face had fallen, and she was terribly worried.

Without more ado, Benjamin picked Eva up, took a blanket from off the bunk, and wrapped it round her over the top of her nightdress. 'Come along,' he said, 'we're going up on deck', and without another word strode out of the cabin. Although there had been no boat drill, he knew the location of the lifeboats because of their walks around the ship, so he headed straight for the lift that was close to their cabin. That took them immediately to the Boat Deck. As he went on deck, Eva said she wanted to go back and fetch her teddy, but she got a sharp reply from her father.

By this time, people were rushing in all directions and for what appeared to be a long time the message was circulated that the lifeboats would not be launched. Eva remembered one of the crew saying 'Well, even if we did launch them and put you in the boats, you'd be back on board for breakfast.' After they had been standing around for a while, Benjamin became apprehensive. He knew a great deal about the sea because he was from Hull and had been brought up in what was mainly a fishing community. He had often been to sea during his life and had an understanding and feel for ships. His first action on deck had been to place them close to one of the lifeboats. 'Now stay right here and don't move', he said to Esther, who was keeping a tight hold of Eva. 'I'm going to see what they are going to do and whether or not they are going to launch these lifeboats.'

They were on the port side at the middle of the ship, where Lifeboats 10, 12, 14, and 16 were hanging on their davits. They waited nervously for his return from the quest for information. During this time, more and more people were coming on deck, but many were also staying in their cabins and bunks, certain that the ship would not sink. Any doubts that there was an impending danger were dispelled when the passengers and crew saw the first of the emergency rockets released into the cloudless sky. Even people unfamiliar with sailing knew that rockets at sea meant that the ship in question was asking for help from any other vessel in the vicinity.

Like Archibald Gracie, Elizabeth Shutes was also on C Deck, in Cabin C125. However such a biting cold air poured in that Elizabeth could not sleep. The air had a strange smell and she had noticed the same odour in an ice cave on the Eiger Glacier, in Switzerland. It all came back to her so vividly that Elizabeth could not sleep, but lay in her berth until the cabin grew so cold that she got up and turned on the electric heater. It threw a cheerful red glow around, and the room was soon comfortable, but she lay waiting. She had always loved both day and night on ship, and was never fearful of anything. But now she was nervous. Suddenly a strange quivering ran under her, apparently the whole length of the ship. Startled by the strangeness of the shivering motion, Elizabeth sprang to the floor, but trusting in the ship she lay down again. Then someone knocked on her door, and the voice of a friend said 'Come quickly to my cabin; an iceberg has just passed our window; I know we have just struck one.'

Now 40, Elizabeth had been born on 30 April 1871, in Newburgh, New York. She had boarded at Southampton with Edith and Margaret Graham. The *Titanic* passenger lists listed the three as 'Mrs Wm G Graham, Miss M Graham, and Miss E. W. Shutes', 'alien' passengers embarked at Southampton, and travelling on ticket number 17582. Elizabeth was the governess to Margaret who was then 19, and had been born in Wheeling, West Virginia. Margaret was the daughter of W. T. Graham, a leading industrialist and founder of the Dixie Cup Company, and his wife Edith, now aged 48. In 1912, the Graham family was living in Greenwich, Connecticut. They had paid a fare of £153 9s 3d for First Class tickets.

There was no confusion, no noise of any kind, and no one believed that any danger was imminent. Elizabeth's stewardess came and said she hadn't found out anything. Looking out into the companionway, Elizabeth saw heads appearing asking questions from half-closed doors. But all was as quiet and still as a tomb, and there was no excitement. Elizabeth sat down again. Edith was by this time dressed, and Elizabeth and Margaret talked on, the girl pretending to eat a sandwich. Her hand shook so much that the bread kept parting company with the chicken. It was then that Elizabeth realized that the girl was frightened, and for the first time she was too, but why get dressed, as no one had given the slightest hint of any possible danger? An officer wearing a cap passed the door. Elizabeth asked him: 'Is there an accident or danger of any kind?' 'None, so far as I know', was his courteous answer, spoken quietly and kindly. The same officer then entered a cabin a little distance down the companionway and, by this time distrustful of everything, Elizabeth listened intently, and distinctly heard 'We can keep the water out for a while.' Then, and not until then, did she realize the horror of an accident at sea. It was too late to dress properly, but she soon put on coat, skirt, and slippers; the stewardess put on their life jackets, and they were just ready when Washington Roebling, Manager of the Mercer Automobile Company, in Hamilton, New Jersey, and whose family had built the Brooklyn Bridge, came to tell them he would take them to Edith, who was waiting upstairs.

They passed the Palm Room, where two hours earlier they had listened to a concert, just as Elizabeth might have sat in her own home—there had been no motion, no engine noise, and nothing that suggested that they were on a ship. There had been happy, laughing men and women constantly passing up and down the broad, strong staircases, and the ship and the music had gone on. How different those staircases were now. There was no crowd of laughing people, but on either side the stewards stood quietly and bravely, all equipped with the white, ghostly life jackets. They were the things Elizabeth always tried not to see even when making a crossing on a ferry. Now there were only pale faces, each form strapped about with those white bars. It was a gruesome scene, and as they passed on there were awful goodbyes, and the quiet look of hope in men's eyes as their wives were put into the lifeboats. Elizabeth and her companions left from the Boat Deck, 75 feet above the water. Washington Roebling and Howard Case, the London Manager of the Vacuum Oil Company, saw them to the lifeboat but made no effort to save themselves, and stepped back onto the deck.

As Pekka Hakkarainen had reached to turn out the cabin light, he and Elin felt the ship make a sudden turn and heard a scraping sound as if someone had pushed a row of glasses from a shelf to a floor. A few moments later, the throb of the engines stopped and the forward motion of the ship came to a halt. Suddenly, there was the sound of steps in the passageway and a man's voice yelling 'Why have we stopped? Is something wrong?' Pekka jumped out of bed, slipped into his clothes, and left the cabin, saying 'I'm going to see what has happened.' Elin fell asleep as soon as he closed the door.

About forty-five minutes later, Elin was awakened by the sound of other passengers walking and talking in the passageway. She dozed off again. She was once more awakened by much louder talking. She didn't know what they were saying. The time was now 1.15 a.m. Something was definitely wrong, because Pekka had not returned and the cabin was tilted at an angle. As Elin stepped out of bed, she fell to the opposite wall. Soon there was a loud knock at the cabin door. As she opened it, Anna Sjöblom, a friend from Munsala in Finland, dashed in saying that the ship had struck something and was sinking. The previous day had been Anna's 18th birthday, and she had also been suffering from seasickness; she had been lying on her bed fully clothed when the collision occurred. 'Where is Pekka?' Anna asked. Elin replied 'He went to see why the ship has stopped, I must have fallen asleep, I don't know where he is.' Elin was dumbfounded, she didn't know what to do next. After a few moments she grabbed her purse and life jacket and ran out to the passageway. Elin finally ran into Anna again. A steward appeared with a small group of women, saying 'You had better come with us.' He said 'There is another way to get to the upper deck.' He directed Elin and her companions to a service ladder, which was used only by the crew. 'Follow me,' said the steward, 'We do not have much time.' They went up the ladder, through the Second Class Dining Room, up another flight of stairs to the Promenade Deck, and finally up to the Boat Deck.

As Elin and her companions arrived on the Boat Deck, she thought to herself 'Why didn't I bring a coat?' The only protection against the biting cold was her nightgown and life jacket. Having been in a warm cabin, she had completely forgotten how cold it had been when Pekka and she had stood on the Fantail. The bow of the ship was down in the water and leaning to port. Due to the angle of the deck, it was very difficult to walk or stand. The loud sound of steam escaping from the funnels, which Elin and her companions had heard below, had stopped before they arrived on deck. It was strangely quiet. Everywhere she looked, she could see groups of men standing, watching, and waiting. She looked for Pekka, because she couldn't understand what had become of him. He should have been able to find her by now.

Frank Goldsmith's parents had also been quickly awakened by the quietness. Both knew they were not due in New York for another forty-eight hours, and so Frank's father decided to dress and discover what was wrong. He left the cabin and was surprised to find their friends, Tom Theobald and the 16-year-old Alfred Rush, walking towards the family's cabin door. Together they went up on the deck to find out why the ship had stopped.

Emily had dressed and became apprehensive the longer her husband failed to return. Then he came back and told her what had happened, calmly—that it was a shame such a great ship had been damaged, but all would be well; she should not worry, but should get Frank dressed. It was this which awakened Frank, and he took over and finished dressing himself. As he was tying his shoelace, a rap came on their cabin door, and it was Dr William O'Loughlin, the Surgeon, who asked if they had any life jackets. He told them they should put them on, and that they might have to get into a lifeboat. This excited Frank. The boys from Third Class had been permitted to go all over the ship in the previous few days, and being finally allowed into one of the lifeboats seemed a fitting climax.

A minute or two after the Surgeon left, Frank's father came back, and it was then that he learnt the ship had struck an iceberg. Frank did not appreciate the true seriousness of the situation. Emily donned her life jacket, and Frank said jokingly 'If we are going out in a lifeboat we'd better take something with us.' He was referring to the Eno's Fruit Salts and bag of Gibson's Fruit Tablets. He proceeded to stuff his overcoat pockets. Frank's life jacket was then put on. Meanwhile, his father had been packing a small suitcase. He had not put on his life jacket. Emily asked him to, but he wouldn't. She said to him that if he wouldn't 'I'll stay here.' Her husband finally did put it on, but took his overcoat off first, donned the life jacket, then put his coat back on to cover it up. Frank's family left their cabin and joined Tom Theobald and Alfred Rush who had been waiting outside their door. They walked slowly forward, and passed through an opened watertight doorway to a stairway leading up to the Second Class Saloon area. Here, everyone was informed that no suitcases were to be carried up to the Boat Deck. Frank's father set theirs down on the floor against the Saloon wall. They passed through a door on to the port side of the deck, the second one below the Boat Deck, from which loaded lifeboats were being lowered.

A few paces brought the family to a gateway, which was overseen by a crewman. Only women and children were being let through. Frank's father put his arm around his mother, kissing her. He then reached down, hugged the boy's shoulders, and said 'So long Frankie, I'll see you later.' Tom Theobald took his wedding ring off his finger, and gave it to Emily saying 'If I don't see you in New York, will you see that my wife gets this?' Frank and his mother were then permitted through the gateway, and the crewman in charge reached out to grasp Alfred Rush's arm to pull him through. But Alfred jerked his arm out of the sailor's hand and, with his head held high said 'No! I'm staying here with the men.'

Emily and Frank were led with the other women and children to a steel ladder located immediately behind the ship's fourth funnel. They all climbed it, and on reaching the floor of the deck the group slowly moved forward, carefully, so as not to be tripped up by the ropes and other things lying on the deck. Just a few minutes before they began climbing the ladder, Frank heard and saw a distress signal rocket being fired from a point up near the ship's Bridge. Eventually they reached a point near the front funnel. A narrow passageway faced them, consisting of a chain of male passengers and crewmen with their arms locked together. It led to the Engelhardt C boat, a collapsible boat with folding sides, which had been swung out on the davits.

Going upstairs with other passengers—no one ran or seemed alarmed—Lawrence Beesley and the others met two women coming down. One seized him by the arm and said 'Oh! I have no lifebelt.

Will you come to my cabin and help me find it?' Beesley returned with them to F Deck—the woman who had addressed him holding his arm all the time in a vice-like grip—and they found a steward who took them in and found their life jackets. Coming upstairs again, Beesley passed the Purser's window on F Deck, and noticed a light was on; when halfway up to E Deck, he heard the heavy metallic clang of the safe door, followed by a hasty step retreating along the corridor towards the First Class quarters. He had little doubt it was the Purser, who had taken all the valuables from his safe and was transferring them to the charge of the First Class Purser, in the hope they might all be saved.

Reaching the top deck, they found many people assembled there. Some were fully dressed, with coats and wraps, others had thrown shawls hastily round them when they were called or heard the summons to put on life jackets. Fortunately there was no wind. Even the breeze caused by the ship's motion had died entirely away, for the engines had stopped again and the *Titanic* lay motionless, not even rocking. Indeed, as they were soon to discover, the sea was as calm as a lake apart from a gentle swell. To stand on the deck many feet above the water lapping idly against the *Titanic*'s sides gave Beesley a wonderful sense of security—to feel her so steady and still was like standing on a large rock in the middle of the ocean. But now there was the roar and hiss of escaping steam from the boilers, issuing out of a large steam pipe high up on one of the funnels—a harsh, deafening boom that made conversation difficult and no doubt increased the apprehension of some people. The unpleasant sound that met them as they climbed out on the top deck sounded like twenty locomotives blowing off steam.

Beesley reflected that locomotives blew off steam when standing in a station, and why should a ship's boilers not do the same when a ship was not moving? He had never heard anyone connect this noise with the danger of explosion, in the event of a ship sinking with her boilers under a high pressure of steam. But he heard very little conversation of any kind among the passengers. No signs of alarm were exhibited by anyone—there were no indications of panic or hysteria, no cries of fear, and no running to and fro to discover what was the matter, why they had been summoned on deck with life jackets, and what was to be done with them now they were there. They stood, quietly watching the work of the crew as they manned the lifeboats, and no one ventured to interfere with them or offered to help. It was obvious they were of no use, and the crowd of men and women stood quietly on the deck or paced slowly up and down waiting for orders from the officers.

All this time people were pouring up from the stairs and adding to the crowd—Beesley thought if they were to embark in lifeboats it would be wise to return to his cabin and get some money and warmer clothing. However looking through the vestibule windows and seeing people still coming upstairs, he decided it would only cause confusion passing them on the stairs, and so he remained on deck.

Beesley was now on the starboard side of the Boat Deck, the time about 12.20 a.m. The passengers watched the crew at work on Lifeboats 9, 11, 13, and 15, some inside arranging the oars, some coiling ropes on the deck—the ropes which ran through the pulleys to lower to the sea—others with cranks fitted to the rocking arms of the davits. As they watched, the cranks were turned, and the davits swung outwards until the lifeboats hung clear of the edge of the deck. Just then Second Officer Lightoller came along from the First Class Deck and shouted above the noise of escaping steam 'All women and children get down to the deck below and all men stand back from the boats.' He had been off duty when the ship struck, and was lightly dressed, with a white muffler twisted hastily around his neck. The men fell back and the women retired below to get into the lifeboats from the next deck. Two women refused at first to leave their husbands, but partly by persuasion and partly by force they were separated from them and sent down. By this time, the work on the lifeboats and the separation of men and women slowly impressed on Beesley and his companions the presence of imminent danger, but it made no difference to the attitude of the crowd; they were just as prepared to obey orders and to do what came next as when they first came on deck.

But if there was anyone who had not by now realized that the ship was in danger, any remaining doubts were to be dispelled in a dramatic manner. Suddenly there was a rush of light from the Forward Deck, a hissing roar that made them all turn from watching the lifeboats, and a rocket leapt upwards to where the stars twinkled above. Up it went, higher and higher, with a sea of faces upturned to watch it, and then an explosion that seemed to split the silent night in two, and a shower of stars sank slowly down and went out one by one. And with a gasping sigh one word escaped the lips of the crowd: 'Rockets!' Everybody knew what rockets at sea meant. And then there was another, and then a third. It was no use denying the terrible intensity of the scene—the calmness of the night, the sudden light on the decks crowded with people in different stages of dress and undress, the background of huge funnels and tapering masts revealed by the soaring rocket, whose flash illuminated at the same time the faces and minds of the obedient crowd, the one with mere physical light, the other with a sudden revelation of what its message was. Everyone knew without being told that they were calling for help from anyone who was near enough to see.

'We Have Collision with Iceberg'

arold Bride hadn't even felt the shock of the collision. He hardly knew it had happened until after the Captain had come to the two Wireless Operators. There was no jolt whatsoever. Bride was standing by Jack Phillips telling him to go to bed when the Captain put his head in the cabin. 'We've struck an iceberg,' the Captain said, 'and I'm having an inspection made to tell what it has done for us. You better get ready to send out a call for assistance. But don't send it until I tell you.' The Captain went away and came back ten minutes later. They could hear a commotion outside, but there was nothing to indicate that there was a problem. The wireless was working perfectly. 'Send the call for assistance', ordered the Captain at 12.15 a.m., barely putting his head in the door. 'What call should I send?' Phillips asked. 'The regulation international call for help. Just that.' Then the Captain was gone. Phillips began to send the 'CQD' signal, giving the *Titanic*'s position as latitude 41° 44' N, longitude 50° 24' W. He and Bride joked while he did so. Both of them made light of the situation. Phillips telegraphed signals for about five minutes. Then the Captain came back. 'What are you sending?' he asked. 'CQD', Phillips replied. The humour of the situation appealed to Bride. He cut in with a remark that made them all laugh, including the Captain. 'Send "SOS",' Bride said, 'It's the new call, and it may be your last chance to send it.' With a laugh, Phillips changed the signal to 'SOS'. The Captain told the two of them the *Titanic* had been struck amidships.

By 12.25 a.m., Fourth Officer Joseph Boxhall had worked out the correct position of the *Titanic* and another message was sent: 'Come at once. We have struck a berg.' This was heard by the liner *Carpathia*, some 58 miles away, which answered saying it was coming to their assistance. Many other messages were sent, but they were heard by steamers too far away to render assistance. At 12.26 a.m., a message was sent about fifteen or twenty times to the *Ypiranga*: 'Here corrected position 41.46 N., 50.14 W. Require immediate assistance. We have collision with iceberg. Sinking. Can hear nothing for noise of steam.' At 12.30 p.m., the *Titanic* gave its position to the *Frankfurt* and said 'Tell your Captain to come to our help. We are on the ice.'

The Captain had earlier left Harold Bride, and Jack Phillips had told him to run and tell him what the *Carpathia* had said. Bride went through a mass of people to his cabin. The decks were full of scrambling men and women, but Bride saw no fighting. He came back and heard Phillips giving the *Carpathia* fuller directions. Phillips told him to put on his clothes. Until that moment Bride had forgotten that he was not dressed. He went to his cabin, dressed, and brought an overcoat to Phillips. It was very cold. Bride slipped the overcoat over him while he worked. Every few minutes Phillips would send Bride to the Captain with little messages. These said that the *Carpathia* was coming their way and gave her speed. Bride noticed as he came back from one trip that they were putting women and children in the lifeboats, and that the list forward was increasing. Phillips told Bride the wireless signal was growing weaker. The Captain came and told them the Engine Room was taking in water and that the dynamos that supplied the power might not last much longer. They sent that message to the *Carpathia*.

When the order to load the lifeboats was given, Archibald Gracie had moved forward with the women towards the boats that were being lowered from the Boat Deck above to A Deck on the port side of the ship. Sixth Officer James Moody, with other members of the crew, prevented male passengers from getting near the lifeboats. All Gracie could do was to hand over the women to the ship's officer; he was no longer responsible for them, and felt they would be safely loaded. A steward rolled a small barrel out of the door of the companionway. 'What have you there?' said Gracie. 'Bread for the lifeboats', was his quick and cheery reply, as Gracie passed inside the ship, searching for two of his dining companions, Helen Churchill Candee, an author from Washington, and Edward Kent, the architect from Buffalo.

Gracie met Frederick Wright, the Racquet Court Attendant, and exchanged a few words on the stairway of C Deck. 'Hadn't we better cancel that appointment for tomorrow morning?' Gracie said rather jokingly to him. 'Yes', Wright replied. His voice was calm, without enthusiasm, but perhaps his face was a little paler than usual. Thinking that it would be sensible to have a supply of blankets for use in the open lifeboats, Gracie went down again to his cabin, but found it locked. On asking why he was told by a steward that it had been done to prevent looting. Telling him what he wanted, Gracie went with him to the Cabin stewards' quarters nearby, where extra blankets were stored. He then went the length of the ship inside on A Deck, looking everywhere for his missing companions. However, no passengers were to be seen except in the Smoking Room, where, all alone by themselves, and seated around a table, were four men. Gracie knew three of them—Archibald Butt, Clarence Moore, and Francis Millet—but not the fourth. All seemed oblivious to what was happening on the decks outside. It was impossible that they did not know of the collision with the iceberg, and had not noticed that the room they were in had been deserted by everyone else. Gracie realized that these men wanted to show their indifference to the danger and that if he told them how serious he thought the situation was, they would laugh at him.

Gracie moved along on the port side, spending some time on the Boat Deck, and some on the deck below it, A Deck. Here he rejoined James Clinch Smith, who reported that Helen Churchill Candee had departed on one of the lifeboats. Gracie was on the Boat Deck when he saw and heard the first rocket, and then successive ones sent up at intervals. These were followed by the Morse red and blue lights, which were signalled from near Gracie and Smith, but they looked in vain for any response. These distress signals indicated to everyone that the ship's fate was sealed, and that she might sink before the lifeboats could be lowered.

On A Deck, Gracie helped in the loading of two lifeboats lowered from the deck above. They were ranged along the ship's rail on the Boat Deck, the odd numbered on the starboard side, and the even on the port. Two of the Engelhardt boats were on the Boat Deck beneath the Emergency Boats suspended on davits above. The other two were on the roof of the Officers' House further forward. They were designated by the letters, A, B, C, and D—A and C on the starboard side, and B and D on the port. They had a rounded bottom like a canoe, but otherwise the name 'collapsible boat', describing the adjustable canvas sides, was misleading.

Gracie no longer held back from approaching the lifeboats, and in fact his assistance and work as one of the crew in loading and getting them away as quickly as possible was accepted, for there was no time to spare. Second Officer Lightoller was in command on the port side, where Gracie was. One of his feet was planted in the lifeboat, and the other on the rail of A Deck, while Gracie and his companions passed women, children, and babies in rapid succession through the windows. Among them was Madeleine Astor, whom Gracie lifted over the four-foot rail. Her husband held her left arm as they carefully passed her to Lightoller, who seated her in the lifeboat. A conversation started between her husband and Lightoller, and Gracie listened to every word of it with great interest. John Jacob Astor was close to him in the adjoining window frame, to his left. Leaning over the rail, he asked Lightoller's permission to get into the boat to look after his wife. In view of the fact that she was pregnant, this seemed a reasonable request. However Lightoller, intent on doing his duty and obeying orders, and not knowing Astor from the rest, replied 'No, sir, no men are allowed in these boats until women are loaded first.' Astor did not disagree, accepted the refusal bravely and resignedly, simply asking the number of the boat so that he could find his wife later in case he was also rescued. 'Number 4', was Lightoller's reply. Nothing more was said, and Astor moved away.

While loading the lifeboats, Gracie saw a young woman clinging tightly to a baby as she approached near the ship's rail, but unwilling even for a moment to allow anyone else to hold the little one while assisting her to board. As she drew back sadly to the outer edge of the crowd on the deck, Gracie followed and persuaded her to accompany him to the rail again, promising that if she would entrust the baby to him he would see that the officer passed it to her after she had got aboard. She agreed and expressed relief when she was safely seated with the baby returned to her. 'Where is my baby?' was her anxious wail. 'I have your baby', Gracie said, as it was gently handed back to her. Gracie wondered how he would have managed with it in his arms if the lifeboats had gone and he had been plunged into the water.

The efforts to load the lifeboats shifted to the Boat Deck above, where Smith and Gracie, with others, followed Lightoller and the crew. On this deck there were some problems in getting the boats ready to lower—it may have been because of lack of drill, an insufficient number of seamen for such an emergency, or because of the new tackle not working smoothly. Gracie and his companions had the hardest time with the Engelhardt boat, lifting and pushing it towards and over the rail. Gracie used his shoulders and the whole weight of his body. Lightoller shouted out his orders in a strong and steady voice, and this inspired confidence and obedience. Gracie claimed that no women shed tears or gave any sign of fear or distress, no men indicated that they wanted to get into the lifeboats and escape with the women, and no members of the crew shirked their duties or left their posts. All the women who were in sight had been loaded, and Gracie ran some distance along the deck on the port side with Smith shouting 'Are there any more women? Are there any more women?' On his return there was a very pronounced list to port as if the ship was about to topple over. The deck was also on a slant. 'All passengers to the starboard side', was Lightoller's loud command, heard by everyone. Gracie thought the final crisis had come, with the lifeboats all gone, and that they were about to be pitched into the sea.

With other male passengers, Gracie and Smith crossed over to the starboard side of the Boat Deck where the officer in command was First Officer William Murdoch. Though the deck was not so noticeably aslant as on the port side, the situation was just as desperate. All the lifeboats had been lowered. There was a crowd congregated along the rail. There was enough light for Gracie to clearly recognize many people that he knew—among them John Borland Thayer and George Widener. They were looking over the ship's gunwale, talking earnestly as if debating what to do. Next to them Gracie was sad to see Caroline Brown and Edith Evans, the two women whom more than an hour previously he had passed to the care of Sixth Officer James Moody on A Deck. They showed no signs of anxiety. Mrs Brown told Gracie how they had become separated from her sisters, Charlotte Appleton and Malvina Cornell. It was a pity that they had not remained on the port side of the ship, or moved forward on A Deck, or the Boat Deck. Instead, they had wandered to the furthest point diagonally from where they had been at first. Gracie had not caught Miss Evans's name, and at this critical moment he thought it was important to ask. Meanwhile the crew were working on the roof of the Officers' Quarters cutting loose one of the Engelhardt boats.

Gracie was on the starboard side, next to the rail, with Mrs Brown and Miss Evans, when a member of the crew said that there was room for more women in the last boat that was being loaded. Gracie immediately seized each woman by the arm, and with Miss Evans on his right and Mrs Brown on his left, hurried towards the port side. However he had not gone halfway, and was near amidships, when he was stopped by a line of crewmen barring his progress. One of the officers told him that only women could pass. With the exception of Astor's plea that he needed to look after his pregnant wife, no men made a move or a suggestion to enter a lifeboat.

Second Officer Herbert Lightoller also noted the quiet orderliness among the passengers, and the discipline of the crew. Many of the passengers came quietly with offers of help. Since the Bosun's Mate and six of the Watch were not there, the work had become very strenuous, and more so as Lightoller instructed two of the remaining Watch to go away with each lifeboat as it was lowered. They lowered each lifeboat until the gunwale was level with the Boat Deck, then, as Gracie has described, standing with one foot on the deck and one in the lifeboat, the women held out their right hands. Lightoller grabbed their wrists with his right hand, hooked his left arm underneath their arms, and so practically lifted them over the gap between the lifeboat's gunwale and the ship's side.

Between one lifeboat being lowered away and the next being prepared, Lightoller usually nipped along to have a look down the long emergency staircase leading directly down to C Deck. Built as a shortcut for the crew, it enabled him to gauge the speed with which the water was rising. By now the Fore Deck was below the surface. The cold, green water, crawling its ghostly way up the staircase, was a sight that stamped itself indelibly on Lightoller's memory. Step by step, it made its way up, covering the electric lights, one after the other, which, for a time, still shone under the surface. The dynamos were still running, and deck lights on, which, though dim, helped considerably with the work. At one point a woman waved an electric light and temporarily blinded Lightoller and the crew as they worked on the lifeboats. Lightoller had by now realized that the ship was doomed, and so he began to load the lifeboats as full as he dared. His plan to fill up at the lower-deck doors had gone by the board—they were under water.

There were many examples of calm courage shown by the passengers—men, women, and children, both individually and collectively. One young couple walked steadily up and down the Boat

Deck throughout the whole proceedings. Once or twice the man asked if he could help. The woman never made the slightest attempt to come towards the lifeboats, much less to be taken on board, although Lightoller looked towards her several times with a sort of silent invitation. But she was not going to be parted from her husband. The order implicitly obeyed was 'Women and children only'. The ship was sinking, and the lifeboats were leaving, yet no adults attempted to get in without being ordered to.

Lightoller was reduced to sending just one seaman away in each lifeboat, and once, after ordering a sailor to take charge, he turned round to find there was only one man left to attend the falls. 'Someone for that after-fall,' Lightoller called, and the next thing Samuel Hemming, a Lamp Trimmer who had sailed with him for many years, replied 'Aye, aye, sir! All ready.' Unknown to Lightoller, Hemming had stepped out of the lifeboat, and back on board. The lifeboat was halfway down when someone halted Lightoller, saying 'We've no seamen in the boat.' He called to the people standing around 'Any seaman there?' There was no reply, and then Major Arthur Peuchen, a Canadian businessman and yachtsman, said 'I'm not a seaman, but I'm a yachtsman, if I can be any use to you.' The boat's falls hung up and down from the davit head, about nine or ten feet away from the ship's side. Lightoller said to Peuchen 'If you're seaman enough to get out on those falls, and get down into the boat, you may go ahead.'

Chief Officer Henry Wilde came over from the starboard side and asked whether Lightoller knew where the firearms were. It was the First Officer's responsibility to receive firearms and navigation instruments. On merchant ships, firearms were regarded as more ornamental than useful, and Lightoller had simply thrown the revolvers and ammunition into a locker in his original cabin. William Murdoch, who had become the First Officer, knew nothing about the firearms, and so couldn't find them. Lightoller told Wilde 'Yes, I know where they are. Come along and I'll get them for you,' and into Lightoller's cabin they went—Wilde, Murdoch, the Captain, and Lightoller himself—where he took them out, still in all their pristine newness and grease. Lightoller was going out when Wilde shoved one of the revolvers into his hands, with a handful of ammunition, and said 'Here you are, you may need it.' On an impulse, Lightoller slipped the gun into his pocket along with the cartridges, and returned to the lifeboats.

As Lightoller returned along the deck, he passed Isidor and Ida Straus leaning up against the deck house, chatting quite happily. He stopped and asked Ida 'Can I take you along to the boats?' She replied 'I think I'll stay here for the present.' Isidor, calling her by her first name said, smilingly 'Why don't you go along with him, dear?' She just smiled, and said 'No, not yet'. Lightoller left them. To another American couple, whom he found sitting on a fan casing, he asked the girl 'Won't you let me put you in one of the boats?' She replied with a frank smile 'Not on your life. We started together, and if need be, we'll finish together.'

Lifeboat after lifeboat was safely lowered into the water, with its cargo of women and children, each with an ever-increasing load as it became more and more evident that the *Titanic* was sinking, and that the ship to which they had looked for help was a false hope. Time and again Lightoller had used the lights of the other ship as a means to buoy up the hopes of the many that he now knew were soon to find themselves struggling in the water. Just before launching the last two lifeboats, Lightoller made his final hurried visit to the stairway. It was clear that not only was the ship sinking, but that she was going to sink very soon, and if they were to avoid the disgrace of going down with lifeboats still hanging in the davits, there was not a moment to lose.

Hurrying back to the two remaining lifeboats, he met Hugh McElroy, the Purser, Reginald Barker, the Assistant Purser, William O'Loughlin, the Surgeon, and John Edward Simpson, the Junior Surgeon. The last was a noted wit—even in the face of tragedy—and couldn't resist saying 'Hello, Lights, are you warm?' The idea of anyone being warm in that temperature was a joke in itself, and Lightoller supposed it struck him as odd to meet him wearing a sweater, and no coat or overcoat. Lightoller had long since discarded his greatcoat, but even in trousers and sweater over pyjamas he was in a bath of perspiration. There was only time to pass a few words, then they all shook hands and said goodbye. Lightoller didn't feel at all like farewell although he knew they wouldn't have the ship under them much longer. The main thing was to get the lifeboats away at all costs. Eventually, and to Lightoller's great relief, they were all loaded and safely lowered.

The last remaining lifeboat having got away, No. 2 Emergency Boat, a small sea boat used for emergencies, remained hanging in the davits. About this time, Lightoller met the engineers, as they came trooping up from below. He knew most of them individually, and had served with them on different ships of the White Star Line. They had all stuck loyally to their duties, long after they could be of any real assistance. Much earlier, the Engine Room telegraph had been 'Rung off'—the last ring made on ships at sea, and which conveyed to the staff the final information that their services below were of no further use, that the case (from whatever cause) was hopeless. At the same time it released the engineers and stokers from duty, leaving them free to make their way to the lifeboats. There was little opportunity to say more than a word or two to the engineers. Up to that time they had known little of what was going on, and it was a bleak and hopeless spectacle that met their eyes. Empty falls hung loosely from every davit head; the lifeboats had gone.

As Lightoller arrived alongside the Emergency Boat, someone spoke out in the darkness and said 'There are men in that boat.' Lightoller vigorously flourished his revolver and ordered them out. He had the satisfaction of seeing them tumbling head over heels onto the deck, preferring its uncertain safety. So much for their imagination—the revolver was not even loaded. 'Any more women and children?' was the cry, and Lightoller and the crew had the greatest difficulty in finding sufficient passengers to fill even this small boat—those who were willing to go and leave others behind. Eventually it was filled, and they lowered it away.

There now only remained the two Engelhardt boats, one on the deck by the davits of the No. 2 Emergency Boat, and one on top of the Officers' Quarters. Both were securely lashed down. The falls of No. 2 were quickly rounded up and one Engelhardt boat was hooked on and swung out ready for lowering. Lightoller stood partly in the boat, owing to the difficulty of getting the women over the high bulwark rail. As they were ready for lowering, Chief Officer Henry Wilde came over to Lightoller's side of the deck and, seeing him in the boat and no seaman available said 'You go with her, Lightoller.' Lightoller had sufficient sense to say 'Not damn likely', and jumped back on board. Not with any idea of self-imposed martyrdom—far from it—it was just pure impulse. As this boat was being lowered, two male passengers jumped into her from the deck below. The boat wasn't full, because the crew couldn't find enough women, and there was no time to wait—the water was lapping round their feet on A Deck.

With one other seaman, Lightoller started to cast adrift the one remaining Engelhardt boat on top of the Officers' Quarters. They cut and threw off the lashings, and jumped round to the inboard side ready to pick up the gunwale together and throw it down to the Boat Deck. The seaman working with Lightoller called 'All ready, sir', and he recognized Samuel Hemming's voice. 'Hello, is that you, Hemming?' 'Yes,

1. Frank Goldsmith (left) and his family, 22 Hone Street, Strood, Kent (19 December 1906). © George Grantham Bain Collection/Library of Congress.

2. Queen's Road, Belfast, with shipyard men leaving work, *Titanic* in the background (May 1911). © National Museums of Northern Ireland.

3. *Titanic*'s anchor leaving the Lloyd's British Proving House at Netherton, West Midlands (1 May 1911). © Dudley Archives and Local History Service.

4. *Titanic* propeller with shipyard workers before launch (31 May 1911). © George Grantham Bain Collection/Library of Congress.

5. White Star Line poster for the *Olympic* and *Titanic*. © Roger-Viollet/Rex Features.

6. Benjamin, Esther, and Eva Hart shortly before sailing on the *Titanic*.
Reproduced by permission of the copyright holder, Ronald C. Denney.

7. Starboard stern view of completed ship in Belfast Lough with tugs (2 April 1912). © National Museums of Northern Ireland.

8. Archibald Gracie IV. From Jack Winocour (ed), *The Story of the Titanic as Told by its Survivors* (New York, 1960, Dover Publications), opposite p. 216.

9. Passenger lists including Elin and Pekka Hakkarainen (10 April 1912).
Images reproduced courtesy of the National Archives, Kew, London, England.

Name of Ship _Titanic_ . Date of Departure _April 10th_ 191 2 . Where bound _New York_

Port of Departure _Southampton_ Steamship Line _White Star Line_.

NÂMES AND DESCRIPTIONS OF **BRITISH** PASSENGERS EMBARKED AT THE PORT OF _Southampton_

(1) Contract Ticket Number.	(2) NAMES OF PASSENGERS.	(3) CLASS.			(4) Port at which Passengers have contracted to Land.	(5) Profession, Occupation, or Calling of Passengers. In the case of First Class Passengers this column need not be filled up.	(6) AGES OF PASSENGERS.								(7) Country of last Permanent Residence.†							(8) Country of Intended Future Permanent Residence.†

10. Passenger lists including Lawrence Beesley (10 April 1912). Images reproduced courtesy of the National Archives, Kew, London, England.

11. Harold Bride at his post in the Marconi Room. © Universal Images Group/Getty Images.

12. Unidentified *Titanic* survivors aboard the *Carpathia* rescue ship. © George Grantham Bain Collection/Library of Congress.

13. Newspaper boy with news of the disaster (14 April 1912). © Private
Collection/Bridgeman Art Library.

14. Chorus girl at baseball game to raise funds for *Titanic* survivors, Polo
Grounds, New York (21 April 1912). © George Grantham Bain Collection/
Library of Congress.

15. Arthur Rostron, Captain of the *Carpathia*, being presented with the cup by survivor Molly Brown (29 May 1912). © George Grantham Bain Collection/Library of Congress.

16. Photograph of the 'Hoffman orphans' before they had been identified as the Navratil children (April 1912). © George Grantham Bain Collection/Library of Congress.

17. Kenneth More as Herbert Lightoller in film poster for *A Night to Remember* (1958). © Mary Evans Picture Library.

18. David McCallum (right) as Harold Bride in *A Night to Remember* (1958). © ITV/Rex Features.

19. Underwater photograph of the *Titanic* bow taken by the Ballard expedition. © EMORY KRISTOF/National Geographic Stock.

20. Edith Haisman (Edith Brown) in later life. From David Haisman, *Titanic: The Edith Brown Story* (Milton Keynes, AuthorHouse 2009), front cover. Reproduced by courtesy of her son, David Haisman.

sir'. 'Why haven't you gone?' Lightoller asked. 'Oh, plenty of time yet, sir', he replied cheerfully. The man had stuck loyally by Lightoller all through, though it had been too dark to recognize him. Lightoller and Hemming had time just to tip the boat over, and let her drop into the water that was now above the Boat Deck, in the hope that some would be able to scramble on to her as she floated off. Then Hemming and Lightoller went over to the starboard side, as every single lifeboat was now away from the port side, to see if there was anything further to be done there. Although all the lifeboats on that side had also been got away, there were still crowds of people on the deck.

At 1 a.m., on the starboard side, Lifeboat 3 began to be lowered down to the sea. This was done amid the greatest confusion. There were seamen all giving different orders, and there was no officer on board. As only one side of the ropes worked, the lifeboat at one time was in such a position that it seemed inevitable they would capsize in mid-air. Finally the ropes worked together, and the lifeboat drew nearer and nearer to the black, oily water. The first touch of their lifeboat on the sea seemed to Elizabeth Shutes and the others on board as a last goodbye to life, and so they pushed off—a tiny boat on a great ocean—and rowed away from what had been a safe home for five days. As her lifeboat was launched, Elizabeth thought there had never been a more brilliant sky, and never had she seen so many falling stars. These tended to make the distress rockets that were being sent up from the sinking ship look small, dull, and futile. The brilliancy of the sky only intensified the blackness of the water, and their utter loneliness on the sea. All of them wanted to stay near.

The crew were now in the lifeboats, the sailors standing by the pulley ropes let them slip through the cleats in jerks, and down the lifeboats went until level with B Deck. Women and children climbed over the rail into the lifeboats and filled them. When full, they were lowered one by one, beginning with Lifeboat 9, the first on the Second Class deck, and working backwards towards Lifeboat 15. Lawrence Beesley and his companions could see all this by peering over the edge of the Boat Deck, which was now quite open to the sea, the four lifeboats which formed a natural barrier having been lowered from the deck.

While waiting on deck, Beesley saw two women come over from the port side and walk towards the rail separating Second Class from First. An officer stood there barring the way. 'May we pass to the boats?' they asked. 'No madam,' he replied politely, 'your boats are down on your own deck', pointing to where they swung below. The women turned and went out towards the stairway.

Almost immediately, a report went round among men on the top deck—the starboard side—that men were to be taken off on the port side. Almost all the men crowded across to the port side and watched the preparations for lowering the lifeboats, leaving the starboard side almost deserted. However, two or three men remained. Soon after the men had left, Beesley saw a bandsman—a cellist—come round the vestibule corner from the staircase entrance and run down the now deserted deck, his cello trailing behind him, the spike dragging along the floor. This was about 12.40 a.m.; the band began to play after this and went on until after 2 a.m.

Looking forwards and downwards, Beesley and his companions could see several of the lifeboats now in the water, moving slowly one by one from the ship's side, without confusion or noise, each stealing away in the darkness which swallowed them in turn as the crew bent to the oars. First Officer William Murdoch came striding along the deck, clad in a long coat, from his manner and face evidently very agitated, but determined and resolute. He looked over the side and shouted to the lifeboats being lowered: 'Lower away, and when afloat, row around to the gangway and wait for orders.' 'Aye, aye, sir', was the reply, and Murdoch passed by and went across the ship to the port side.

Almost immediately after this, Beesley heard a cry from below of 'Any more ladies?' and looking over the edge of the deck, saw Lifeboat 13 swinging level with the rail of B Deck, with the crew, some stokers, a few men passengers and the rest women—the latter being about half the total number. The boat was almost full and just about to be lowered. The call for 'ladies' was repeated twice, but apparently there were none to be found. Just then one of the crew looked up and saw Beesley looking over. 'Any ladies on your deck?' he said. 'No,' Beesley replied. 'Then you had better jump.' Beesley sat on the edge of the deck with his feet over, threw his dressing-gown (which he had carried on his arm all the time) into the boat, dropped, and fell into the lifeboat near the stern.

As Beesley picked himself up, he heard a shout 'Wait a moment, here are two more ladies', and they were pushed hurriedly over the side and tumbled into the lifeboat, one into the middle and one next to him in the stern. They told him afterwards that they had been assembled on a lower deck with other women, and had come up to B Deck, not by the usual stairway inside, but by one of the vertically upright iron ladders, meant for the use of the crew, that connected each deck with the one below it. Other women had been in front of them and had got up quickly, but these two were much delayed by the fact that one of them was not at all physically fit; it had been almost impossible for her to climb a vertical ladder.

It was now 1.35 a.m. As they tumbled in, the crew shouted 'Lower away'. But before the order was obeyed, a man with his wife and baby came quickly to the side. Albert Caldwell from Iowa and his wife

Sylvia handed their 9-month-old son Alden to steward Frederick Ray in the stern. Sylvia got in near the middle, and Albert at the last moment dropped in as the lifeboat began its journey down to the sea. For Beesley, the lowering of the lifeboats was strangely thrilling. It was exciting to feel Lifeboat 13 drop by jerks, foot by foot, as the ropes were paid out from above and shrieked as they passed through the pulley blocks, the new ropes and gear creaking under the strain of a lifeboat laden with people. The crew called to the sailors above as the lifeboat tilted slightly, now at one end, then at the other, 'Lower aft!' 'Lower stern!' and 'Lower together!' as she came level again—but they did not feel much apprehension about reaching the water safely. It was thrilling to see the black hull of the ship on one side and the sea, 70 feet below, on the other, or to pass down by cabins and saloons still brilliantly lit. The ropes were new and strong, and the lifeboat did not buckle in the middle as an older one might have done.

One reason why Beesley felt little sense of the unusual in leaving the *Titanic* in this way was that it seemed the climax to a series of extraordinary events; the magnitude of the whole thing dwarfed others that in the ordinary way would seem to be full of imminent peril. It is easy to imagine it—a voyage of four days on a calm sea, without a single incident; the assumption that they should be ashore in forty-eight hours and so complete a splendid voyage; and then to feel the engine stop, to be summoned on deck with little time to dress, to tie on a life jacket, to see distress rockets shooting aloft, and to be told to get into a lifeboat. After all these things, it did not seem much to feel the lifeboat dropping down to the sea—it was the natural sequence of previous events, and they had learnt in the last hour to take things as they came. As they dropped down her side, Beesley and his companions were thankful that the sea was calm and the *Titanic* lay so steadily and quietly. They were spared the bumping which so often accompanied the launching of lifeboats.

As they went down, steward Frederick Ray shouted 'We are just over the condenser exhaust: we don't want to stay in that long or we shall be swamped; feel down on the floor and be ready to pull up the pin which lets the ropes free as soon as we are afloat.' Beesley had often looked over the side of the *Titanic* and noticed this stream of water coming out of the side just above the waterline. In fact the volume of water was so large that as they ploughed along and met the waves coming towards them, this stream caused a splash that sent spray flying. As well as they could in the crowd of people, they felt, on the floor, along the sides, with no idea where the pin could be found. And all the time they were getting closer to the sea and the exhaust was roaring nearer and nearer—until finally they floated with the ropes still holding them from above, the exhaust washing them away, and the force of the current driving them back against the side.

The result of these forces was that they were carried parallel to the ship, directly under the place where Lifeboat 15 would drop from her davits into the sea. Looking up they saw her already coming down rapidly from B Deck; she must have filled almost immediately after theirs. They shouted up 'Stop lowering 15', and the crew and passengers in the lifeboat above, hearing them shout and seeing their position immediately below them, shouted the same to the sailors on the Boat Deck. However apparently they did not hear, for she dropped down foot by foot—20 feet, 15, 10—and Beesley in the bows along with Frederick Barrett, the stoker who had been in No. 6 Boiler Room at the time of the collision, reached up and touched her bottom swinging above their heads, trying to push away their boat from under her. It seemed now as if nothing could prevent her dropping on them, but at this moment Robert Hopkins, an Able Seaman from Belfast, sprang with his knife to the ropes that still held them and Beesley heard him shout 'One! Two!' as he cut them through. The next moment they had swung away from underneath Lifeboat 15, and were clear of her as she dropped into the water in the space they had just occupied. They were washed clear by the force of the stream, and floated away as the oars were got out. They all felt this was the most exciting thing they had yet been through, and a great sigh of relief and gratitude went up as they swung away. Beesley heard no one cry aloud during the experience—not a voice was raised in fear or hysteria.

As Elin Hakkarainen and a group of women huddled against the Deck House on the starboard side of the ship, an officer motioned for them to get into a lifeboat. Elin didn't move, for she was still scanning the faces in order to find Pekka. Lifeboat 15 was being guarded by the ship's officers standing in a semicircle around it. Occasionally a man would try to get through the circle, but would be scared off by the officers' revolvers. There was a lot of cursing and yelling from one group of men, and some fighting amongst them. One of the officers pointed at Elin saying 'Room for one more, lady. Come on. Hurry!' As she stepped into the lifeboat, it was already moving downwards. The time was now 1.35 a.m. She lost her balance, almost falling between the lifeboat and ship until someone grabbed her arm and pulled her into a seat. On the way down they stopped at a lower deck and picked up one more woman. As Lifeboat 15 continued its descent, the stern of the ship rose higher and higher. They wondered if the ropes lowering the lifeboats would be long enough to reach the water. When they reached the water, they could feel the boat rising with the stern before the ropes were released. 'Row, row, row!' someone yelled. 'We will be swamped as the ship goes under!' When they reached a safe distance, they stopped rowing and looked back.

Over on the port side of the ship, Edith Brown found that most of the women and children destined for Lifeboat 14 were already in the boat. Elizabeth and Edith were ushered along by a crew member saying 'Come on ladies! Quick as you can!' Elizabeth, very tearful by this time, turned her head around and shouted at Thomas 'Get into another boat, Tom!' She implored him to go around to the other side of the Boat Deck to find a lifeboat there. Almost falling as she was helped in, she started to cry again as she sat alongside Edith on one of the cross benches. Seeing Elizabeth in this state and looking back towards her father, Edith sat with her hands in her lap as tears streamed down her face. Thomas was making no effort to find another lifeboat. He just stood there, gently puffing on his cigar and never taking his eyes off them.

Looking up towards Thomas, Elizabeth shouted again to her husband. Edith joined in, crying out in desperation 'Do what mother says! Find a boat, father!' Tears streamed down her face as Thomas gave them both a little wave and blew a kiss. As the lifeboat continued its descent down the ship's side, Thomas, almost out of sight now, stepped forward and shouted down to both women 'I'll see you in New York!' Edith could see, through the lighted portholes, that some people were still in their cabins, grabbing what bits and pieces they could. The lights from some could be seen shining up through the icy water. Just before reaching the water, one end of the lifeboat stopped as the other continued to descend. Fifth Officer Harold Lowe knew what the problem was; he shouted up as hard as he could to the men on deck to clear the falls and stop one end lowering.

Amid the din, the poor lighting, and the inability to be heard back up on deck, it was futile. The falls had jammed, and with the weight of the boat and its occupants, it was impossible to free. As the boat was almost touching the water, there was only one solution, and that was to cut the falls. 'Get your knife out and cut the bloody falls!' shouted

Lowe to Able Seaman Joseph Scarrott sitting in the bow. With a few slices of the seaman's knife, the lines parted and the boat crashed into the sea, splashing the occupants and shipping a great deal of icy water. Passengers fell about at the impact, screaming, shouting, and fearing they would all be dumped in the sea. There was another shout; water was spouting up from the bottom of the boat, where the impact had forced out the plug. With some luck, the bung was quickly replaced, but not before several inches of water had pooled in the bottom of the boat. Elizabeth and Edith looked down at their feet. The beautiful boots that Thomas had bought for them in London were ruined.

Once the lifeboat had settled in the water, the hooks at each end were released and cleared, and the boat was pushed away from the ship's side with oars. Elizabeth raised her head and looked back. She tried to fix her gaze on the place on the Boat Deck where she had last seen Thomas, but due to the poor light it was impossible to make out where he was. Edith, as though reading her thoughts, tried to comfort her mother by saying that he had probably gone to the other side of the ship and had most likely found another lifeboat. 'Oh, God, I hope so!' Elizabeth said. 'But he never even had a life jacket on!' Again she broke down, with Edith doing her best to comfort her as her own tears fell down her cheeks.

Another distress rocket streaked up from the *Titanic*'s Bridge, arcing over and lighting up the immediate vicinity with its starburst. As soon as Lowe decided they were far enough from the ship, he ordered the rowers to 'Rest oars!' They stopped rowing and leaned forward on their oars, looking back at the ship, her bow almost completely submerged. They hardly believed what they were witnessing; in the lifeboats, there was a sob or a cough now and then as they continued to look back.

Violet Jessop found that there were officers and men briskly getting lifeboats ready to lower, but also that their tense faces were strangely in contrast to the well ordered groups wandering about, people who were curious but with not very much to do. She felt chilly without a coat, so went down again for something to cover her shoulders. She picked up a silk eiderdown from the first open cabin that she came to. It was strange to pass all the rooms lit up so brilliantly, their doors open and contents lying around in disorder. Jewels sparkled on dressing tables, and a pair of silver slippers were lying where they had been kicked off. Violet gathered up the eiderdown and went up. On her way she passed Captain Smith, J. Bruce Ismay, Purser McElroy, and Dr O'Loughlin, still in their mess jackets, hands in pockets, chatting quietly. They smiled at her and she waved back. As she turned, she ran into Jock Hume, the musician, and his crowd with their instruments. Jock smiled in passing, looking unusually pale, remarking 'Just going to give them a tune to cheer things up a bit', and passed on. Soon the strains of the band reached Violet faintly as she stood on deck watching a young woman excitedly remonstrating with an embarrassed young officer. He wanted her to get into the lifeboat, but she refused to go without her father. 'He must wait', responded the officer, 'till, the decks are cleared of women and children'.

Up one of the emergency stairs, two young figures struggled, laughing as they nearly dropped their load. It was the two stewards from the pantry. One of them stumbled and partly fell over another object lying in their path. The man who had brought it up came from the Purser's Office. He was taking a breather, for it was very heavy and he had yet to get it into a lifeboat. Somebody else passed by hurriedly and kicked the bag in passing. Some of its precious contents scattered, to the mortification of the man in charge. As he tried to rescue the coins from under moving feet, his mate came up with a heavy dispatch box and joined him.

Out on deck, the first arguments started over who would and who wouldn't go into the lifeboats which were suspended miles above the yawning blackness below. Nobody was anxious to move, as the ship seemed so steady. To justify their reluctance, some pointed to the lights of another ship on the horizon. People were reassured, content to bide their time. One boat was already being lowered with very few people in it. When this was pointed out by the officer near Violet as an example for those who were reluctant to get in, the crowd surged forward to embark. The lifeboat was lowered, almost too full this time. Some people held back and had to be coaxed, while others were too eager. A steward stood waiting with his back to the bulkhead, cigarette in mouth, and hands in pockets. It struck Violet forcibly as the first time she had ever seen a steward standing in this way among a group of First Class passengers.

A woman standing near Violet gave an approving glance as John Jacob Astor helped his wife into a lifeboat, waving encouragingly to her as he stepped back into an ever-increasing crowd of men. Elizabeth Leather, still silent and unmoved, dragged a little behind Violet. Violet suggested they keep together and they stood to watch for a while. There was nothing else they could do. Dimly Violet heard a shot. Glancing forward, Violet caught her breath as a white rocket shot up, then another. Distress rockets! They went very high with much noise. The lights on the horizon seemed to come nearer. That cheered up the group around them, who had slowly started to fill a lifeboat. Young officers urged them to hurry, showing unlimited patience. Another rocket went up into the night.

A few women near Violet started to cry loudly when they realized a parting had to take place, their husbands standing silently by. They were Polish migrants and could not understand a word of English. Violet thought it was a terrible plight, to be among a crowd in such a situation and not be able to understand anything that was being said. Lifeboats were now being lowered more rapidly, and more migrants were brought up by a steward from Third Class. They dashed eagerly over to a boat, almost more than the officer could control. But he regained order and managed to get it away. It descended slowly, uncertainly at first, first one end up and then the other; the falls were new and difficult to handle. Some men nearby, among them Thomas Andrews and Ernest Freeman, the Chief Deck Steward, were throwing things over the side—deck chairs, rafts, and any other wooden objects lying nearby.

Suddenly, the crowd of people beside Violet parted. A man dashed to the ship's side, and before anyone could stop him, hurled himself into the descending boat. There was a murmur of amazement and disapproval. Violet turned to say something to Elizabeth. Looking along the length of the ship, she noticed the forward part was much lower now. For a fraction of a second, her heart stood still, as is often the case when faith, hitherto unshaken, gets its first setback. One of the mailmen from the Sorting Office joined them. His work was finished, he remarked unemotionally. Violet tried not to hear what he said, not wanting to believe what he accepted so stoically. Instead, she listened to the faint sounds of music from the band.

Violet's arm was suddenly jerked and she turned to see Sixth Officer James Moody who had been busy filling a lifeboat. His face looked weary and tired, but he smiled brightly, calling out 'Good luck!' as they stepped in, helped by his willing, guiding hand. Violet nearly fell over the tackle and oars as she tried to help Elizabeth Leather in beside her. Violet could see that she was suffering with her feet, and she found her life jacket prevented her from moving freely. Before Violet could do anything, Moody hailed her and held up something, calling, as he prepared to throw it, 'Look after this, will you?' and she reached out to receive a baby in her arms. It started to whimper as Violet pressed it to her, the hard cork surface of the life jacket being anything but a comfort. The lifeboat was full now of people with dull, enquiring faces. Violet spoke to one woman but she shook her head, not understanding a word the stewardess said.

Groaning, Lifeboat 16 descended a long way into the inky blackness beneath, the dark intensified as the lights fell on it occasionally. 'Surely it is all a dream,' Violet thought as she looked up the side of the ship, beautifully illuminated, each deck still alive with lights. She tried to make herself believe it could not be true. She even noticed a few people leaning over a rail, watching in an unconcerned manner; perhaps they also were persuading themselves it was a bad dream. The lifeboat touched the water with a bone-cracking thud—the baby started crying in earnest. Somebody in the front ordered them to get the oars out, and they slowly pulled away from the side of the ship. Violet noticed a fireman who had evidently just come up from the stokehold, his face still black with coal dust and eyes red-rimmed, wearing only a thin singlet to protect himself from the icy cold. George Pelham was a trimmer. Normally on ships the job of trimmers was to bring coal from the bunkers to the boiler rooms in wheelbarrows; with the greasers they were among the lowest wage earners among the crew. But on the *Titanic*, Pelham's job was to haul away the ash from the boilers, cool it with a hose, and then cart it to the ash ejectors which fired it into the sea using a high pressure jet of water. Taking a cigarette from his trouser pocket, Pelham offered Violet half.

Fascinated, Violet's eyes never left the ship, as if by looking she could keep the ship afloat. She reflected that only four days earlier she had wanted to see her from afar, to be able to admire her under way; now there she was, her *Titanic*, her splendid lines outlined against the night, and every light twinkling. Violet started subconsciously to count the decks by the rows of lights. One, two, three, four, five, six; then again—one, two, three, four, five. She stopped.

Surely she had miscounted. She went over them again more care-fully, at the same time hushing the whimpering baby. No, she had not made a mistake—there were only five decks now. Then Violet started all over again—only four now. She could no longer deny that the ship was getting lower in the water.

When Benjamin Hart eventually returned to his cabin, he was able to tell Esther and Eva, and the other passengers around them, that the lifeboats were going to be launched. A short time later, under the supervision of the ship's officers, loading of the boats started. Eva and her parents saw some frantic pushing and shoving by people now anxious to get off the ship as fast as possible. Fifth Officer Harold Lowe, who was directing the filling of their lifeboat, drew his revolver and fired a shot into the air, shouting 'If anybody tries to get here in front of women and children, I'll shoot.' And nobody had any doubt that he meant what he said. Eva heard her father say 'I'm not trying to get in, but for God's sake look after my wife and child.' He made sure they were safely in Lifeboat 14, and then continued to help other mothers and children.

As the lifeboat was being filled with people, they could feel that the deck was sloping more, and throughout it all they could hear the piercing shriek of steam being released from the boilers. While they waited on the Boat Deck they all became conscious of music being played close at hand by a group of musicians. Eventually their life-boat was ready for lowering, and they could see over to the smooth, cold, black water below. As their boat was ready to drop, Benjamin said 'Stay with your Mummy and hold her hand tightly like a good girl.' Esther held the girl closely to her before they dropped below the level of the Boat Deck.

It was 1.30 a.m., and the lowering of the lifeboat was itself a hair-raising experience. As the Boat Deck was at least 70 feet above the water level, it was the equivalent of being lowered down the side of a nine- or ten-storey building in a series of sharp jerks as the ropes were paid out from the davits. But eventually they were on the water, which remained unusually smooth and still. Then they were rowed away from the ship to wait with the others, while the *Titanic* sank lower and lower at the bows.

So far, Frank Goldsmith had not become apprehensive. There was little panic. Almost the very next second, a passenger forced his way into the passage right in front of Emily, who was holding the boy's left hand and leading him behind her. Emily dropped the boy's hand, forced her hands around the man's shoulders, and jerked him to one side. The passageway guards cheered her, and a crewman shouted 'That's the way lady! Don't give up!' Seconds later, they were helped aboard the Engelhardt C boat, which was almost full. They were seated on the port side, close to the front.

As the lifeboat reached the point of lowering, shots from a pistol rang out, and Frank quickly saw that Fifth Officer Harold Lowe, at the davit near him, holding a pistol aimed at the sky, had fired three shots. They were being fired as warnings to people who were trying to force their way past guards and trying to rush to the lifeboat that Frank and Emily were in. Passengers knew this was their last chance. Officers felt they had to block such action to ensure the safety of Frank's lifeboat, and to prevent its being capsized. The crewmen at the davits began lowering. Frank looked into the windows and open spaces of the two decks they were being lowered past. On one, he saw men and women sitting in chairs or slowly walking around together, on the other, teenage boys who were playing games and smoking cigarettes, something normally forbidden. As they passed this deck, the large rivets attached to the plates of the ship's side began to appear. Due to the severe list, the gunwales of D Deck quickly began to catch on their lifeboat. The lowering continued, and they would all have been tipped out had it not been for the women who were able to force the loaded boat free of the rivets. This happened twice more before they finally hit the water safely.

A man with a beard had helped the Touma family into the same boat; there were twenty-five people in that boat altogether. Hanna also found that the descent was terrifying. It was now 1.40 a.m. The water was 70 feet below and the sailors let out the rope a little at a time causing the boat to rock and sway. She prayed. The children wanted to know what had happened to the ship, and what they were doing in the lifeboat. Hanna said that the ship had something wrong with it, and that was why they were in the lifeboat.

The *Titanic* carried fourteen standard 30-foot lifeboats (capacity 65 people); four Engelhardt boats, just over 27 and a half feet long (capacity 47); and two Emergency Boats, or cutters, just over 25 feet long (capacity 40). The lifeboats were stowed on the Boat Deck, by groups of three at the forward, and four at the after ends, nearer the stern. On each side of the Boat Deck the cutters were arranged forward of the group of three, and fitted to lash outboard as Emergency Boats. The Engelhardt boats were stowed abreast of the cutters, one on each side of the ship, and the remaining two on top of the Officers' House, immediately abaft or behind the navigating Bridge. Overall, while the *Titanic* carried 2,201 passengers and crew, the lifeboats were sufficient for 1,178 people. The keels were of elm, while the stems and stern posts were of oak. They were all clinker-built of yellow pine, double fastened with copper nails, their ends broken down over roves. The timbers were of elm, and the seats pitch pine. The boats had a depth of four feet when rowing, so wooden foot rests were inserted between the seats; this helped during rowing. The buoyancy tanks in the lifeboats were of 18 oz copper, and of capacity to meet the Board of Trade's requirements. The name of the ship 'SS Titanic' was placed on a metal plaque on the outboard side, the port name 'Liverpool' on the inboard. Below the port nameplate was the company flag plate, and the draft plate with dimensions of length, breadth, depth, and capacity, in this case '30'-0, 9'-0 x 4'-0, 64P'. The lifeboat numbers began with the forward-most starboard boat and alternated from starboard to port starting at Lifeboat 3 and ending at Lifeboat 16.

The davits used on the *Titanic* were the latest invention. An article in the journal *Engineering*, published in July 1910, noted that this type of davit was superior to the older type, but also saved deck space. The most obvious way of achieving this was by 'double banking' the lifeboats on convenient parts of the deck. But the Board of Trade had refused to recognize the inward boat as fulfilling the clause in its regulations that required a boat to be 'under davits'. Double banking had been practised, but only in respect of lifeboats above the regulation complement. This did not help to reduce the long row of lifeboats. However the Board of Trade amended its rules, so that the inboard lifeboat of the two double banked boats could count as forming part of the regulation complement when fitted efficiently. The modified pattern of davit brought out by the Welin Davit and Engineering Company (1901) complied with these new conditions. Designed by the Swedish inventor and industralist Axel Welin, the special 'Quadrant, Double-Acting' design was supposed to enable the stowage and lowering of up to four lifeboats per davit. The 'Welin

Quadrant' davit became the industry standard for many years, with a reported 4,000 units sold. Although early designs of the ship allowed for this, when the *Titanic* sailed she had only one lifeboat per davit (apart from Boat Stations 1 and 2, which also accommodated the Engelhardt boats).

The collision took place at 11.40 p.m., and at about 12.05 a.m. the order was given to uncover the fourteen lifeboats. This work proceeded slowly at first under the supervision of the five officers; the crew arrived gradually on the Boat Deck, and there was an average of only three hands per lifeboat. The stewards were rousing the passengers in their different quarters, helping them to put on life jackets, and getting them up to the Boat Deck. At 12.20 a.m., the order was given to swing out the lifeboats, and about 12.30 a.m. the order was given to put women and children in them. At about 12.45 a.m. First Officer William Murdoch gave the order to lower Lifeboat 7 on the starboard side to the water. Fifth Officer Harold Lowe dealt with Lifeboats 1, 3, 5, and 7; Murdoch dealt with 1 and 7, and with A and C; Sixth Officer James Moody looked after Lifeboats 9, 11, 13, and 15, and Murdoch also saw to Lifeboats 9 and 11. Second Officer Lightoller saw to Lifeboats 4, 6, 8, and B and D, while Chief Officer Henry Wilde saw to Lifeboats 8 and D. Lightoller and Moody saw to Lifeboats 10 and 16, and Lowe to 12 and 14. Wilde assisted at Lifeboat 14, while Fourth Officer Joseph Boxhall helped generally. The odd-numbered lifeboats were launched from the starboard side, and the even-numbered ones from the port. The Engelhardt boats C and D were properly lowered, but it was difficult to get the boats A and B down from the roof of the Officers' House given the listing of the ship.

The boats that were carried on the *Titanic* in addition to the main lifeboats were a new type of collapsible lifeboat developed by a Danish Captain called V. Engelhardt. The first prototypes had been shown at the World's Fair in Paris in 1900. After this, a company was founded in Copenhagen called 'The Engelhardt Collapsible Life Boat Co', and the invention was patented in many countries. The first boat had been put on display in Copenhagen in 1901, and the Danish Navy, several ship insurance companies, and various nautical magazines predicted that the boat would have a great future.

In the United States, the boat was used on the warship *Illinois*, while the British Admiralty ordered a 20-foot boat which was delivered to the shipyard in Portsmouth in May 1903. Following trials on the *Illinois*, the American Navy ordered two further boats. The main advantages were that several boats of this type took up as much room on the deck of a ship as a normal lifeboat, while the number of people that the Englehardt boat could carry, regulated by the Board of Trade, was higher than for conventional boats of the same size. The boat could be unfolded quickly on the deck or in the water. And it was claimed that the boat was unsinkable. In an emergency, conventional lifeboats on the windward side were useless, whereas the Engelhardt boats could be carried to the leeward side and be put into the water without using the davits. And unlike conventional lifeboats, the Engelhardt boats would float even if they were damaged. The Engelhardt boats used on the *Titanic* were slightly different to those described above. They had a real hull, possibly a later invention to give them better stability at sea. In general, it seems likely that the Engelhardt boats were better than they are generally represented as having been in the *Titanic* literature. They were as safe as a conventional lifeboat, and not merely a weak substitute.

'**Latitude 41° 46' N, Longitude 50° 14' W**'

The crew of Lifeboat 13 was made up of cooks and stewards, the white jackets of the former showing up in the darkness as they pulled away, two to an oar. They had not done much rowing before, and their oars crossed and clashed; fortunately the safety of the passengers did not depend on speed or accuracy in keeping time. Shouting began from one end of the boat to the other as to what they should do, and where they should go. No one seemed to know. At last they asked 'Who is in charge of this boat?' but there was no reply. They agreed that Frederick Barrett, who stood in the stern with the tiller, should act as 'Captain', and from that time he directed their course, shouting to other boats and keeping in touch with them. Not that there was anywhere to go or anything they could do. Their plan of action was simple—to keep all the boats together as far as possible and wait until they were picked up by other liners. The crew had heard of the wireless messages before they left the *Titanic*; it was the *Olympic* that was coming to their rescue. They thought they even knew how far away she was, and making a calculation, came to the conclusion that there might be a chance of other steamers coming near enough to see the lights of the lifeboats. Everyone thought they would be picked up the next day. They knew that wireless messages would go out from ship to ship, and as one of the stokers said, 'The sea will be covered with ships tomorrow afternoon: they will race up from all over the sea to find us.'

Almost immediately after leaving the *Titanic*, they saw what they all said was a ship's lights down on the horizon on the ship's port side: two lights, one above the other, and obviously not one of their lifeboats. They even rowed in that direction for some time, but the lights drew away and disappeared below the horizon. But at first they had no eyes for anything but the ship they had just left. As the oarsmen pulled slowly away they all turned and took a long look at the mighty vessel towering above their tiny boat. It was the most extraordinary sight—language was inadequate to convey what Lawrence Beesley and the others saw.

First of all, the weather was extraordinary. The night was one of the most beautiful Beesley had ever seen, the sky without a single cloud to mar the perfect brilliance of the stars, clustered so thickly together that in places there seemed almost more dazzling points of light set in the black sky than background of sky itself. Each star seemed, in the keen atmosphere, free from any haze, to have increased its brilliance tenfold and to twinkle and glitter with a staccato flash that made the sky seem nothing but a setting made for them. They seemed so near, and their light so much more intense than ever before, that it seemed as if they saw this beautiful ship in dire distress below and all their energies had awakened to flash messages across the black dome of the sky to each other—telling and warning of the calamity happening in the world beneath. The complete absence of haze produced a phenomenon Beesley had never seen before. Where the sky met the sea, the line was as clear and definite as the edge of a knife, so that the water and the air never merged gradually into each other and blended to a softened rounded horizon, but each element was so separate that where a star came low down in the sky, near the clear-cut edge of the waterline, it still lost none of its brilliance. As the earth revolved and the water edge came up and covered partially the star, it simply cut it in two, the upper half continuing to sparkle as long as it was not entirely hidden, and throwing a long beam of light along the sea.

Secondly, there was the cold air. Here again was something quite new—there was not a breath of wind to blow keenly round them as they stood in the lifeboat, and to make them feel cold. It was just a bitter, icy, motionless cold that came from nowhere and yet was there all the time. The stillness of it—if one could imagine 'cold' being motionless and still—was what seemed new and strange. These—the sky and the air—were overhead, and below was the sea. Here again something was unusual—the surface was like a lake of oil, heaving gently up and down with a quiet motion that rocked their lifeboat dreamily to and fro. They did not need to keep her head to the swell—often Beesley watched her lying side on to the tide, and with a boat loaded as they were, this would have been impossible had it not been so calm. The sea slipped away smoothly under the boat, and they never heard it lapping against the sides, so oily in appearance was the water. When one of the stokers said he had been to sea for twenty-six years and never yet seen such a calm night, they believed him. Just as expressive was the remark of another—'It reminds me of a bloomin' picnic!' It was quite true; it did—a picnic on a lake, a quiet inland river like the Cam, or a backwater on the Thames.

And so in these conditions of sky, air, and sea, they gazed side-on at the *Titanic* from a short distance. She was absolutely still—indeed from the first it seemed as if the blow from the iceberg had taken all the courage out of her and she had just come quietly to rest and was settling down without an effort to save herself, without a murmur of protest. For the sea could not rock her—the wind was not there to howl noisily round the decks, and make the ropes hum. From the first what impressed all as they watched was the sense of stillness about her and the slow, insensible way she sank lower and lower in the sea, like a stricken animal. The sheer bulk alone of the ship viewed from the sea below was an awe-inspiring sight. A ship nearly a sixth of a mile long, 75 feet high to the top decks, with four enormous funnels above the decks, and masts again high above the funnels; with her hundreds of portholes, all her saloons and other rooms brilliant with light, and all round her, little boats filled with those who until a few hours before had walked her decks and read in her libraries and listened contentedly to the music of her band; and who were now looking up in amazement at the enormous mass above them and rowing away from her because she was sinking.

Some 58 miles away, on the steamship *Carpathia*, Captain Arthur Rostron's door had suddenly opened—the door near the head of his bunk which communicated with the Chart Room. He had only recently turned in and was not asleep, and drowsily he thought to himself: 'Who the dickens is this cheeky beggar coming into my cabin without knocking?' Then First Officer Horace Dean was blurting out the facts and Rostron was immediately wide awake, with thoughts for nothing but doing everything that was in the ship's power to render the necessary aid. The news seemed so incredible that, having at once given orders to turn the ship around, Rostron got hold of Harold Cottam, the Marconi operator, and assured himself there could have been no mistake. 'Are you sure it is the *Titanic* that requires immediate assistance?' Rostron asked him. 'Yes, sir.' But he had to ask again: 'You are absolutely certain?' 'Quite certain', Cottam replied. 'All right,' Rostron said, 'Tell him we are coming along as fast as we can.'

At 12.25 a.m., Cottam had been about to turn in for the night but waited at the headphones for a bit longer to hear news of the coal strike in England. The Marconi operator was keen on his job, and ignored the regulation time to stop work. He was, in fact, in the act of bending down to undo his boots when the call came, for he had kept the earphones on. 'SOS. *Titanic* calling. We have struck ice and require immediate assistance.' Cottam jerked upright, the alarm growing in his mind. It was the *Titanic*, a huge ship, proud of her size and power, carrying over 2,000 people, and making her maiden voyage from England to America. That was enough to impress on Cottam the magnitude of the danger and, throwing the earphones onto the table, he raced to Dean who was on watch at the time. If the signal had been two or three minutes later they would not have picked it up.

The passenger liner *Carpathia* had been built for Cunard by C. S. Swan & Hunter Ltd, in Newcastle, and was launched in August 1902. At 13,555 tons, it was 540 feet long, and 64½ feet wide. Its crew were quite proud of their Marconi equipment, though it had a normal range of only 130 miles, and just over 200 in exceptionally favourable conditions. And the ship carried only one operator. Cottam had been born in January 1891, in Southwell, Nottinghamshire. He had attended Minter Grammar School, and later studied the Marconi wireless system in London, becoming the youngest ever graduate from the School of Telegraphy, finishing when he was 17. He had gone to sea straightaway, but returned to work at one of the shore stations belonging to the Post Office. It was there that he had met the young Harold Bride. He returned to sea aboard the White Star liner *Medic*, on the Liverpool to Sydney route, before transferring to the *Carpathia* in February 1912.

Arthur Rostron had left New York on Thursday 11 April, the day after the *Titanic* had left Southampton, with many tourists among the 125 First Class, 65 Second Class, and 550 Third Class passengers. For nearly four months he had been taking the ship on her regular service between New York and Fiume on the Adriatic coast, taking migrants west to America, and holidaying Americans east to the ports of Europe. Rostron's home address was 52 Victoria Road, Great Crosby, near Liverpool. He had been born at Astley Bridge, Bolton, Lancashire, on 14 May 1869, the son of James and Nancy. He was educated at Astley Bridge High School, and at the age of 13 went to sea, on the Naval training ship *Conway*. After two years he was apprenticed to the Waverley Line on board the *Cedric the Saxon*; his work took him to America, India, and Australia. After three years, Rostron joined the barque *Red Gauntlet* as Second Mate; he was promoted to Mate before leaving the Waverley Line to join the *Camphill*, a barque trading to the west coast of South America. Rostron served as Second Mate on the steamship *Concord*, and joined the Cunard Line in 1895, serving on various ships. Rostron was made First Officer of the *Lusitania* in 1907, but was transferred to the Mediterranean service. His first command was the passenger steamer the *Pennonia*. As a Royal Naval Reserve, Rostron had to leave Cunard to serve in the Royal Navy during the Russo-Japanese War; after his return he was given command of the *Carpathia*.

Rostron went into the Chart Room, having got the *Titanic's* position from Cottam. It was latitude 41° 46' N, longitude 50° 14' W. He immediately worked out the course and issued orders. Within a few minutes of the call, the *Carpathia* was steaming as fast as it could to the rescue. One of the first things Rostron did was to wake up A. B. Johnson, the Chief Engineer, explain the urgency of the situation and, calling out an extra Watch in the Engine Room, get every ounce of power from the boilers and use every particle of steam for the engines, diverting it from all other uses, such as heating. The *Carpathia* was a 14-knot ship, but for three and a half hours she worked up to 17 knots. Fortunately it was night, and all the passengers were in their bunks. One of Rostron's first instructions was that, as far as possible, absolute silence should be maintained, while every crew member was told to instruct any passengers seen out to return to their cabins and stay there.

There was much to be done. All hands were called, and then began three hours of restless activity and never-ending anxiety. For although it was fortunate that the passengers were asleep, the fact it was night added to the risks. Racing through the dark towards unknown dangers from icebergs, standing on the Bridge with everyone keeping a look out, Rostron was fully conscious of the dangers his own ship and passengers were facing. The spring of that year had been phenomenal as far as ice was concerned. The *Titanic* was on the correct course, one where ice might sometimes be seen, but that night was exceptional and unique in everyone's memory. Two summers before, the season had been unusually warm in the far north. Islands of ice had broken adrift from the Arctic and drifted south. It took two years for these giant remnants to work their way so far south. The *Carpathia* raced into that zone of danger, and every nerve was strained watching for ice.

Before he could take command of the Bridge, however, there were a thousand and one things to be done. They started at once. Even as Rostron stood in the Chart Room working out the position, he saw the Bosun's Mate pass having finished his Watch to wash down the decks. Rostron called him, told him to stop routine work and, without making any noise, get all the lifeboats out ready for lowering. He looked very surprised. 'It's all right,' Rostron assured him, 'We are going to another vessel in distress.' The first officer that Rostron had called was the Engineer. Speed was the imperative need. When he had gone to turn out his extra Watch—and as soon as the men heard what was wanted and went to work, many without waiting to dress—Rostron summoned the English doctor, Purser, and Chief Steward.

Dr Frank McGee, the *Carpathia*'s Surgeon, was instructed to remain in the First Class Dining Room; Vittorio Risicato, an Italian doctor, in the Second; and Árpád Lengyel, a Hungarian doctor, in the Third. All were to get ready supplies of hot drinks, medicines, and other things. The Purser, with his Assistant Purser and Chief Steward, was to receive the rescued at the different gangways, managing the *Carpathia*'s stewards in assisting the *Titanic* passengers to the different dining rooms for accommodation and attention. They were also to get, as far as possible, the names of survivors, so that these could be sent by wireless. The Inspector, Third Class stewards, and Masters-at-Arms were to control the *Carpathia*'s Third Class passengers, keep them out of the Dining Hall, and stop them from going on deck. The Chief Steward was to call all hands and have coffee ready for the *Carpathia*'s crew, with soup, coffee, tea, and other drinks for the rescued. Blankets were to be placed ready near gangways, in saloons and public rooms, with others handy for the lifeboats. All spare berths in Third Class were to be prepared for the *Titanic*'s passengers, while the *Carpathia*'s own Third Class occupants were to be grouped together.

It was made clear to everyone that the strictest silence and discipline was to be maintained, while a steward was to be stationed in each gangway to reassure the *Carpathia*'s passengers if any heard noises and asked questions—such people were to be asked politely but firmly to return to, and remain, in their own cabins. Rostron's friends, Lewis M. Ogden and his wife, were on board that night. They occupied a deck cabin and because of its location it was inevitable that they would hear some of the preparations that were being made. Their experience was replicated many times by other passengers, though while all these things were being done the great majority of those on board slept peacefully, unaware of the efforts of the crew. During the night, Ogden's wife awoke and roused him. 'What's that noise on deck?' she asked. 'Don't worry, go to sleep,' Ogden replied. But Mrs Ogden was not to be so summarily silenced. 'Open the door and see what's wrong.' Ogden obeyed the order. Outside was a steward. Ogden called him. 'What's the noise all about?' he asked. 'Nothing, sir, doing work with the boats.' 'What for?' 'I can't tell you, sir.'

Ogden went back to bed, and naturally his wife's suspicions only increased. She waited for a few minutes listening to the noises which were inevitable as the *Carpathia*'s lifeboats were swung out on their davits. 'Try again,' she requested at length. This time Ogden, peeping out, encountered the Surgeon. 'What's the trouble?' 'There's no trouble. Please return to your cabin. It is the Captain's orders.' That didn't allay the doubts. Going back and repeating the conversation to his wife, the Ogdens both began to dress, putting their valuables in their pockets. Then Mrs Ogden's insistence began again. 'Try again.' Once more Ogden opened the door—and, surprisingly, he again looked into the face of Frank McGee, the Surgeon. There was no need for questions, and McGee ordered him back and told him on no account to leave the cabin until the Captain gave instructions. But the passenger was urgent and at length, as the only method of satisfying him, the Surgeon said 'We are going to the *Titanic*. She's in distress.' 'But isn't this ship in distress?' 'No, sir, it's the *Titanic*, she's struck ice.' But then Ogden saw stewards in line carrying pillows and blankets. 'There's something wrong,' he concluded. And somehow he and his wife reached the deck. They found a nook and remained there.

Meanwhile, the *Carpathia* was ploughing on through the night—a brilliant night of stars. Rostron had been able to go to the Bridge. Harold Cottam reported to Rostron that he had picked up a message from the *Titanic* to the *Olympic* asking the latter to have all her lifeboats ready. The sense of tragedy was growing. But the *Olympic*, bound for home, was hundreds of miles away, very much further than the *Carpathia*. The *Titanic* had also called the *Carpathia*. They asked how long she would be getting there. 'Say about four hours,' Rostron told Cottam, 'and tell her we shall have all our boats in readiness and all other preparations necessary to receive the rescued'.

Rostron then gave the following orders to First Officer Dean. All lifeboats were to be prepared and swung out; all gangway doors to be opened; there were to be electric clusters at each gangway and over the side; a block—with line rope—was to be hooked in each gangway; a chair—slung—was to be at each gangway for getting up sick or injured; there should be pilot ladders and side ladders at gangways and over the side; there should be cargo falls, with both ends clear and secured, along the ship's side on deck, for boat ropes or to help people up; lines and gaskets were to be distributed about the decks to be handy for lashings; the forward derricks were to be rigged and topped and with steam on winches—to get mail or other goods on board; oil was to be poured down both sides to quieten the sea; canvas ash-bags should be near gangways for hauling up children or the helpless; and the company's rockets were to be fired from 3 a.m. every quarter of an hour to reassure the *Titanic*. Beyond these, there were detailed instructions as to the various duties of the officers in case the situation required the use of the *Carpathia's* lifeboats.

At about 2.35 a.m.—roughly two hours after the first call—the doctor came to the Bridge and reported that all instructions had been carried out and everything was ready. While they were talking together, Rostron saw a green flare on the port bow. 'There's her light,' Rostron cried, pointing. 'She must be still afloat.' This looked like good news. An hour earlier, Harold Cottam had brought Rostron a message from the *Titanic* that the Engine Room was filling. That had looked fatal. It left little doubt that the ship was sinking. So to catch that green flare brought renewed hope. At almost the same time, the Second Officer reported the first iceberg, on the port bow. Rostron saw it towering into the sky quite near—saw it because a star was reflected on its surface—a tiny beam of warning which guided them safely past. The crew of the *Carpathia* grew more and more anxious. Icebergs loomed up and fell astern, but the ship never slowed, though sometimes it altered course suddenly to avoid them. It was an anxious time with the *Titanic's* fateful experience uppermost in the minds of the crew. The *Carpathia* had 700 passengers and crew, and these lives, as well as those of the survivors of the *Titanic*, depended on a sudden turn of the wheel.

As the *Titanic's* passengers watched the ship sink lower and lower in the water from the safety of their lifeboats, they knew only too well that many crew and passengers were still aboard. When Archibald Gracie first realized that every lifeboat had gone, his voice had died in his throat. But he also knew that he needed to think quickly, act, and stay composed. Gracie hoped and prayed for escape. His mind was ready to do what might be necessary, and his muscles seemed to be hardened in preparation for the coming struggle. When he learned that there was another boat, the Engelhardt, on the roof of the Officers' Quarters, he felt encouraged with the thought that here was a chance of getting away before the ship sank. But what was one boat among so many eager to board her?

John Borland Thayer and George Widener had disappeared, but Gracie didn't know where. They must have gone towards the stern. Gracie was now working with the crew at the davits on the starboard side, adjusting them, ready for lowering the Engelhardt boat from the roof of the Officers' House to the Boat Deck below. One of the crew on the roof called out 'Has any passenger a knife?' Gracie took his out of his pocket and tossed it to him, saying 'Here is a small penknife, if that will do any good.' Gracie noted that it was more difficult than it ought to have been to remove the canvas cover and cut the boat loose; it should have been possible to do this without any delay. Meanwhile, four or five oars were placed diagonally across the walls of the Officers' House to break the fall of the boat. It was pushed from the roof and slipped with a crash down onto the Boat Deck, smashing several of the oars. Gracie and James Clinch Smith scurried out of the way and stood leaning with their backs against the rail, watching and feeling anxious in case the boat had been damaged.

About this time, an officer on the roof of the House called down to the crew 'Are there any seamen down there among you?' 'Aye, aye, sir', was the response, and quite a number left the Boat Deck to assist in cutting loose the other Engelhardt boat up there on the roof. Again Gracie heard a request for a knife. He thought he recognized the voice of Second Officer Lightoller working up there with the crew. The crew had thrown the Engelhardt boat on to the deck, but Gracie did not understand why they were so slow in launching it, unless they were waiting to cut the other one loose and launch them both at the same time. Two young crewmen, dressed in white, one tall and the other smaller, were coolly debating whether the watertight compartments would keep the ship afloat. They were standing with their backs to the rail looking at the rest of the crew, and Gracie asked one of them why he wasn't helping.

At this time there were other passengers around, but Smith was the only one who stayed with Gracie. Now, fifteen minutes after the launching of the last lifeboat on the port side, Gracie heard a noise that spread anxiety among all of them. This was the water striking the Bridge and gurgling up the forward hatchway. It seemed for a moment as if it would reach the Boat Deck. It appeared as if it would take the crew a long time to turn the Engelhardt boat right side up and lift it over the rail, and there were so many passengers and crew ready to board her that she would have been swamped. Realizing this, Smith proposed that he and Gracie should leave and go towards the stern, still on the starboard side.

They had only taken a few steps when a crowd of people several ranks deep, from the decks below, arose in front of them, covering the Boat Deck, facing them, and completely blocking their path towards the stern. There were women in the crowd, as well as men, and they seemed to be Third Class passengers. Instantly, when they saw Gracie and Smith and the water on the deck chasing them from behind, they turned in the opposite direction towards the stern. This brought them right up against the iron fence and railing which divided First and Second Class. Smith and Gracie immediately realized that they could make no progress ahead, and that, with the water following behind them over the deck, they were in a desperate situation. Smith was immediately on Gracie's left, and their backs were turned towards the ship's rail and the sea. Looking up towards the roof of the Officers' House, Gracie saw a man above and to his right, lying on his stomach, with his legs dangling over. Smith jumped to reach the roof, and Gracie followed him. They both failed to make it—Gracie was loaded down with a long overcoat, Norfolk jacket, and clumsy life jacket. As he came down, the water struck his right side. He crouched down into it before jumping with it, and rose as if on the crest of a wave. He was able to reach the roof and the iron railing along its edge, and pulled himself on his stomach over on top of the House near the base of the second funnel. He had no time to advise Smith to do the same. To his dismay, a quick glance to left and right showed that Smith had not followed him, and that the wave had completely covered him, as well as people on both sides.

It was on Smith's suggestion that Gracie had left the point on the starboard side of the Boat Deck where the crew, under Chief Officer Wilde and First Officer Murdoch, were in vain trying to launch the Engelhardt boat which had been thrown down from the roof of the Officers' Quarters forward of the first funnel on the Boat Deck. Smith and Gracie got away from this point just before the water reached it, drowning Wilde, Murdoch, and others who were not successful in getting on the boat as it was swept off the deck. The force of the wave that struck Smith and the others knocked most of them unconscious.

Gracie held on to the iron railing and this saved him from the same fate. He pulled himself over on the roof on his stomach, but before he could get to his feet he was in a whirlpool of water, swirling round and round, as he still tried to cling to the railing as the ship plunged to the depths below. Down, down, he went; it seemed a great distance. He noticed the pressure on his ears, though there must have been plenty of air that the ship carried down with it. As soon as he could, he swam away from the starboard side as if his life depended on it. Gracie was frightened by the thought of boiling water, or steam, from the explosion of the ship's boilers, and that he would be scalded to death, like sailors he had read about. Because of that, the plunge in the icy water produced no sense of coldness, and he did not think about it until later on. Gracie struck out and swam faster and further underwater than he had ever done before. He held his breath for what seemed forever until he could stand it no longer.

Just at the moment when he thought he would have to give in, he found his second wind.

With this, Gracie had a new lease of strength, until he finally noticed it getting lighter and he was coming to the surface. Though it was dark, the clear starlit night made a noticeable difference to the degree of light immediately below the surface of the water. As he was rising, Gracie bumped into wreckage, but the only sizeable object he struck was a small plank, which he tucked under his right arm. When his head at last rose above the water, he eagerly seized a wooden crate. Looking around, he could not see the *Titanic*. She had entirely disappeared beneath the calm surface of the ocean and without a sign of any wave.

What impressed Gracie was a thin light-grey smoky vapour that hung like a pall a few feet above the broad expanse of the sea that was covered with a mass of tangled wreckage. It may have been caused by smoke or steam rising to the surface around the area where the ship had sunk. At any rate it produced a supernatural effect. Added to this there rose to the sky agonizing death cries, the wails and groans of the suffering, the shrieks of the terror-stricken, and the awful gaspings for breath of those in the last throes of drowning. 'Help! Help! Boat ahoy! Boat ahoy!' and 'My God! My God!' were the heart-rending cries and shrieks of men, which floated continuously for the next hour to Gracie and the others over the surface of the dark waters. As time went on, they grew weaker and weaker until they died out entirely.

As Gracie clung to the wreckage, he noticed just in front of him, a few yards away, a group of three bodies with their heads in the water, faces downward, and another body just behind him to his right. There was no one alive or struggling in the water or calling for aid in the immediate vicinity. Gracie threw his right leg over the wooden crate in an attempt to straddle it, but he turned in a somersault, underwater and up to the surface again. He thought of the accounts of shipwreck he had read and pictures he had seen. He looked around, but he knew the thought of a rescuing boat was a vain one—for hadn't all the lifeboats, loaded with women and children, departed from the ship fifteen or twenty minutes before he sank with it? And had he not seen them leaving from the port side, and fading away from his sight?

But Gracie's prayers and hopes were answered in an unexpected way. He saw to his left the same Engelhardt boat that he had tried to launch until the water had broken on the ship's deck. On top of this upturned boat were more than a dozen members of the crew. He discarded the crate, struck out through the wreckage, and after a considerable swim reached its port side. There was a member of the crew at the bow with an improvised paddle, and another at the stern. When Gracie reached the side of the boat, he grabbed a young member of the crew nearest and facing him. At the same time he threw his leg over the boat, pulled himself aboard, and then lay with the others on the bottom of the capsized boat. About a dozen other swimmers followed and were helped aboard. Among them was one who was completely exhausted. Gracie pulled him in and he lay face downwards in front of him. The moment of getting aboard this upturned boat was one of huge mental relief. Gracie now felt for the first time since the lifeboats had left the ship that he had a chance of not drowning. He had received a blow on the top of his head, but at the time he noticed neither it nor his other wounds.

There was an anxious moment on the Engelhardt boat when about thirty men clambered out of the water on to it. The weight of each additional body submerged the boat more and more. There were men swimming in the water all around them. The situation was a desperate one, and was only saved by the refusal of the crew, especially those at the stern of the boat, to take another passenger aboard. After pulling aboard the exhausted man, Gracie turned his head away. Though he did not see, he could not avoid hearing what took place. The men with the paddles, forward and aft, steered the boat to avoid contact with those struggling for their lives. Gracie heard the constant explanation made as they passed men swimming in the wreckage: 'Hold on to what you have, old boy; one more of you aboard would sink us all.' He heard no word of rebuke from a swimmer because of a refusal to give assistance. There was no violence. But there was one case of heroism that he remembered. One man replied 'All right, boys, good luck and God bless you.' Their nearly submerged boat was among the wreckage and was quickly being paddled out of the danger zone. The expressions used by some of the crew sounded harsh to Gracie's ears.

Earlier, at about 12.30 a.m., Assistant Wireless Operator Harold Bride had gone out on the *Titanic*'s deck and looked around. The water was close up to the Boat Deck. There was a great scramble aft, towards the stern, and Bride noted later that he did not know how his colleague Jack Phillips worked through it. Bride suddenly felt a great respect to see him standing there bravely sticking to his work while everybody else was trying to save themselves. He thought it was about time to look around and see if there was anything detached that would float. Every member of the crew had a special life jacket and he ought to know where it was. His was under his bunk, and he went and got it. Then he thought how cold the water was. He had some boots, and he put those on, along with an extra jacket. He saw Phillips standing still sending messages, giving the *Carpathia* details of how they were doing.

Jack Phillips had been sending messages as quickly as possible, saying the *Titanic* had struck an iceberg and required immediate assistance. At 1.10 a.m., Phillips telegraphed the *Olympic*: 'We are in collision with berg. Sinking Head down. 41.46 N., 50.14 W. Come as soon as possible', and again at 1.10 a.m. saying 'Get your boats ready. What is your position?' At 1.25 a.m., the *Olympic* asked 'Are you steering southerly to meet us?' Phillips explained 'We are putting the women off in the boats.' At 1.35 a.m., Phillips said 'Engine room getting flooded'. Then, at 1.45 a.m., there was a final plea from Phillips to the *Carpathia*: 'Come as quickly as possible old man: our engine-room is filling up to the boilers.' As Phillips was sending the message, Bride strapped his life jacket to his back. He had already put on his overcoat. He wondered if he could get Phillips into his boots. Phillips suggested with a sort of laugh that Bride look out and see if all the people had gone in the lifeboats, or if any were left.

Bride saw an Engelhardt boat near a funnel and went over to it. Twelve men were trying to lift it down to the Boat Deck, but they were having a desperate time. It was the last boat left, and Bride looked at it longingly for a few minutes. Then he gave them a hand, and over the boat went. They all started to scramble in on the Boat Deck, and he walked back to Phillips. He told him the last raft had gone. Then they heard the Captain's voice: 'Men, you have done your full duty. You can do no more. Abandon your cabin. Now it's every man for himself. You look out for yourselves. I release you. That's the way of it at this kind of a time. Every man for himself.'

When Bride next looked out, the Boat Deck was awash. Jack Phillips had continued sending messages for about ten or fifteen minutes after the Captain had released him. At 2.17 a.m., Phillips sent the faint message 'C.Q.', but the water was already coming into the Wireless Cabin. While Phillips worked, Bride was back in his room getting Phillips's money. As he looked out the door he saw a stoker, or someone from below decks, leaning over Phillips from behind. Phillips was too busy to notice what the man was doing. The man was slipping the life jacket off Phillips's back. He was a large man whereas Bride was very small. So Bride got hold of something. He remembered in a flash the way Phillips had continued sending the messages, how Bride had had to fix his life jacket in place because Philips had been too busy to do it for himself. Bride knew that the man from below decks had his own life jacket and should have known where to get it. He suddenly felt furious. Bride did what he regarded as his duty. When he and Phillips left the wireless cabin, the stoker was on the floor and was not moving.

From behind came the tunes of the band. It was a ragtime tune, but Bride didn't know exactly what it was. Then he recognized Archibald Joyce's tune 'Songe d'automne'. Phillips ran aft, towards the stern, to the place where he had seen the Engelhardt boat and the men trying to push it off. There wasn't a sailor in the crowd, and they couldn't do it. Bride went up to them and was just lending a hand when a large wave came awash on the deck. The big wave carried the boat off the ship. Bride had hold of an oarlock, and he went overboard with it. The next thing Bride knew he was in the boat. But that was not all. He was in the boat, and the boat was upside down, and he was under it. He realized he was wet through. And he knew that, whatever happened, he must not breathe, for he was underwater. He knew he had to fight. He did not know how he got out from under the boat, but he felt a breath of air at last. There were men all around him—hundreds of them. The sea was dotted with them, all relying on their life jackets. Bride felt he simply had to get away from the ship.

The *Titanic* was a beautiful sight, and smoke and sparks were rushing out of her funnel. Bride and the others did not hear an explosion. They only saw a big stream of sparks. The ship was gradually turning on her nose—just like a duck does when it goes down for a dive.

Bride had only one thing on his mind—to get away from the suction. He swam with all his might. He was 150 feet away when the *Titanic* began to settle slowly, on her nose, with her after-quarter sticking straight up in the air. Bride found that when at last the waves washed over the rudder, he couldn't feel the least bit of suction. She must have kept going just as slowly as she had been. Apart from the *Olympic* and the *Carpathia*, Bride and Phillips had spoken to a German ship, the *Frankfurt*, and had told it about the predicament of the *Titanic*. They had also spoken to the *Baltic*. Bride began to figure out which ships would be coming towards them.

He felt, after a little while, like sinking. He was very cold. He saw a boat of some kind near him, and put all his strength into an effort to swim to it. It was hard work. He was nearly exhausted when a hand reached out from the boat and pulled him aboard. It was the Engelhardt boat, and there was just room for Bride to roll on the edge. He lay there, not caring what happened. Someone sat on his legs. They were wedged in between the slats and were being wrenched. Bride had not the heart to ask the man to move. It was a terrible sight around the boat—men swimming and sinking. Bride lay where he was, letting the man twist his feet out of shape. Others came near, but nobody gave them a hand. The upturned boat already had more men than it could hold and was sinking. At first the larger waves splashed over Bride's clothing. Then they began to splash over his head, and he had to breathe when he could. As they floated around on their upturned boat, and he kept straining his eyes for a ship's lights, someone said 'Don't the rest of you think we ought to pray?' The man who made the suggestion asked what denomination the others were. Each man called out his religion; one was a Catholic, one a Methodist, and one a Presbyterian. It was decided the most appropriate prayer for everyone was the Lord's Prayer. They said it together with the man who suggested they pray as the leader.

'She's Gone, Lads;
Row Like Hell'

Second Officer Herbert Lightoller was also still aboard the ship. Just then the ship took a slight but definite plunge—probably a bulkhead went—and the sea came rolling up in a wave, over the steel-fronted Bridge, along the deck below him and Samuel Hemming, washing the people back in a dreadful huddled mass. Those that didn't disappear under the water right away instinctively started to clamber up that part of the deck still out of the water, and work their way towards the stern, which was rising steadily out of the water as the bow went down. A few of the more agile leapt up on top of the Officers' Quarters. It was a sight that didn't bear dwelling upon —to stand there, above the Wheelhouse, and on their Quarters, watching the frantic struggles to climb up the sloping deck, completely unable to even hold out a helping hand.

Lightoller knew, only too well, the utter futility of following that instinct of self-preservation and struggling up towards the stern. It would only be postponing the plunge, and prolonging the agony— even lessening his already slim chances, by becoming one of a crowd. It came home to him very clearly how fatal it would be to get among those hundreds of people who would shortly be struggling for their lives in the water. There was only one thing to do, and Lightoller decided he might as well get it over with. So turning to the fore part of the Bridge, he dived. Striking the water was like a thousand knives being driven into his body, and, for a few moments, he completely lost grip of himself—and no wonder for he was perspiring freely, while the temperature of the water was 28° Fahrenheit, or 4° Celsius below freezing.

Ahead of him the Crow's-Nest on the foremast was visible just above the water—normally it would have been 100 feet above. Lightoller struck out blindly for this, but only for a short time, until he got hold of himself again and realized the futility of seeking safety on anything connected with the ship. He then turned to starboard, away from the ship altogether. For a time he wondered what was making it so difficult for him to keep his head above water. Time and again he went under, until it dawned on him that it was the Webley revolver, still in his pocket, that was dragging him down.

The water was now pouring down the stokeholds, by way of the gratings abaft the Bridge, and round the forward funnel. On the Boat Deck, above the Officers' Quarters, on the forward funnel, was a huge rectangular air shaft and ventilator, with an opening about 20 by 15 feet. On this opening was a wire grating to prevent rubbish being drawn or thrown down. This shaft led directly to No. 3 Hold, and was therefore a sheer drop of nearly 100 feet, right to the bottom of the ship. Lightoller suddenly found himself drawn by the sudden rush of the surface water now pouring down this shaft, and held flat and firmly up against the wire. The pressure of the water glued him there while the ship sank slowly beneath the surface. He knew what would happen if this gave way.

Although Lightoller struggled and kicked for all he was worth, it was impossible to get away, for as fast as he pushed himself off he was irresistibly dragged back, every instant expecting the wire to give way, and to find himself shot down into the bowels of the ship. Apart from that, he was drowning. He was still struggling and fighting when suddenly a blast of hot air came up the shaft, and blew him away and up to the surface. The water was now swirling around, and the ship sinking rapidly, when once again he was caught and sucked down by an inrush of water, this time pinning him to one of the gratings. He didn't know how he got clear, but he eventually came to the surface, this time alongside the Engelhardt boat which Samuel Hemming and he had launched from the Officers' Quarters on the opposite side—Lightoller was now on the starboard side, near the forward funnel. There were many other men in the water, some swimming, others drowning—a nightmare to see and hear. In the circumstances, Lightoller made an effort to get on top of the upturned boat, but was content to remain floating alongside, just hanging on to a small piece of rope.

The bow of the *Titanic* was now rapidly going down and the stern rising higher and higher out of the water, piling the people into helpless heaps around the steep decks, and by the score into the water. Organized help, or even individual help, was quite impossible. All Lightoller could do was wait on events, and try and forget the icy grip of the water. The terrific strain of bringing the after-end of that huge hull clear of the water caused the expansion joint abaft No. 1 Funnel to open up. This threw an extraordinary strain on the two wire stays to this funnel, eventually carrying away the wire guy on the port side, to be followed almost immediately by the starboard. Instantly the port one parted, the funnel started to fall, but the fact that the starboard one held a moment or two longer gave this huge structure a pull over to that side of the ship, causing it to fall, with all its weight, onto the people already in the water. It struck the water between the Engelhardt boat and the ship, missing Lightoller by inches. The wash that was created flung the Engelhardt clear of the sinking ship.

Lightoller was 50 yards from the ship. The piece of rope was still in his hand, and the Engelhardt boat upturned and attached to the other end, with several men standing on it. Lightoller scrambled up. Lights on board the *Titanic* were still burning, and the ship made an awe-inspiring spectacle, standing out black and massive against the starlit sky, with myriads of lights still gleaming through the portholes from that part of the decks still above water.

The fore part and up to the second funnel was by this time completely submerged, and as they watched, suddenly all the lights went out and the huge bulk was left in black darkness, clearly silhouetted against the sky. Then, the next moment, the massive boilers left their moorings and went thundering down with a hollow rumbling roar, through the bulkheads, carrying everything with them. The tragedy now rapidly approached its finale, as the huge ship slowly but surely reared itself on end and brought rudder and propellers clear of the water, until, at last, she assumed a perpendicular position. She remained poised for about half a minute. Then, with impressive majesty and ever-increasing momentum, the *Titanic* silently took her last dive. Almost like a benediction, everyone around Lightoller on the upturned boat breathed the two words 'She's gone'. Although the scene that followed was shrouded in darkness, the calm, still night carried every sound with startling distinctness. The sounds were heart-rending and never-to-be-forgotten.

Lawrence Beesley had often wanted to see the *Titanic* from a distance, and only a few hours before, in conversation at lunch with a fellow passenger, he had vowed to get a proper view of her lines and dimensions when they arrived in New York—to stand some distance away to take in a full view of her beautiful proportions, which the narrow approach to the dock at Southampton had made impossible. Little had Beesley thought the opportunity would be found so quickly and so dramatically. The background, too, was different to what he had planned—the black outline of her profile against the sky was bordered all round by stars studded in the sky, and all her funnels and masts were picked out in the same way—her bulk was seen where the stars were blotted out. And another thing was different—the thing that stole all sense of the beauty of the night, the ship's lines, and her lights. That was the awful angle made by the level of the sea with the rows of porthole lights along her side in dotted lines, row above row. The sea level and the rows of lights should have been parallel—should never have met—and now they met at an angle inside the black hull of the ship. There was nothing else to indicate she was injured; nothing but this apparent violation of a simple geometrical law—that parallel lines should never meet. It meant that the *Titanic* had sunk by the head until the lowest portholes in the bow were under the sea, and those in the stern were lifted above the normal height. Beesley and his companions rowed away from her in the quietness of the night, hoping and praying that she would sink no more, and the day would find her still in the same position.

The crew of Lifeboat 13, however, did not think so. Frederick Barrett—the same man that had pushed Lifeboat 15 away from above them—told them how he was at work in the stokehole, and in anticipation of going off duty in a quarter of an hour had a pan of soup near him on some part of the machinery keeping hot. Suddenly the whole side of the compartment had come in, and the water had rushed him off his feet. Picking himself up, he had sprung for the compartment doorway and was just through the aperture when the watertight door came down behind him, as he said, 'like a knife'. He had gone up on deck but was ordered down again at once and with others was told to draw the fires from under the boiler. They did this, and were then free to go on deck again. This group of stokers must have known as soon as anyone the extent of the damage. He added mournfully, 'I could do with that hot soup now'—and indeed he could—he had been clad at the time of the collision in trousers and singlet, both very thin on account of the intense heat in the stokehole, and although he had added a short jacket later, his teeth were chattering with the cold. Barrett found a place underneath the tiller, and there he lay all night with a coat belonging to another stoker thrown over him; he was almost unconscious. A woman next to him, who was warmly clad with several coats, tried to insist that he should have one of hers—a fur-lined one—but he absolutely refused while some of the women were insufficiently clad. So the coat was given to an Irish girl with auburn hair standing near, leaning against the gunwale and so more exposed to the cold air. The same woman was able to distribute more of her wraps to the passengers, a rug to one, a fur boa to another. Beesley had not seen his dressing-gown since he had dropped into the boat, but some time in the night a Third Class passenger found it on the floor and put it on.

In Lifeboat 13 there was one First Class passenger, Dr Washington Dodge, a banker from San Francisco; twelve passengers from Second; and twenty-six other passengers, mostly women, from Third. The rest of the lifeboat's occupants, about twenty-four, were crew, mainly Able Seamen, firemen, stewards, scullions, and plate washers. Near to Beesley was a group of three Swedish girls, Anna Nysten, Helmina Nilsson, and Aurora Landergren, warmly dressed, standing close together to keep warm, and very silent. There was very little talking. Alden Caldwell, the baby who had been handed down at the last moment, had been received by a woman next to Beesley—the same one who shared her wraps and coats. Alden's mother Sylvia had found a place in the middle of the lifeboat and was too tightly packed to come through to the child, and so he slept contentedly for about an hour in a stranger's arms. Then he began to cry and the temporary nurse said: 'Will you feel down and see if the baby's feet are out of the blanket? I don't know much about babies but I think their feet must be kept warm.'

Wriggling down as well as Beesley could, he found the baby's toes exposed to the air and wrapped them up. He immediately stopped crying. Having recognized the woman by her voice—it was much too dark to see faces—as one of the people he had met at the Purser's table, Beesley said 'Surely you are Miss Hilda Slayter?' 'Yes,' she replied, 'and you must be Mr Beesley; how curious we should find ourselves in the same boat!' Remembering that she had joined the boat at Queenstown, he said 'Do you know Clonmel? A letter from a great friend of mine who is staying there at [giving the address] came aboard at Queenstown.' She replied 'Yes, it is my home: I was dining at [place] just before I came away.' Hilda Slayter had been born in Halifax, Nova Scotia, in 1882, the daughter of a doctor. She had left home to study music in Italy, but had returned to Canada and become engaged to Harry Reginald Dunbar Lacon of Ottley, son of a British MP. She had been shopping in England for her wedding trousseau, and had shared a cabin with Fannie Kelly, a widow from London who was going to visit her son in New York. It seemed that Hilda knew Beesley's friend, and they agreed that of all places in the world to recognize mutual friends, a crowded lifeboat afloat in mid-ocean at 2 a.m., 1,200 miles from their destination, was one of the most unexpected.

And all the time, as they watched, the *Titanic* sank lower and lower by the head and the angle became wider and wider as the stern port-hole lights lifted and the bow lights sank, and it was clear she was not to stay afloat much longer. Barrett now told the oarsmen to row away as hard as they could. This seemed sensible for two reasons. First, that as she sank the *Titanic* would create such a wave of suction that the lifeboats, if not sucked under by being too near, would be in danger of being swamped by the wave her sinking would create. They all knew their lifeboat was in no condition to ride big waves, crowded as it was and manned with untrained oarsmen. Second, that an explosion might result from the water getting to the boilers, and debris fall over a wide radius. At about 2.15 a.m., they were between a mile to two miles away. They had been afloat an hour and a half, the boat was heavily loaded, the oarsmen unskilled, and their course erratic. Following one light and then another, sometimes a star and sometimes a light from a port lifeboat which had turned away from the *Titanic* in the opposite direction and lay almost on the horizon, they could not have gone very far.

About this time, the water had crept in up almost to the *Titanic*'s sidelight and the Captain's Bridge, and it seemed a question only of minutes before she sank. The oarsmen lay on their oars, and all in the lifeboat were motionless as they watched her in absolute silence—apart from some who would not look and buried their heads on each other's shoulders. The lights still shone with the same brilliance, but not so many of them—many were now below the surface.

And then, as they gazed awestruck, the *Titanic* tilted slowly up, revolving apparently about a centre of gravity just astern of amid-ships, until she was vertically upright, and there she remained—motionless. As she swung up, her lights, which had shone without a flicker all night, went out suddenly, came on again for a single flash, and then went out altogether. And as they did, there was a noise. It was the engines and machinery coming loose from their bolts and bearings, and falling through the compartments, smashing everything in their way. It was partly a roar, partly a groan, partly a rattle, and partly a smash, and it was not a sudden roar as an explosion would be. It went on successively for some seconds, possibly fifteen to twenty, as the heavy machinery dropped down to the bottom of the ship. But it was a noise no one had heard before, and no one wished to hear again. It was stupefying, stupendous, as it came to them across the water. It was as if all the heavy things Beesley could think of had been thrown downstairs from the top of a house, smashing each other and the stairs and everything in the way.

When the noise was over, the *Titanic* was still upright like a column. They could see her now only as the stern and some 150 feet of her stood outlined against the star-speckled sky, looming black in the darkness, and in this position she continued for some minutes—perhaps as many as five. Then, first sinking back a little at the stern, she slid slowly forwards through the water and dived slantingly down. The sea closed over her, and Beesley had seen the last of the beautiful ship on which he had embarked four days earlier at Southampton.

And in place of the ship on which all their interest had been concentrated for so long and towards which they looked most of the time because it was still the only object on the sea which was a fixed point, they had the level sea now stretching in an unbroken expanse to the horizon, heaving gently just as before, with no indication on the surface that the waves had just closed over the *Titanic*. The stars looked down just as before, and the air was as bitterly cold.

There seemed a great sense of loneliness when they were left on the sea in a small boat without the *Titanic*—not that they were uncomfortable (except for the cold) nor in danger—but the ship was no longer there. They waited head on for the wave which they thought might come—the wave they had heard so much of from the crew and which they said had been known to travel for miles—and it never came. But the *Titanic* did leave them something they would willingly forget forever, something which it was as well not to let the imagination dwell on—the cries of many hundreds of their fellow passengers struggling in the water.

Beesley and his companions were utterly surprised to hear this cry go up as the waves closed over the *Titanic*. They had heard no sound of any kind from her since they had left her side, and they did not know how many lifeboats or rafts she had. The crew had never told the passengers. So, unprepared as they were for such a thing, the cries of the drowning floating across the quiet sea amazed them. They longed to return and rescue at least some, but they knew it was impossible. Lifeboat 13 was filled to standing-room, and to return would mean swamping them all, and so Barrett told his 'crew' to row away from the cries. They tried to sing to keep everyone from thinking of them, but they had no heart for it.

The cries, which were loud and numerous at first, died away gradually one by one, but the night was clear, frosty, and still, the water smooth, and the sounds must have carried for miles on its level surface free from any obstruction. The last of them must have been heard nearly 40 minutes after the *Titanic* sank. Life jackets would keep the survivors afloat for hours, but the cold water was what ended the cries.

In Lifeboat 14, Edith Brown also noted that puffs of vapour marked the breaths of the occupants; the night air was icy cold. Edith had turned her head away to comfort her mother, but now she looked back as the grating, crashing, and creaking noises of twisted, tortured metal and woodwork grew louder. Despite those sounds from across the water, music could be heard now and again, coming from somewhere up on the Boat Deck. The ship's deck lights shone down on the water, and lights from many portholes as the stern of the *Titanic* continued to rise slowly out of the water. People were making their way along the decks towards the stern, as there were now no lifeboats left on the ship. The only option left for the crew and passengers was to get onto the highest part of the ship and hope that some miracle might save them.

As the lifeboats circled the stricken liner at a safe distance, the occupants could see that the forward section of the ship had now completely disappeared below the sea. There were thunderous noises coming from deep within the hull, followed by screeches, screams, and shouts that grew louder across the water. The crashing of broken glass and the booming noises of bulkheads giving way were followed by tremendous thuds as huge sections of machinery crashed through the ship towards the submerged end. Edith and her mother watched and listened in horror. They put their hands over their ears to block out the sounds of human suffering. Suddenly there was a shout from one of the boat's crew. 'The funnel is falling over!' With that, there was a gasp from the lifeboats as the foremost funnel appeared to teeter over and the wire stays snapped. It crashed into the sea amid clouds of steam, smoke, and a shower of sparks. At this time, people were jumping into the sea as the stern continued to rise. Then it appeared to settle back slightly, before finally following the forward end down into the depths. The screams and cries for help were drowned out briefly as huge underwater explosions erupted, sending towering spumes to the surface as the flagstaff at the *Titanic*'s stern finally disappeared below the sea.

Edith noted that the gurgling and bubbling noises had begun to abate as the surface of the water began to settle, leaving a slight mist. 'Make way together!' shouted Fifth Officer Harold Lowe. Once more, hundreds of cries for help could be heard from people in the water. They were scattered over a wide area. Lifeboat 14 returned to an area of concentrated cries and moans, and managed to pull four people out of the water. One of them died soon after; another appeared to be in a very bad way but was quickly wrapped in a blanket in an attempt to keep him warm. Edith and her mother remained cuddled together, looking down once in a while at the water in the bottom of the boat. Their sodden boots had left them with no feeling in their feet.

As the stern of the ship rose higher and higher, Elin Hakkarainen saw from Lifeboat 15 that everything within the ship broke loose and went crashing downward to the bow. There was a mad rush of passengers and crew to the rear of the Well Deck and Poop Deck. There seemed to be a similar rush of people from below. Many hundreds more must have been trapped below decks and crushed by the breaking up of the ship. One of the giant funnels toppled to the deck crushing many passengers as it slid into the water. The screaming and moaning of the trapped passengers was beyond description. The *Titanic* was standing straight up, and its three huge propellers glistened in the starlight.

They were all hypnotized by the sight of the giant ship standing on end, going down slowly, as if an invisible hand was holding it back. Hundreds of people were holding on to the railings, stairs, and ladders, capstans, and framework of the rear Docking Bridge. The ship's lights, which had remained on during the entire episode, finally went out. It was still possible to see the *Titanic* in its death plunge. There was no suction whatsoever when it disappeared beneath the water. Only a haze of mist hung over the spot where the ship had gone under. The screams of people struggling in the water continued for about half an hour. Suddenly, Elin realized that Pekka was somewhere out there. She stood up to look at the people in the water. She called 'Pekka, Pekka I am here, come this way, please come this way.' Her calls were in vain, and she felt sure he was trapped within the passageway in the ship.

Elin's lifeboat did not return to the spot where the *Titanic* went down. Everyone in the boat was afraid that they would be swamped with additional people. The screams and sounds of the people in the water soon stopped. Complete silence prevailed, including among the occupants of the lifeboat. They could see the lights of another ship not too far away. They rowed towards it, but it soon disappeared beyond the horizon. Elin was colder than she had ever been. She didn't know if she was falling asleep or slowly freezing to death. Her thoughts went back to everything that had happened in her life so far. She remembered her childhood in Finland, her parents, friends, and her brothers and sister, who were living in America, and whom she had hoped to see very soon. Foremost in her mind was Pekka, who had so quickly disappeared without a trace.

Frank Goldsmith found that when the lowering cables for the Engelhardt C boat were released, the rowing started at once, heading the boat straight out in an angular direction slightly towards that in which the *Titanic*'s bow was aimed. The rowers then stopped, and the passengers could see the ship very clearly, badly down by the head. Although all the lights seemed to be on, suddenly they all went out, and a loud explosion was heard. His mother Emily grasped him and roughly forced his head onto her breast. Frank began to hear a loud noise of human voices. Emily continued to hold his head so that he could not witness the sinking until many of the women in their boat began to exclaim 'Oh, its going to float!' Emily then released him, and now beginning to be fearful about his father, Frank lifted himself to look past her shoulder and saw the tail end of the ship aimed straight up towards the stars. It seemed to stay that way for several minutes. Then another slight noise was heard, and it very slowly began to go lower and then completely disappeared. Frank and many of the others wept.

Hanna Touma covered Georges and Maria with her cloak so that they would not see the ship break up and sink. She cried for her fellow villagers. She watched people jump off the *Titanic* into the water. There were screams, then silence. It was freezing cold, and the view was something Hanna would never forget. The enormity of the ship looked unreal, with hundreds of portholes all lit up and slowly being extinguished one by one. The cries of the people in the water soon stopped and it became very quiet. The sky was black with millions of stars all the way into the distance where the sky and waterline became one. It was so black you could not see who else was in the lifeboat. They were all in a state of shock.

As if everyone could read Violet Jessop's mind, the women in Lifeboat 16 started to weep, some silently, some unrestrainedly. Violet closed her eyes and prayed for everyone. She dared not visualize those people she had just left, warm and alive as she was. She tried to busy herself with the baby, but could not refrain from looking up again. There were only three decks now, and still not a list to one side or the other. Desperately, Violet turned to where the other ship's lights shone on the horizon; surely they should be getting nearer by now. It was such a long time since they had first seen their comforting glow. They should have been with them by now, taking off the patient, waiting people. But the ship did not seem nearer, and in fact seemed further away.

A tiny breeze, the first they had felt on this calm night, blew an icy blast across Violet's face; it felt like a knife in its penetrating coldness. She sat paralysed with cold and misery, as she watched the *Titanic* give a lurch forward. One of the huge funnels toppled off like a cardboard model, falling into the sea with a fearful roar. A few cries came to them across the water, then silence, as the ship seemed to right herself like a hurt animal with a broken back. She settled for a few minutes, but one more deck of lighted portholes disappeared. Then she went down by the head with a thundering roar of underwater explosions. One awful moment of empty, misty blackness enveloped Violet's lifeboat in its loneliness, then an unforgettable, agonizing cry went up from those in the water.

Sitting beside Elizabeth Shutes in Lifeboat 3 were two women, Clara Hays from Montreal, Quebec, and her daughter Orian Davidson from Calgary, Alberta. Charles Hays was General Manager of the Grand Trunk Pacific Railway, and he and his entourage were travelling as guests of J. Bruce Ismay. Clara had left her husband Charles on the ship, and Orian both her father and her husband Thornton. While they were near the other lifeboats these two stricken women would call out a name and ask 'Are you there?' 'No' would come back the answer. These women never lost heart, but forgot their own sorrow and told Elizabeth to sit close to them to keep warm. Now

Elizabeth began to wish for the velvet suit she had left hanging in her cabin. She had thought of it for a minute, and then had quickly thrown on a lighter skirt. She knew the heavier one would make the life jacket less effective. Had she only known how calm the sea was that night, she would have felt that death was not so certain, and would have dressed for life rather than for the end. The life jackets helped to keep Elizabeth and the others warm, but the night was bitterly cold, and it grew colder and colder.

Elizabeth and her companions all felt much safer near the ship. Surely such a vessel could not sink. She thought the danger must be exaggerated, and they could all be taken on board again. But the outline of the ship was growing less, and the bow of the *Titanic* was getting black. Light after light was disappearing, and now the seamen put to their oars and the passengers were told to hunt under seats, any place, anywhere, for a lantern or a light of any kind. Nothing was to be found. There was no water—no drink of any kind. Not a biscuit—nothing to keep them alive if they drifted for a long time. The men knew nothing about the position of the stars, and hardly knew how to row together. Two oars were soon overboard. The men's hands were too cold. They stopped while the men beat their hands and arms, then started again. The sea, calm as a pond, kept their boat steady, and now the *Titanic* was fast disappearing. Only one tiny light was left—a powerless little spark, a lantern fastened to the mast. Fascinated, Elizabeth watched that black outline until the end. Then across the water swept an awful wail, the cry of the drowning people. Elizabeth heard: 'She's gone, lads; row like hell or we'll get the devil of a swell.'

The other boats had drifted away from them; they had to wait for the dawn and they dared not think what the day might bring. To see if she could make the night seem shorter, Elizabeth tried to imagine herself back in Japan, where she had lived previously. She had twice departed at night and had been unafraid; now the Atlantic was calmer than the Inland Sea had been. This helped a little, but her hands were freezing cold. Two men had jumped into Lifeboat 3 as they were about to lower, and they kept striking matches and lighting cigars until Elizabeth feared they would have no matches left. She asked them not to use any more, but they kept on. She did not know what they looked like—it was too dark to distinguish people's features clearly.

Like Edith Brown and her mother, Eva Hart found that Lifeboat 14 was heavily laden, and when they reached the water the seaman in charge, Fifth Officer Harold Lowe, had it rowed well clear to avoid the expected drag or wash if the ship finally sank. They could see other lifeboats on the water around them, all staying well clear of the liner as she slipped lower and lower at the bow. And so they waited, with the clear sky above and the calm, cold sea around. Slowly they could see the liner getting lower in the water. As the slope of the decks became even greater there was an increasing amount of noise, from the people still on board, loose articles sliding along the decks, and the boilers as they eventually tore loose from the ship's body and fell through the length of the hull. Then, for a short time, the ship seemed to hang almost vertically as if suspended from the sky with her stern clearly above the water. Eva and her companions all held their breath for what they knew would be the end.

The horror of seeing the ship sink was unbelievable. One minute it was there with its lights still ablaze and illuminating the sea all around, and the next minute it was gone and the only light was from the stars. At the same time there was a great noise from the screams and cries of hundreds of people plunged into the water with little hope of being saved. For the first time, those in the lifeboat realized that there had been many people left on the ship without access to lifeboats. Eva's father was a champion swimmer and in warmer water could have remained afloat a long time, but he was not overweight and probably succumbed very quickly to the coldness of the water. Before the ship sank they could clearly hear the noise of people shouting and screaming on board. When the ship had gone, those in charge started to try and collect the lifeboats into groups. This was not easy, as they had become scattered and only two or three had any lights. But eventually some did manage to come together, and Eva's lifeboat was in a group of four or five. It was then realized that some had left the *Titanic* before they had been completely filled.

Eva and Esther were initially in Lifeboat 14 which, with sixty passengers, was heavily laden. This made it unsuitable for picking up any additional survivors. But in their group of lifeboats Lowe took command and made himself responsible for redistributing the survivors in order to make one boat almost completely empty to pick up people still swimming in the water. Lowe called over to each boat in turn 'How many can you take?' They in their turn called back 'We can take three in this boat,' another said 'Well, we can manage to take another six,' whilst a third replied 'We can't take any, we're already overcrowded.' So they went through the distressing experience of being transferred in the dark from one lifeboat to another while people were crying and dying around them. Eventually, Lowe managed to reduce the numbers in Eva's lifeboat; he clearly considered that their safety was his first priority. The lifeboat was then able to return to seek other survivors. But the transferring of survivors had taken a long time during which the cries for help from the water had subsided.

Due to a combination of coldness and fright, Eva had been clinging as firmly as possible to Esther, who was still very cold despite her sheepskin coat. At the same time Eva was pulling her blanket tightly around her, as much for security as for warmth. But they became involved in the mid-Atlantic transfer between the lifeboats, and as a result they became separated. For Eva, that was the most terrifying thing of all. Eva started screaming for Esther, and no doubt added to the misery around her. She cried and cried, on and off throughout the whole of the remainder of the night; somebody else tried to comfort her. Esther, for her part, was panic-stricken when she found Eva was not in the same boat. She kept trying to find out into which lifeboat Eva had been transferred, but had no success. From where they were on the water, they could see the lights of another ship some miles away. They all hoped she had seen the distress rockets, but as they watched she made no movement towards them and the occupants of the lifeboats felt despair. Some of the survivors in other lifeboats tried to row towards the ship, but she was too far away to be easily reached.

Archibald Gracie and his companions prayed that the calm would last. Towards morning, the sea became rougher, and it was to avoid the ice-cold water and attract attention that they all stood up in a column, two abreast, facing the bow. The waves broke over the keel, and they maintained their balance by shifting their weight to port and then to starboard. They were anxious that some of the air con-fined between the sea and the upturned boat would escape, and it would sink. If the boat had been completely turned over, so that they would have had to cling to the submerged gunwale, it would not have supported their weight and they would have frozen to death in the water. Gracie's efforts had been so continuous and strenuous before he got aboard that he had not noticed the temperature of the water. They all suffered severely from cold and exposure. The boat was so loaded down that the water washed up to their waists as they lay. Several of their companions near the stern of the boat, unable to stand the exposure and the strain, gave up the struggle and fell off.

Fortunately, the majority were not exhausted or desperate. On the contrary, they had plenty of strength and purpose to battle for their lives. There were lights forward, and on the port side. These were the lights of the *Titanic*'s other lifeboats. The suffering on the boat from the cold was intense. But an uncommunicative little member of the crew beside Gracie did not seem to suffer much. He, like others, had a cap. The upper part of his body seemed to be comparatively dry. He seemed so dry and comfortable while Gracie felt so damp in his waterlogged clothing, his teeth chattering, and his hair wet, that the American asked if he could borrow his cap for a short time. 'And what would I do?' was his curt reply. 'Ah, never mind,' said Gracie, as he thought it would make no difference. It seemed that all the man's possessions had been lost when his kit went down with the ship. Not far from Gracie and on the starboard side was a more talkative member of the crew. He had been drinking before he left the ship. Most of the conversation, as well as the excitement, came from behind Gracie.

After they paddled away from the wreckage and the swimmers in the water, their undivided attention until the dawn of the next day was concentrated on scanning the horizon in every direction for the lights of a ship that might rescue them before the sea grew rougher. It was shortly after they had emerged from the scene of men swimming in the water that Gracie noticed among them Second Officer Lightoller with whom he had helped to lower the boats on the *Titanic*'s decks. Gracie identified him at once by his voice and appearance, but did not know his name. As soon as he was recognized, the talkative member of the crew astern volunteered and called out to him

'We will obey what the officer orders.' The results were noticeable immediately. They now felt the presence of a leader among them, and that gave them purpose and courage. The excitement at the stern was demonstrated by the frequent suggestion of 'Now boys, all together', and then in unison they shouted 'Boat ahoy! Boat ahoy!' This was kept up for some time until it was seen to be a waste of time.

On the Engelhardt boat, human endurance was taxed to the limit during the long hours of exposure in a temperature below freezing, the survivors standing motionless in their wet clothes. Hour by hour, the compartments in the Engelhardt were filling with water due to the rough-and-ready treatment she had received when dumped from the top of the Officers' Quarters on to the Boat Deck. Second Officer Lightoller and the others were painfully conscious of the cold water, slowly but surely creeping up their legs. Some people quietly lost consciousness, fell back into the water, and slipped overboard, as there was nothing on the smooth flat bottom of the boat to hold them. No one was in a condition to help, and the fact that a slight but distinct swell had started meant that those still alive were unable to help those in the water. It was only through being huddled together that many more did not die.

With the rising sea, Lightoller realized that, without concerted action, they were all going to be pitched headlong into the water, and that would be the end of everyone. So he made everyone face one way, and then, as he felt the boat under their feet lurch, one way or the other, he corrected it by the orders 'Lean to the right', 'Stand upright', or 'Lean to the left.' In this way, they managed to maintain their footholds on the slippery planks that were by now well under water. Lightoller and his companions knew that ships were racing to their rescue, though the chances of their keeping up their efforts of balancing until one came along seemed very remote. Jack Phillips, who was standing near Lightoller, told him the different ships that had answered their distress calls. Of these, the *Carpathia* was the nearest and by daylight should be where the *Titanic* had sunk. In order to encourage the people around him, Lightoller passed on to them his rough calculations, and it helped them keep up their spirits.

Jack Phillips hung on until daylight came and they sighted one of the *Titanic*'s lifeboats in the distance. They could not make her hear their shouting, but Lightoller still had his whistle in his pocket. This piercing sound carried, and also indicated that it was an officer making the call. Slowly the lifeboat made its way towards them. Meanwhile the Engelhardt showed unmistakable signs of sinking altogether. Phillips suddenly slipped down, sitting in the water, and although they held his head up, he never recovered. Lightoller insisted on taking him into the lifeboat with them, hoping he might still be alive, but it was too late.

Stories of survival in lifeboats abound in history and literature. During the Second World War, in particular, there were many stories of people surviving long periods in lifeboats. With the *Titanic*, the move into the lifeboats immediately upset the conventional order of First, Second, and Third Class, and also relationships between passengers and crew. Crew members who would have been more or less anonymous for the earlier voyage now assumed great significance, as they took charge of the loading of the lifeboats. The Engelhardt B boat was different, in that its passengers were all male, though still a mixture of passengers and crew. More generally, each lifeboat had a mix of passengers from the three Classes, there was at most one officer, and of course there was a preponderance of women and children. Lifeboat 13 had a stoker as Captain, Frederick Barrett, and on other lifeboats it was the cooks and stewardesses who took up the oars. Third Class passengers for the first time encountered their counterparts from First Class, with migrants, many from Finland and Sweden and speaking little English, sitting next to British and American passengers. Passengers shared material possessions such as furs, overcoats, blankets, warm clothes, rugs, cigarettes, caps, and bits of food. They exchanged information, including stories about the collision (especially from the stokers), tales of other voyages, the time, the positions of the stars and navigation, how to row, and thoughts about the possibility of rescue. Together they discussed how to care for the babies and young children. But class conventions quickly reasserted themselves. People were told off for smoking, and passengers (such as Lawrence Beesley) slowly found mutual friends. If it was a kind of egalitarianism, it was also only a temporary break in the conventional hierarchy of class relationships.

'A Dark Speck on the Horizon'

Someone in Lifeboat 13 had a watch that gave the time shortly after the *Titanic* sank as being 2.30 a.m. Its passengers were then in touch with three other boats: one was Lifeboat 15, on their starboard side. They never got into close touch with each other, but called occasionally across the darkness and saw them looming near and then drawing away again. Lawrence Beesley and his companions called to ask if any officers were aboard the other three, but there weren't. So in the absence of any plan of action, they rowed slowly forward—or what they thought was forward, for it was in the direction the *Titanic*'s bow was pointing before she sank.

None of the other three lifeboats near them had a light—and they needed lights badly. They could not see each other in the darkness, and they could not signal to ships which might be rushing up full speed to their rescue from any direction. They had been through so much that it seemed hard to have to face the additional danger of being run down. They felt again for a lantern beneath their feet and along the sides. Beesley finally managed to reach the locker below the tiller and open it. However he found nothing but the zinc air tank which rendered the lifeboat unsinkable. They also felt around for food and water, and found none. Not that they wanted any food or water—they thought rather of the time that might elapse before the *Olympic* might pick them up in the afternoon.

Towards 3 a.m., they saw a faint glow in the sky ahead on the starboard side, the first gleams, they thought, of the coming dawn. They were not certain of the time and were eager perhaps to accept too readily any relief from darkness—only too glad to be able to look each other in the face and see who their fortunate companions were, and to be free from the hazard, invisible in the darkness, of lying in the path of a steamer. But they were doomed to disappointment— the soft light increased for a time, and died away a little, glowed again, and then remained stationary for some minutes. Beesley suddenly realized that it was the Northern Lights—soon the light arched fanwise across the sky, with faint streamers reaching towards the Pole Star. He had seen lights of about the same intensity in England some years earlier. A sigh of disappointment went through the boat as they realized that it was not yet daylight.

All night long, they had watched the horizon with eager eyes for signs of a steamer's lights. They heard from Frederick Barrett that the first appearance would be a single light on the horizon, the masthead light, followed shortly by a second one, lower down, on the deck. If these two remained in vertical alignment and the distance between them increased as the lights drew nearer, they could be certain it was a steamer. But what a night to see that first light on the horizon! They saw it many times as the earth revolved, and some stars rose on the clear horizon and others sank down to it—there were 'lights' in every direction. Some they watched and followed until they realized they were mistaken; others were lights from the lifeboats that were fortunate enough to have lanterns, but these were generally easily detected, as they rose and fell in the near distance. The lights raised the hopes of the occupants of the lifeboat, only to dash them again. Near what seemed to be the horizon on the port side they saw two lights close together, and thought this must be their double light. However as they gazed across the miles that separated them, the lights slowly drew apart and they realized that they were two lifeboats' lanterns at different distances from them, in line, one behind the other.

But notwithstanding these hopes and disappointments—the absence of lights, food, water, and the bitter cold—Beesley and his companions were not unhappy in those early morning hours. The cold that settled on them like a garment was the only real discomfort, and they could keep that at bay by not thinking too much about it, as well as by vigorous rubbing and gentle stamping on the floor. There were many things to be thankful for—so many that the temporary inconvenience of the cold, the crowded boat, the darkness, and the hundred and one other things that normally they would have regarded as unpleasant seemed insignificant. The quiet sea, the beautiful night, and above all the fact of being in a boat at all when so many of their fellow passengers and crew—whose cries no longer came across the water to them—were silent. The dominant feeling of those in Lifeboat 13 was one of gratitude.

About 3.30 a.m., someone in the bow called their attention to a faint faraway gleam in the South East. They all turned quickly to look and there it certainly was, streaming up from behind the horizon like a distant flash of a warship's searchlight—then a faint boom like guns far off, and the light died away again. Barrett, who had been lying all night under the tiller, sat up suddenly as if from a dream, the overcoat hanging from his shoulders. He stared across the sea, to where the sound had come from, and shouted 'That was a cannon!' They knew now that something was not far away, racing up to their help, and signalling to them a preliminary message to give them hope until she arrived.

With every sense alert, gazing intently at the horizon, and with ears open for the least sound, the survivors in Lifeboat 13 had waited in absolute silence in the quiet night. And then, creeping over the edge of the sea where the flash had been, they saw a single light, and then a second below it, and in a few minutes the lights were well above the horizon and remained in line. But they had all been deceived before, and waited a little longer before they allowed themselves to believe they were safe. The lights came up so rapidly it seemed only a few minutes between first seeing them and finding them well above the horizon and bearing down rapidly on their lifeboat. They did not know what sort of a vessel was coming, but they knew she was coming quickly, and they searched for paper, rags, and anything that would burn, even their coats if necessary. A paper torch was hastily twisted out of letters found in someone's pocket, lit, and held aloft by Barrett standing on the tiller platform. The little light shone in flickers on the faces of the occupants of the boat, ran in broken lines for a few yards along the black, oily sea, and spluttered away to blackness again as he threw the burning remnants of paper overboard. It was here that Beesley for the first time saw what had caused the disaster—ice—in little chunks the size of a fist, bobbing harmlessly up and down.

With their torch extinguished and in darkness again, they saw the headlights stop, and realized that the rescuer had stopped. A sigh of relief went up when they thought no hurried scramble had to be made to get out of her way, with a chance of just being missed, and having to meet the wash of her propellers as she tore by them. They waited and she slowly swung round and revealed herself to them as a large steamer with lights in all her portholes. The way the lights came slowly into view was one of the most wonderful things that Beesley and his companions had ever seen. It meant immediate deliverance—that was the amazing thing to them all. They had thought that it would be the afternoon when they were rescued, and here only a few hours after the *Titanic* had sunk, before it was light, they were to be taken aboard. It seemed almost too good to be true, and everyone's eyes filled with tears, men's as well as women's, as they saw again the rows of lights one above the other shining kindly to them across the water. 'Thank God!' was murmured in heartfelt tones round the lifeboat. The lifeboat swung round and the crew began their long row to the steamer; Barrett called for a song and led off with 'Pull for the Shore'. The crew took it up quaveringly and the passengers joined in, but one verse was all they sang. It was too early, and gratitude was too deep and sudden in its overwhelming intensity for them to sing very lustily. Shortly afterwards, finding the song had not gone very well, they tried a cheer, and that was more successful. It was easier to relieve their feelings with a noise, and timing and tune were not necessary ingredients.

In the midst of their thankfulness for having survived, one name was mentioned with the deepest feeling of gratitude—that of Marconi. Beesley wished that he had been there to hear the chorus of gratitude that went out to him for the invention that had spared them many hours, and perhaps many days, of floating on the sea in hunger, storm, and cold. All around, they saw lifeboats making for the ship and heard their shouts and cheers. Their new crew rowed hard in friendly rivalry with other boats to be among the first, but Beesley's lifeboat was eighth or ninth at the side. They had a heavy load aboard, and had to row round a huge iceberg on the way.

And then, as if to make their happiness complete, came the dawn. First a beautiful, quiet shimmer away in the East, then a soft golden glow that crept up stealthily from behind the skyline as if it were trying not to be noticed as it stole over the sea and spread itself in every direction. It did this so quietly as if to make them believe it had been there all the time and they had not observed it. Then the sky turned faintly pink and in the distance the thinnest, fleeciest clouds stretched in bands across the horizon and close down to it, becoming more and more pink with every moment. And next the stars died, slowly— apart from one which remained long after the others, just above the horizon. Nearby, with the crescent turned to the North, and the lower horn just touching the horizon, was the thinnest and palest of moons.

And with the dawn came a faint breeze from the West, the first breath of wind they had felt since the *Titanic* stopped her engines. Barrett shouted 'A new moon! Turn your money over, boys! That is, if you have any!' along Beesley's lifeboat to the 'crew', as they strained at the oars—two pulling and an extra one facing them and pushing to try to keep pace with the other boats. They laughed at him for the quaint superstition at such a time, and it was good to laugh again. However he showed his scepticism of another superstition when he added 'Well, I shall never say again that 13 is an unlucky number. Boat 13 is the best friend we ever had.'

Looking towards the ship in the faint light, they saw what seemed to be two large fully rigged sailing ships near the horizon, with all sails set, standing up near her. They decided that they must be fishing vessels off the Banks of Newfoundland which had seen the ship stop and were waiting to see if she wanted help of any kind. But in a few minutes more, the light shone on them and they stood revealed as huge icebergs, peaked in a way that readily suggested a ship. When the sun rose higher, it turned them pink. Sinister as they looked, towering out of the sea like rugged white peaks of rock, and terrible as was the disaster one of them had caused, there was an awful beauty about them which could not be overlooked. Later, when the sun came above the horizon, they sparkled and glittered in its rays; deadly white, like frozen snow rather than translucent ice. As the dawn crept towards them, there lay another iceberg almost directly in the line between their lifeboat and the ship, and a few minutes later, another on her port side, and more again on the southern and western horizons, as far as the eye could see—all differing in shape, size, and tone of colour depending on whether the sun shone through them or was reflected off them.

They drew near their rescuer and soon could make out the bands on her funnel, by which the crew could tell she was a Cunard ship. Already some lifeboats were at her side, and passengers were climbing up rope ladders. Beesley and his companions had to give the iceberg a wide berth and make a detour to the South; they knew it was sunk a long way below the surface with such things as projecting ledges. Not that it was very likely there was a ledge so near the surface as to endanger their small boat, but they were not inclined to take any risks for the sake of a few more minutes when safety was so close at hand. Once clear of the iceberg, they could read the name of the ship—*Carpathia*—a name they were not likely to forget—the way her lights climbed up over the horizon in the darkness, the way she swung and showed her lit portholes, the moment when they read her name on her side, the scene of rescue, and the same thrill of gratitude for all she brought them.

In the Engelhardt C boat, the survivors began to row. There were only two crewmen aboard, and they asked the women who were rowing to stop. However, one crewman talked to them and explained they should stay where they were because rescue ships were on their way. The surface of the water was exceedingly calm except for the normal swell of the ocean, and Frank Goldsmith's fellow passengers were quite calm too. Frank himself was not frightened. As they floated, one of the passengers saw lights in the distance. They all looked and studied them, and a crewman recognized them as being a ship's lights. The three women and one crewman who were handling the oars began to row rapidly towards them. The other women began to cry out, loudly, in an effort to attract its attention. Frank's mother Emily suggested setting light to the straw hat she was wearing, raising it on one of the oars. Several other women sacrificed their petticoats to be burned for the same purpose. But all was to no avail. The lights slowly got fainter, and some of them disappeared. The women continued rowing, and Frank heard Emily saying to them finally they should stop, because the ship had ignored them and they had better save their strength. The ship's lights gradually dipped below the horizon. Soon after this, Frank leant against Emily's breast and became increasingly sleepy. The gentle movement of the lifeboat ensured he was soon fast asleep.

The next thing that Frank recalled was awakening to find that it was daylight and that their four rowers were forcing them across the water towards a ship; it had become a bit rough with waves about two feet high. It was the *Carpathia*. It took them quite a while to reach the side of the vessel, but they eventually did. Georges Touma was placed in a sack and pulled up on deck. He was the first to set foot on the ship. Frank was helped into a rope sling or Bosun's Chair and hauled up the side to an entrance door and then onto the deck. Alongside the sling was a rope ladder up which Emily climbed so that she could keep close to Frank. When the Engelhardt C boat was picked up by the *Carpathia* at 7.30 a.m., many survivors were already aboard. They were studying Frank and his companions hoping to see friends or family members, and Frank and Emily started to do likewise, then waited for others to be taken aboard. It was not very long after that that Frank and Emily began to become upset. However they were told by the friendly and sympathetic *Carpathia* crew to not give up hope, that there was a reasonable possibility that Frank's father, Tom Theobald, and Alfred Rush could have been taken aboard by another lifeboat.

In Lifeboat 16, Violet Jessop found that dawn broke slowly when the Watch was long and hazardous. It seemed to her as if it never would come that April morning. After a night of calm sea and floating mists, the wind rose to an icy keenness, cutting through the numbed bodies of Violet and her companions, paralysing senses already dulled by shock and cruel disappointment. The light that they had followed with so much hope from 2 a.m. was finally discovered to be retreating further and further away from them. For hours, it had drawn them off their course. Their lifeboat seemed all too tiny as the sea began to lash itself against it. Huddled into grotesque heaps by the violence of its movements, they prayed, sobbed, and stared into space. Violet tried desperately to counter the nausea that threatened to overcome her, and strove vainly to keep her mind focused.

A weak cry from the baby in her numbed arms helped her regain control of herself. The hard edge of her life jacket was not comforting to its poorly-clad body, and its little face looked old and pinched in the dim light. Violet tucked the eiderdown tightly round it, for she feared, suddenly, that this stranger's child might die in her arms.

After the horrors they had experienced, the prospect of a child's death still shook her. Finally, the baby stopped whimpering and slept, while Violet's mind drifted back to what had happened. Elizabeth Leather sat stoically by Violet's side. As Violet saw again with her mind's eye the crowds walking the decks aimlessly after their lifeboat had been lowered, a fresh horror was borne home to her—there had been no more boats to take those people off. She felt she had no right to comparative safety when so many must have perished; she knew that no one could have lived long in the water.

The sea became more violent, tossing their overloaded lifeboat helplessly about. Only four people could row and they were too cold, totally unequipped to resist the strength of the waves. They had no light, water, or food; nothing to keep body and soul together or help them battle the elements. Violet recalled that in the dim past there had always been inspections by officials in Southampton for everything that they now lacked, and she was perplexed. As the faint streaks of dawn lit the horizon, the majestic shapes of icebergs crossed their vision, passing in panoramic procession. But what once had for them been objects of interest now appeared sinister monsters of destruction; appreciation of their beauty had changed to dread of the damage they could do. There was nothing in sight, none of the *Titanic*'s boats, just water and ice everywhere. Violet and her companions realized how far off their course they had gone by following that elusive ship.

Elizabeth never moved her position, remaining silent. The men in charge of the lifeboat tried to cheer everyone with a few feeble songs but these soon died away; their lips were too frozen to move, and they needed all their strength to row. Violet's mind wandered for a few minutes from the tragedy, fastening onto something irrelevant. She thought of the things she had done recently. She regretted having started to buy a piano before they sailed—she had always longed to have one but could never quite save the little extra that represented the first instalment. Now she might never need such an instrument.

Then, suddenly, a flicker of hope revived. Somebody woke and pointed a trembling finger at a dark speck on the horizon. There was a ship, not going away from them this time, but getting closer and becoming more distinct every minute. While there were three Second Class passengers, the vast majority of the women in Violet's lifeboat were Third Class, and migrants who had left their men on board. Many of the people, murmuring prayers in a soft monotone, were overcome with emotion when they sighted the ship. They were thinking more of their loved ones than of themselves, hoping that there might yet be a chance that they could have been picked up by the approaching vessel. One woman sitting beside Violet, who had kept her head buried in her arms since they had got into the lifeboat, thought as she looked up that they were nearing the *Titanic*, still afloat, and that she would soon regain her husband and two sons.

As the ship loomed nearer, they saw her stop and realized she was doing so in order that the lifeboats might make their way to her, and she would avoid the risk of so much floating ice. As kind hands helped Violet and her companions aboard, they searched for familiar faces, but mostly in vain. As they reached the deck, glasses of neat brandy were poured down their throats; it went down like molten fire. While Violet stood, still clutching the baby in her frozen arms, a woman rushed up, snatched the child and ran away with it. In the confusion, the baby had slipped from Violet's thoughts, but when things became more settled in her mind she wondered why the mother had not expressed one word of gratitude for her baby's life.

Then the saddest search that it had ever been Violet's lot to witness began. Tragically, very few survivors were reunited with their loved ones. Violet and her companions looked similarly without success for Thomas Andrews, Dr William O'Loughlin, members of the crew, and good friends in all departments. But when the roll was called, they were all among the missing. No engineers answered their names. Fifth Officer Harold Lowe had some difficulty with the people in his lifeboat and had asserted his authority with the help of a revolver. Those were the shots Violet had heard just before they were lowered.

The rescuers worked tirelessly, and held out hope to everyone, reminding them that many ships, even the *Titanic's* sister ship *Olympic*, had received the distress call and might have picked up survivors. The *Carpathia's* crew did everything to relieve suffering and anxiety, attending to the injured, and tenderly caring for the dead. But there was little that could be done to comfort those who had lost members of their families. So the *Carpathia*, having searched vigilantly, turned back to New York. She seemed weighed down with her extra load of human cargo. As there were not enough cabins, Violet and her companions slept on benches on the deck. They watched the stars at night and were thankful.

As soon as there was a chance that they were in view, Arthur Rostron and the crew of the *Carpathia* had started sending up rockets at intervals of about a quarter of an hour and, when nearer, fired Cunard's Roman candles (night signals) to let them know it was the *Carpathia* that was approaching. Occasionally they caught sight of a green light, and knew they were getting near the spot. By this time the hope that the green signals had at first inspired in the crew of the *Carpathia* was gone. There was no sign of the *Titanic* herself. By now— it was about 3.35 a.m.—they were almost up to the position and had the giant liner been afloat they would have seen her. The skies were clear, the stars gleaming with that brightness which only a keen frosty air brought to them, and the visibility was as good as it could be on a moonless night. Rostron put the engines on 'stand by' so that the engineers should be on the alert for instant action. At 4 a.m., Rostron stopped the engines; they were there.

As if to prove that was correct, Rostron saw a green light just ahead of them, low down. He knew it must be a lifeboat and, just as he was planning to come alongside, he saw a big iceberg immediately in front of them—Second Officer James G. P. Bisset reported it at the same moment. Rostron had meant to take the lifeboat on the port side, which was the lee side, though there was not much wind or sea. But the iceberg altered the plan. It was necessary to move with the utmost caution. Rostron swung the ship round and so came alongside the first of the *Titanic*'s lifeboats on the starboard side. He was thankful that the long race was over. Every minute had brought its risk—a risk that only keen eyes and quick decisions could counter—but with that feeling was the pain which the now-certain knowledge of the liner's loss brought. There was no sign of her—and below was the first lifeboat containing survivors.

A shout came up from the lifeboat: 'We have only one seaman in the boat and cannot work very well.' They were a little way off the *Carpathia*'s gangway. 'All right,' Rostron told them and brought the vessel alongside. Then they started climbing aboard. Obviously they had left the *Titanic* in a hurry, for there were only twenty-five of them, whereas the capacity of the boat was forty. They were in charge of one officer. Rostron asked that he should come to him as soon as he was on board and Rostron put the question to him, knowing what his answer would be. 'The *Titanic* has gone down?' 'Yes,' he said—one word that meant so much, so much that the man's voice broke on it.

'She went down at about 2.30.' An hour and a half ago! Tragic that they had not been nearer!

But there was no time for vain regrets. Daylight was just setting in and what a sight that new day gradually revealed. Everywhere were icebergs. About a third of a mile on their starboard beam was the one that a few minutes ago had faced them, and less than 100 feet off their port side was a growler—a broken-off lump of ice 10 to 15 feet high and 25 feet long. But stretching as far as the eye could see were masses of them. Rostron instructed a junior officer to go to the Wheel-House Deck and count them. There were twenty-five over 200 feet in height, and dozens ranging from 150 feet down to 50. And amid the tragic splendour of them as they lay in the first rays of the rising sun floated the lifeboats of the lost ship. From that moment the *Carpathia* went on picking them up. As the rescued came aboard, their thankfulness for their safety was always mixed with the sense of their loss and the chattering cold that possessed them. Many of the women had been hours in these open lifeboats, shielded from the cold only by a coat hastily thrown over nightclothes. They told of the urgency with which they had left the ship, suggesting the long drawn-out anxiety before the lifeboats were launched and were on the water and away.

In Lifeboat 15, Elin Hakkarainen had also suddenly noticed that it was daylight. She was warmer and she was alive. Someone had covered her with a steamer rug, which probably saved her life, since she was dressed only in a nightgown. Everyone in the lifeboat sat in a trance-like state, not saying a word and staring into space. The sea was much rougher than it had been when they left the *Titanic*. In the distance, they could see a ship with several lifeboats near her, and the other lifeboats were headed in that direction. The fact that they would soon be rescued, warm again, and safe aboard another ship did not register with Elin. Her only thought was of Pekka and what had become of him. Perhaps he was on another lifeboat? Perhaps he was already on the rescue ship and waiting for her? This thought kept her from giving up completely.

Elin's lifeboat reached the side of the *Carpathia* at 7.30 a.m. They were one of the last boats to be picked up. A large group of survivors and *Carpathia* passengers watched Elin and the others intently as they climbed or were lifted aboard. As they stepped onto the *Carpathia*, the survivors' eyes searched them for loved ones. To feel a solid ship under their feet, instead of a small lifeboat, was a wonderful feeling. It took at least an hour to get rid of the bobbing sensation. A crewman helped Elin off with her life jacket and draped a blanket over her shoulders. She was directed to a dining area and given food and coffee. Both the passengers and crew on the *Carpathia* did their best to console Elin and the other survivors. They were given clothes which had been donated by the ship's passengers. A memorial service was also later held for those who had died. This turned out to be one of the most heart-breaking scenes Elin had ever witnessed. She stood at the rail for hours, looking out to sea, hoping upon hope that she would discover just one more lifeboat from the *Titanic*.

On Lifeboat 3, someone had asked: 'What time is it?' When a match was struck they found it was 4 a.m. Where had the hours of the night gone? Dawn would soon be there, and it came, surely and strong with hope. The stars slowly disappeared, and in their place came the faint pink glow of another day. Then Elizabeth Shutes heard 'A light, a ship'. She could not look while there was a bit of doubt, but kept her eyes averted. All night long she had heard 'A light!' Each time it had proved to be one of the other lifeboats, someone lighting a piece of paper, anything they could find to burn, and now she could not believe it. Someone found a newspaper, and it was lit and held up. Then Elizabeth looked and saw a ship bright with lights; strong and steady she waited, and they were to be saved. A straw hat belonging to Orian Davidson was offered—it would burn longer. The same ship that had come to save them might run them down. But no—the ship was still. The two, the ship and the dawn, came together, like a living painting. The ship was white, but whiter still were the horribly beautiful icebergs. As they drew nearer to the ship, they also drew nearer to those mountains of ice. They rose as far as the eye could see, each one more fantastically chiselled than its neighbour. The floe glistened like a never-ending meadow covered with new-fallen snow. And near those white mountains, marvellous in their purity, stood the ship which had come in such quick response to the *Titanic's* call for help.

From the *Carpathia,* a rope forming a tiny swing was lowered into Elizabeth's lifeboat, and one by one they were lifted up to safety. The woman pulled up just ahead of Elizabeth was very large, and Elizabeth felt herself being jerked terribly, when she heard someone say: 'Careful, fellers, she's a lightweight.' Elizabeth bumped against the side of the ship until she felt she was like a bag of meal. Her hands were so cold she could hardly hold on to the rope, and she was afraid of letting go. Again she heard: 'Steady, fellers, not so fast!' She felt she would let go and bounce out of the ropes. Finally, she found herself at an opening of some kind and there a kind doctor wrapped her in a rug and led her to the Dining Room, where warm drinks were immediately given, and everything possible done for them. Lifeboats kept coming in, and the sights were heart-rending, women who were now widows being brought aboard. Each hoped a lifeboat ahead of hers might have brought her husband safely to this waiting ship, but it was never the case.

Elizabeth was still so cold that she had to get a towel and tie it around her waist. Then she went back to the Dining Room and found Louis Hoffman, the French child, lying alone; his cold, bare feet had become unwrapped. She put a hot water bottle against the little boy. He smiled his thanks. Knowing how much better she felt after taking the hot drink, Elizabeth tried to get others to take something, but often they just shook their heads and said 'Oh, I can't'. Towards night they remembered they had nothing—no comb or brush of any kind—so they went to the barber's shop. Barbers always had everything, but now he had only a few toothbrushes left. Elizabeth bought a cap, and she was very glad to have something to cover her head. There were also a few silk handkerchiefs left, and on the corner of each was embroidered in scarlet 'From a friend'. They bought these, and so they were now fitted out for their remaining three days at sea. Patiently through the dismal, foggy days they lived, waiting for land and possible news of the lost.

Before dawn, on the upturned Engelhardt B boat, Archibald Gracie found that when they realized Assistant Wireless Operator Harold Bride was at the stern, Second Officer Herbert Lightoller called out questions from his position in the bow about the names of the steamships with which he had been in touch for assistance—the *Baltic*, *Olympic*, and *Carpathia*. Gracie and his companions had assumed that most of the lights they saw belonged to the *Titanic*'s lifeboats, but they were fooled by the green lights and rockets directly ahead of them, which from time to time loomed up especially bright. Their boat headed towards this ship as quickly as possible, but they realized that the light was going away from them, rather than approaching. Some time before dawn, a call came from the stern of the boat: 'There is a steamer coming behind us.' At the same time, a warning cry was given that they should not all look back at the same time in case they capsized the boat. Lightoller cried out 'All you men stand steady and I will be the one to look astern.' They were tightly packed, and when standing up Gracie once or twice had to hold on to the life jacket of the passenger in front in order to keep his balance. In the same way, the man behind held on to him.

Gracie was one of the first to see, far in the distance, the unmistakable mast lights of a steamer about four or five points away on the port side. They were anxious that this ship would not see them and run their boat down. To Gracie's disappointment, the lights seemed to make no progress towards them. She had come to a stop in sight of the lights of their lifeboats. The first boat to come to her sides was Fourth Officer Boxhall's Lifeboat 2, with its green lights. Finally dawn appeared, and there, on the port side of their upturned boat, they saw the steamer *Carpathia* about four or five miles away, with other *Titanic* lifeboats rowing towards her. On their starboard side, they saw four lifeboats strung together in line, surprising because they had seen no lights on that side. Meanwhile the sea had got rougher, and was washing over their keel. They had to move to keep their balance.

As daylight increased, those on board the boat had the welcome sight of the *Carpathia* cautiously picking her way through the ice towards them. They saw lifeboats in turn go alongside, but the question was, would she come their way in time? Both the sea and the wind were rising. It was survivors in Lifeboat 12 who saved those on the Engelhardt B boat. They had a lifeboat which was right-side-up, and it was full to its capacity. Lightoller put a whistle to his lips and blew a shrill blast, attracting the attention of the lifeboats about half a mile away. 'Come over and take us off,' he cried. 'Aye, aye, sir' was the ready response, as two of the lifeboats cast off from the others and rowed towards them. Just before they reached them, Lightoller ordered them not to scramble, but to take it in turns, so that the transfer might be made safely. When Gracie's turn came he went carefully, hands first, into the rescuing lifeboat. The Second Officer remained to the end, lifting a lifeless body into the boat beside Gracie. Gracie worked on it for some time, rubbing the temples and the wrists, but when he turned the neck it was stiff; *rigor mortis* had set in and the man was dead. He was wearing a uniform and grey woollen socks. He had dark hair. Gracie's lifeboat was so over-crowded that he had to rest on this dead body.

In the lifeboat were sixty-five or seventy people, and it was low in the water. Lightoller took command and steered at the stern. Gracie recognized Jack Thayer, son of John B. Thayer, amidships, and there was a French woman in the bow near them, seasick but brave. She was very kind in lending an extra steamer rug to Algernon Bark-worth, a magistrate from Yorkshire, beside Gracie, who shared it with him and a member of the crew. It was a great comfort as they drew it over their heads and huddled close together to get some warmth. For a short time another *Titanic* lifeboat was towed by theirs. Gracie's life jacket was wet and uncomfortable, and he threw it over-board. Harold Bride felt the pain in his feet and didn't care what happened. He just lay and gasped. Gracie recalled that when they were first transferred, some survivors took it hard, that only two of the lifeboats had come to their rescue, and when they saw how few survivors two of the other lifeboats had on board. However Fifth Officer Harold Lowe in Lifeboat 14 had cleverly rigged up a sail and, towing an Engelhardt boat astern, made his way to the *Carpathia* well ahead of them. On his way he picked up survivors from another Engelhardt boat which had shipped a lot of water.

It seemed a long time before Gracie and his companions reached the *Carpathia*. Ranged along her sides were other *Titanic* lifeboats. In one of these on the port side, standing up, Gracie noticed Third Officer Bert Pitman, with whom he had made a trip across the Atlantic aboard the *Oceanic*. Rope ladders were strung all along the sides of the *Carpathia*. Leaning over the rail of the port side, Gracie saw anxiously gazing down upon them many fellow survivors, and among them friends and acquaintances to whom he waved as he stood up in the bow of his boat. Now the task was to get the lifeboat safely alongside. They couldn't last many minutes longer, and round the *Carpathia*'s bow was a flurry of wind and waves that looked like defeating all Lightoller's efforts after all. One wave lopped over the bow and the next one was far worse. The following one she rode, and then, to Lightoller's relief, she came through the flurry into calm water under the *Carpathia*'s lee. Quickly the Bosun's Chairs were lowered for those unable to climb a swinging rope ladder, and old and young, fat and thin, were bundled on to the Chair. Then the word was given to 'hoist away', and up into the air they went. There were a few screams, but on the whole, the survivors took it well; in fact many were by now in a condition that rendered them barely able to hang on, much less scream. This was the last to reach the *Carpathia*; her passengers were transferred at about 8.30 a.m.

Harold Bride found that Jack Phillips had died from exposure and the cold. He had been exhausted from his work even before the disaster happened, but then he had continued working and had finally collapsed. Bride passed the body and went to the ladder, although his feet hurt terribly. But he hardly thought about that then, or about anything else for that matter. Bride tried the rope ladder, but he got to the top and felt hands reaching out to him. The next thing he knew, a woman was leaning over him in a cabin, and he felt her hand pushing back his hair and rubbing his face. Bride felt somebody at his feet, and felt the warmth of a jolt of liquor. Somebody got him under his arms. Then he was hustled down below to the ship's hospital.

There was no one around needing Archibald Gracie's help, so he mounted the rope ladder and climbed up as fast as he could. He entered the first hatchway he came to, and felt like falling down on his knees and kissing the deck in gratitude that his life had been saved. He made his way to the Second Class Dispensary, where he was handed a hot drink. He then went to the deck above and got a warm reception in the Dining Room. Nothing exceeded the kindness of the women, who did everything possible for Gracie's comfort. His wet clothing, overcoat, and shoes were sent down to the ship's large ovens to be dried. Having no clothing, he lay down in a corner of the Dining Room under rugs and blankets, waiting for a complete outfit of dry clothing. Gracie was particularly grateful to various people on the *Carpathia* who lent him clothes, but especially to his friends Lewis M. Ogden and his wife, and Frederic and Daisy Spedden. The Speddens had left the United States in late 1911 for Algiers, in Algeria, on the *Caronia*. Having visited Monte Carlo and Paris, they had embarked on the *Titanic* at Cherbourg, and had been rescued in Lifeboat 3. They gave Gracie hot cordials and coffee which soon warmed him up.

When all were on board, they counted the cost. Apart from four junior officers in charge of lifeboats, Herbert Lightoller found that he was the most senior survivor of over fifty officers and engineers. Nearly everyone among the hundreds of surviving passengers had lost a close family member. Then came the torment of being unable to hold out a vestige of hope. Some asked 'Could not another ship have picked them up?', others 'Could they not possibly be in some boat overlooked by the *Carpathia*?', and still others 'Was it not possible that he might have climbed on to an iceberg?' After think-ing about it, it seemed kindest to be frank and to give the only reply possible. There was no kindness in holding out hope, knowing full well there was not even the shadow of hope. Cold comfort, and possibly cruel, but Lightoller could see no alternative.

Lawrence Beesley and his companions rowed up to the *Carpathia* at about 4.30 a.m., and sheltering on the port side from the swell, were held on by ropes at the stern and bow. Women went up the side first, climbing rope ladders with a loop round their shoulders to help their ascent, male passengers scrambled next, and the crew last of all. Alden Caldwell, the baby, went up in a bag with the opening tied up—he had been quite well all the time, and never suffered any ill effects from his cold journey in the night. They set foot on the deck with very thankful hearts, grateful beyond what they could express to feel a solid ship beneath them once more. Beesley believed that no novelist would have dared portray such an array of beautiful weather conditions—the rosy dawn, the morning star, the moon on the hori-zon, and the sea stretching in level beauty to the skyline. Nor on this sea would they have placed an ice field like the Arctic regions and everywhere icebergs in numbers—white and turning pink and deadly cold—and near them, rowing round the icebergs to avoid them, little boats coming suddenly out of mid-ocean, with rescued passengers. No artist would have conceived such a picture—it would have seemed so highly dramatic as to border on the impossible, and would not have been attempted. Such a combination of events went beyond the limits of the imagination of authors and artists.

The passengers on the *Carpathia* crowded the rails and looked down at Beesley and his companions as they rowed closer in the early morning. They stood quietly aside while the crew at the gangways below took the survivors aboard, and watched them as if the ship had been in dock. Both the passengers, and the survivors as they came aboard, were very quiet. There was very little excitement on either side—just people who were in the presence of something so big they were unable to grasp its significance, and which they could not yet discuss. And so the passengers and crew politely asked the survivors to have hot coffee, which they drank, and food, which they generally declined—they were not hungry—and they said very little at first about the *Titanic* and their adventures in the night. Judging feelings as far as they were revealed by expressions, it was joy, relief, and gratitude that were the dominant emotions written on the faces of those who climbed the rope ladders and were hauled up in cradles.

One of the first things the survivors did was to crowd round a steward with a bundle of telegraph forms. He was the bearer of the welcome news that passengers might send messages to their relatives free of charge, and soon he bore away to the operator the first sheaf of hastily scribbled messages. By the time the last boatload was aboard, the pile must have risen high in the Marconi cabin. Then, a roll-call of the rescued was held in the *Carpathia*'s Saloon, and this was sent by wireless to land before any other messages. The last boatload of passengers was taken aboard at 8.30 a.m., the lifeboats hauled on deck and the Engelhardts abandoned, and the *Carpathia* proceeded to steam round the scene of the sinking in the hope of picking up anyone floating on wreckage. Before this, Captain Rostron arranged in the Saloon a service over the spot where the *Titanic* had sunk—a service, as he said, of respect to those who had been lost and gratitude for those who had been saved.

The *Carpathia* cruised round the scene, but found nothing to indicate there was any hope of picking up more survivors, and as the liner the *Californian* had arrived, followed shortly afterwards by the *Birma*, a Russian tramp steamer, Rostron decided to leave any further search to them and to make all speed with the rescued to land. As they sailed round, there was surprisingly little wreckage to be seen—wooden deckchairs and small pieces of wood, but nothing of any size. Covering the sea in huge patches was a mass of reddish-yellow seaweed.

From Lifeboat 14, as the early hours of the morning approached, there was silence across the water, broken only by a cough now and then, a whimper from a child, and the water gently lapping the planking around the sides. The cold had its searching effects on all of them as they waited for daybreak and possible rescue. As daylight approached, they could see that they were in the middle of a vast ice field with several small icebergs scattered around a wide area. At 6 a.m., a shout from one of the lifeboat's crew roused many of the occupants of the lifeboats. 'I can see a steamer's lights!' the man shouted. Fifth Officer Harold Lowe, in the stern of the lifeboat, shouted back 'Where do you see it?' Pointing ahead of them, the seaman shouted 'You can see her mast-head light!' Lowe, now standing up on a seat, exclaimed 'By Christ, you're right! It's the *Carpathia*!' To many in the lifeboats, it appeared that the ship was hardly moving at all.

As dawn broke at about 4 a.m., Eva Hart could see other lifeboats ringed about by huge icebergs as far as the horizon. Between two of these huge, jagged peaks the survivors on Lifeboat 14 saw what seemed at first to be a very small ship moving steadily towards them. All this time the sea had been calm and smooth, but now as the day brightened they could feel a swell beginning to develop. They were overwhelmed with relief at the sight of that ship which offered hope of warmth and comfort to those who had survived the ordeal. The *Carpathia* started to pick up the survivors as quickly as possible, but it was a long job and some of the lifeboats had to row three or four miles to reach her. Eva Hart's was one of the last to be emptied, and it was about 8.30 a.m. before she was actually on board. The adults had to climb up rope ladders, but that was too terrifying for the younger children. They were almost hysterical with fright. Eva and the other children were each put into a large canvas bag with their head poking out at the top, and several bags were then put into a lifting net which was winched up very quickly by a wheel on the deck. And so they arrived wet and cold amongst the crew and passengers of the *Carpathia*. Eva was more frightened by this experience than by almost anything else that had happened.

As soon as they were on board, they were taken below to one of the rooms where they were each wrapped in a blanket and given something hot to drink. Eva had all sorts of odd clothes piled around her, including a man's coat. All this time her mother was frantically searching everywhere for her, hoping she would be on the ship somewhere. By now it was very crowded and finding anyone was not easy; the number of passengers had doubled in a matter of a few hours. As a result there were throngs of people in all the companionways. While Eva was still crying for Esther, between dozing and being comforted by strangers her mother was going from one part of the ship to another asking everyone if they had seen her daughter. It was much later in the day before she discovered Eva, still miserable and huddled under borrowed clothing. They clung to each other with tears of relief, sharing their suffering and gaining much comfort from being together again. Esther didn't let the girl out of her sight for the rest of the journey to New York.

The *Carpathia* was a much smaller and slower ship than the *Titanic*, and only had a single funnel. But despite her size and lack of speed, she was paradise after the exposure and bleakness of the lifeboats. She gave Eva and the other survivors warmth, comfort, and dryness; above all, she gave them back life and hope. The people on board the ship couldn't have been kinder. Some were migrants to the United States who were going home; many were naturalized American citizens returning to Europe on vacation. Despite this disruption to their own plans, and although many of them were fairly poor, they still found the *Titanic* survivors articles of clothing. In some cases, they gave up their cabins to the survivors and did their best to comfort and help them. Although some of the *Titanic* survivors were fortunate enough to be given empty cabins, most of them had to sleep on straw mattresses in either the Dining Room or the Library. Eva's bed was made up on one of the dining tables. Apart from food, warmth, and sleep, some people needed to have medical attention for frostbite. Eva and Esther had both suffered from exposure. Despite the foresight shown by Benjamin in giving Esther his coat, most of their clothing had been inadequate against the penetrating damp and cold. The blanket had helped prevent Eva from suffering serious injury.

Once on board the *Carpathia*, Edith and Elizabeth Brown had great difficulty in walking as they waited for the circulation to slowly return to their legs and feet. Its crew had been well briefed on what to expect during their voyage to the wreck site, and had organized bedding and clothing for those coming on board. The passengers could never have anticipated the sort of mercy mission they were going to be involved in. Many survivors, including Edith and Elizabeth, were offered clothing and, in some cases, cabins. As the circulation returned slowly, they began talking to other survivors about their ordeals over the past eight hours. Their stories were similar, with many women fearing for the safety of their husbands and fathers. Their conversations were interrupted every time another lifeboat came alongside, with everyone rushing to the ship's side to see if any of their loved ones had been saved. Edith and Elizabeth followed them to the ship's rail in the hope that Thomas might be one of the few men who had been rescued, but each time the boats were loaded with women and children and one or two crew. Of all the women rescued that morning, only four were found to still have husbands, but there was hope that more would be found in hospitals in New York.

The rescue had come only just in time. Shortly after the *Carpathia* picked them up the weather deteriorated and by the afternoon of that day was quite bad. It took Captain Rostron four hours to navigate the *Carpathia* out of the ice field, and then they ran into fog. Every few minutes they had the monotonous blaring of the fog horn while the wet, clammy fog swirled around them. The ship could only make slow progress. Then, as if they had not suffered enough—as if the sea was reluctant to lose its prey—the fog was followed by a terrible thunder storm. Their new ship was unable to go very fast under these conditions. She was slow and heavily overladen as she slowly limped back to New York.

During the work of getting the lifeboats alongside, Arthur Rostron had happened to look down from the Bridge and saw his friend Lewis Ogden. The day before, he had been trying out a new camera. So Rostron cupped his hands and shouted down: 'What about that new camera?' Ogden glanced Rostron's way, threw up his hands as if to say he had never thought of it, sped off, and in a few minutes was taking snaps of the lifeboats as they came alongside. An amateur photographer never had a more thrilling scene. The *Carpathia* had stopped in mid-Atlantic. It was a beautiful morning, with a clear sun burning on the sea and glistening on the icebergs. On every side were dozens of these monsters, so wonderful to look at, so dreadful to touch. Some lifeboats containing the survivors were alongside; people were climbing up the ship's side, others were pulled up. All were wearing life jackets, and it was the wearing of these that protected those who had been so long exposed in the boats and prevented many from dangerous chills. And then, from every direction, lifeboats were pulling in, all making for the same place—the *Carpathia*.

The *Carpathia* cruised slowly from lifeboat to lifeboat, and as he neared the end of his task, Rostron began to appreciate the enormity of the disaster. So many hundreds lost whom a few hours before had been members of a happy and privileged crowd, halfway through the maiden voyage of the world's largest liner! One thing stood out in Roston's mind about it all—the quietness. There was no noise, no hurry. When the *Carpathia*'s passengers finally came on deck it was some time before they realized the nature of the tragedy; it was too big to take in all at once. Their hardly-awakened senses could not respond to the immensity of the scene. But as soon as reality dawned, the passengers realized that they must not remain spectators, and that here was an unparalleled situation in which they must play a part. They set about comforting the rescued, persuading them to take food and drinks, and seeking to soften the grief which enveloped them. The *Carpathia*'s doctors were relieved to see the passengers using their persuasion and common sense so successfully. They saw that the survivors required dry and warm clothing, so they took them to their own cabins to fit them out with everything they could. All the male passengers gave up their cabins and many of the women doubled up in order to leave their own quarters free for the survivors. Every officer gave up his accommodation.

Except for the lifeboats beside the ship and the icebergs, the sea was strangely empty. Hardly a bit of wreckage floated—just a deckchair or two, a few life jackets, and a lot of cork. No more flotsam than Rostron often saw on the seashore drifted in by the tide. The *Titanic* had sunk taking everything with her. Rostron saw only one body in the water; the intense cold made it impossible for anyone to live long in it. Staying on the scene was not an option for the crew of the *Carpathia*, especially as about this time—8 a.m.—they saw another ship coming up. This was the *Californian* which all night had been lying not many miles away, stationary because of the ice. The *Carpathia* signalled her now, asking her to continue searching as they were about to make for New York. The sea was rising and Rostron was anxious to get away from that danger zone in good daylight. Once all the *Titanic*'s lifeboats were emptied, they were hoisted on board by the ship's derricks and stowed away, some remaining suspended in their davits, others hauled on the Forecastle Head, and they proceeded on.

Soon after the rescue, the *Carpathia*'s Purser, Ernest Brown, interviewed each survivor. He had a difficult time writing the names of the 100 or so of the survivors who spoke very little English or none at all. The Scandinavian names, especially the Finnish ones, were full of spelling errors. Brown did the best he could by writing what the name sounded like in English. Due to Elin Hakkarainen's physical and mental state at the time, Brown wrote down the information incorrectly.

In the afternoon, Lawrence Beesley visited Third Class along with another passenger, to take down the names of all who had been saved. They grouped them into nationalities—English, Irish, and Swedish mostly—and learnt from them their names and homes, the amount of money they possessed, and whether they had friends in

America. Very few of the Irish girls had any money, and were going to friends in New York or places nearby, while the Swedish passengers, among whom there were many men, had saved most of their money and in addition had railway tickets through to their destinations in America. Beesley noticed these curious national differences, but could offer no explanation for them. It was likely the Irish girls never had very much money but they must have had the amounts stipulated in the immigration laws. There were some pitiful cases of women who had lost their children and husbands, and some with one or two children saved and the others lost. In one case, a whole family was missing, and there was only one friend left to tell their story. Among the Irish migrants Beesley noted a girl of remarkable beauty, with black hair, deep violet eyes with long lashes, and perfectly shaped features. She was quite young, not more than 18 or 20 years old.

The full impact of what had happened did not become clear until the second day after the rescue. Surely this was a bad dream and she would soon wake up and this nightmare would be over? Elin Hakkarainen kept searching every face in hope of locating her husband. She read the survivor list over and over again, looking for his name. She finally located her 18-year-old friend, Anna Sjöblom, who had knocked on her cabin door to awaken her. Anna had been travelling to visit her father, Gabriel Gustafson, who worked for the Simpson Timber Company, in Olympia, Washington State. Elin and Anna had become separated in the rush up to the Boat Deck and had got into separate lifeboats. Other than Anna, very few of Elin's friends from Finland were rescued. During the voyage to New York, Elin finally resigned herself to the fact that Pekka had gone down with the *Titanic*. Over and over again, she tried to reconstruct what had happened to him. When he left the cabin he would have had to go directly to the exit that would have been to the Rear Well Deck, since this was the allotted deck space for Third Class passengers. From this area, he could have gone to the Poop Deck where they had been earlier that evening. On returning to the cabin, and after he had discovered why the ship had stopped, he must have become disorientated. In desperation, he may have tried another route to their cabin, becoming lost in the maze of passageways.

'Arranged for Your Exclusive Story'

In Arthur Rostron's cabin on the *Carpathia* were three First Class passengers, Eleanor Widener, Madeleine Astor, and Marian Thayer, each of whom had been bereaved. Their husbands George Widener, John Jacob Astor, and John B. Thayer had perished, and Eleanor had lost her son Harry as well. On the other hand, Marian had a son Jack, aged 17, who had been saved in dramatic fashion. Jack had been separated from his mother, but later found a place on the Engelhardt B boat. Much later, Lifeboat 4 was hailed, and the boy was taken on board. His mother Marian was in it also, but the two did not notice each other until they were reunited aboard the *Carpathia*. But Rostron heard other stories that matched that one. Some of the first lifeboats that left the *Titanic* had not been filled to capacity, but others were overloaded, and there were heart-rending moments when they encountered men swimming in the sea. In one case, a boat's gunwale was seized by a swimmer. It was well before dawn. No one could see who it was, but many voices were raised protesting against him being hauled in. 'We are full, we are full,' they cried, 'Don't let him come in!' One woman in the stern, however, grieving for a husband left behind on the sunken ship, begged for the swimmer to be taken in. Her pleading prevailed and she knew the swimmer had been saved before she sank back unconscious. Hours passed, but finally dawn lit up the haggard faces of those who huddled and shivered in the boat. Only then did the woman see the features of the man she had saved from drowning. It was her husband.

Rostron's heart was stirred to see the fortitude of the bereaved, just as it gave him a glow of pride to listen to some of the tales of the survivors. There were tales of bravery and self-sacrifice in every Class. Rostron wondered, looking into the troubled and sometimes vacant faces of those who had been saved, whether they or those left behind had the harder part to play. Over the next few days, he heard stories of both the famous and the unknown. One concerned a young girl. A lifeboat full of women had been ready for lowering from the ship. It was found to be too full, and the order was given for someone to get out. The overfull boat endangered the lives of everyone. A young girl got up to leave the lifeboat. At once some of the others protested, pleading that she should stay. 'No,' she said, 'you are married and have families. I'm not, it doesn't matter about me.' She stepped out of the lifeboat, returned to the deck, and went down with the ship.

The *Carpathia* had sailed from New York on Thursday 11 April. It had been a pleasant and smooth passage apart from the intense cold, which everyone had remarked upon. On Sunday 14 April— three days out—the ship was within reach by wireless of the *Titanic*. At dinner that night, a message was received from the *Titanic*—a private communication. It came from the three sisters who were aboard, Charlotte Appleton, Malvina Cornell, and Caroline Brown, and was addressed to their uncle and aunt—Charles H. Marshall and his wife—who were on the *Carpathia*. Just a cheery greeting, saying how they were enjoying the crossing on the new ship. The Marshalls knew nothing about the disaster. They had retired to their cabin, and had gone to sleep. The night was calm, the sea smooth, and they slept on, all through the preparations that were being made on board. But in the morning among the first of the survivors who came up the gangways were their nieces. It was about 6.30 a.m. when the Marshalls awoke. A steward knocking on their door roused them. 'What is it?' asked Mr Marshall. 'Your nieces wish to see you, sir,' replied the steward. No wonder he was dumbfounded, hardly believing his eyes when he opened the door and looked at the three women, and not believing his senses as he listened to their story.

Rostron was struck by the silence on board. There was no excitement. At first, no doubt, the scale of the tragedy stunned the passengers, while the rescue came solemnly, dumbly, and out of a shivering shadow. Afterwards everyone was too busy to think. The women very quickly appointed themselves as nursing sisters, getting the newcomers to lie down, or rest on deck, and doing what they could to console and ease suffering. As many of the Second and Third Class passengers were poorly clothed, blankets and sheets were collected and many of the women started to make clothes. Others went to the Third Class and busied themselves, nursing, clothing, and feeding the children. Through it all the quietness reigned—as though the disaster was so great that it silenced human emotion. It seemed incredible that people who had undergone the experience did not become hysterical. Indeed on the morning of Tuesday 16 April, Dr Frank McGee, the Surgeon, went to Rostron and reported that all the survivors were physically well.

This was the result of endless attention on the part of Rostron and the crew. Loyally and cheerfully every member, both officers and men, gave of their best. Doctors, Pursers, stewards—even the bellboys—all entertained no thought of rest from the moment Rostron issued his first orders until they landed the survivors in New York and resumed their interrupted voyage to the Mediterranean. Rostron heard of only one case of selfishness. One man who had come aboard bedded down in one of the Smoking Rooms. With an acquisitive eye, and disregard of others, he had obtained several blankets for his own comfort. These were draped round his portly figure while other men found they didn't have any. He was asked to share them, but adopted the motto of 'What I have I hold.' There was a council of war among a few men. But the war was soon over—and the blankets were distributed. Another man, having given up his cabin, didn't have a bed. He wandered about the ship looking for somewhere to curl up until he saw an empty mattress with some blankets nearby. With a sigh of relief he lay down, pulled the blankets over his head, and went to sleep. In the morning, he woke up to find himself entirely surrounded by women—he had camped in a part of the ship which had been reserved for the rescued, and had lain there unnoticed through the night. He beat a hurried retreat.

When Harold Bride was first dragged aboard the *Carpathia*, he went to the ship's hospital and stayed there for ten hours. Then somebody brought word that the ship's Wireless Operator, Harold Cottam, was getting 'queer' from the work. They asked Bride if he could go up and help. He could not walk and both his feet were broken, but he went up on crutches with somebody helping him. Bride started work, and he claimed he never left the Wireless Cabin after that.

Their meals were brought to them, and they kept the wireless working all the time. He didn't know what happened to the passengers as he saw nothing of Madeleine Astor or any of the others. All he did was operate the wireless. They worked all the time; sometimes Cottam sent messages, and sometimes Bride. There was a bed in the Wireless Cabin, and sometimes while sending Bride could sit on it and rest his feet. The splutter of the telegraph never died down. For Bride it soothed the pain, and felt like a link with the world of friends and home.

While he was operating the wireless, Bride sometimes let a newspaper ask a question and he got a long string of questions asking for full particulars about everything. Bride claimed that he refused to send press dispatches because there were so many personal messages with touching words of grief. Whenever he started to take such a message he thought of the poor people waiting for their messages to go—hoping for answers to them. Bride found that the Navy operators were a great nuisance, and only knew American Morse; they needed to learn the Continental Morse and become quicker. The man on the light cruiser, the USS *Chester*, thought he knew it, but he was very slow. The naval wireless operators taxed Bride's endurance to the limit. Finally he had to cut them out, they were so slow, and he went ahead with the messages of grief to relatives.

By midnight on Monday 15 April, Bride and Cottam had given the *Olympic* the names of the First and Second Class survivors, and by dawn the Third Class and the crew. They sent 50 personal messages on Wednesday 17 April, and 199 the following day. Nevertheless Frederick Sammis, Marconi's Chief Engineer in New York, had been contacted by the *New York Times* which said that it would pay Bride and Cottam for their stories. Sammis relayed this to the two on the *Carpathia*: 'Arranged for your exclusive story for dollars in four figures Mr Marconi agreeing Stop say nothing until you see me.' Bride claimed he was still sending his personal messages when Marconi and reporter Jim Speers arrived to ask that he prepare a statement. Bride dictated his story to him after the *Carpathia* had docked. At that stage there were perhaps 100 messages left. Bride wished he had been able to send them all, because he would have rested easier if he had known all those messages had gone to the friends waiting for them.

Frank and Emily Goldsmith were assigned to the Second Class Saloon along with several other women and children. Officers and crewmen later dropped by to see if any special help was needed. By that time, Emily had become concerned about some of the women. Several had very young children with them, and the clothes they were wearing were the nightclothes which they had quickly covered with their heavy coats. Dressmaking had been Emily's hobby for several years, and she asked the men if they could collect together any cloth or ship's blankets, scissors, needles, thread, and buttons so that she and some of the other women could make emergency clothes. The men shortly returned with everything they had been able to find. A few hours later, several more crewmen came to offer assistance, and Emily asked if they would look after the children.

One of the rescued men took Frank under his wing, and for a walk around the ship. Samuel Collins, originally from Ramsgate, in Kent, had been a stoker on the *Titanic*. He introduced Frank to fellow crewmen and tried to cheer the boy up. Several times he saw tears on Frank's cheeks. He pleaded with the boy: 'Don't cry, Frankie. Your Daddy is surely on another boat and may get to New York before we do. You'll see him, and he will be so glad to see you.' Several times on Monday afternoon he tried to calm Frank, and by noon the next day he had completely succeeded. Sam took Frank all over the ship, from the Captain's Bridge to down into the boiler rooms. Then it all came back to Frank—those wonderful nights when the young boys aboard the *Titanic* had looked down upon the boilers, and the wonderful singing they had listened to as those firemen were doing their job.

Late in the afternoon, Sam took Frank into a room where a group of crewmen were sitting around, listening to first one then another telling interesting stories about experiences they had gone through on board ships they had served upon. Frank sat there listening, fascinated, with his eyes and mouth wide open. The sailor talking at the time suddenly went silent while his gaze was in Frank's direction. Then he quickly spoke up, saying 'Say, fellers, if little Frankie is being in here with us, he'd better be a sailor too, hadn't he?' One of the others spoke up and said 'He sure should!' The first one said 'Frankie, are you willing?' Frank said yes. He was told that he would have to be initiated by repeating certain words after him. After completing this formality, he would be accepted as a fellow sailor by drinking a 'Bombay Oyster'. This turned out to be a glass about two thirds full of water, slightly flavoured with vinegar and with an egg yolk floating on top. Frank was told he had to drink it and swallow the egg yolk without breaking it. From then on, Frank had all his meals with the crewmen. Each morning, prior to reaching New York, Frank would waken, quickly dress, and rush down to have breakfast with Sam Collins and the other crewmen. Since Frank was under Sam's wing most of the day, and Emily trusted him, she was able to work for the other women.

On the evening of Thursday 18 April, Frank was sitting next to Sam in the crew's dining room, eating supper. Just in front was one of the portholes. Suddenly Frank saw a light glide past. Excitedly he cried 'Oh, that ship nearly hit us!' Sam said 'Why Frankie, we are in New York Harbour! That was a harbour light you saw, not a ship.

We'll soon be docking.' The crewmen had given Frank such kind and wonderful treatment that it had driven from his mind any thought of landing. Frank had even stopped worrying about his father, Alfred Rush, and Tom Theobald, whom Frank and Emily hoped were safe. Frank dashed away from the table, rushed up to the open deck, and tore over to the ship's rail to gaze upon his new land. Just as he stretched to lean over the rail, one of many small boats was almost directly below him and standing on its deck was a man with a megaphone shouting 'How many were saved?' Frank shouted right back at him '710', as 712 people had reached the side of the *Carpathia*, but 2 had died. Shortly after, mother and son prepared to land. The ship docked, and when they walked down the gangplank they were taken in hand by Major Cowan of the Salvation Army.

Some days earlier, Lawrence Beesley had found that the problem of where the survivors were to be landed had to be settled next. The *Carpathia* was bound for Gibraltar, and Captain Rostron could have continued his journey there, landing Beesley and the others at the Azores on the way. However he required more linen and provisions, and the survivors were mostly women and children, ill-clad, dishevelled, and in need of much attention he could not give them. In addition, the ship would soon be out of the range of wireless communication. Rostron soon decided against that course. Halifax, Nova Scotia, was the nearest port, but that meant steaming north through the ice, and he thought his passengers did not want to see any more of that. Therefore he headed back to New York, which he had left the previous Thursday, working all afternoon along the edge of the ice field which stretched away north as far as the naked eye could see. Beesley found it an extraordinary sight to stand on deck and see the sea covered with solid ice, white and dazzling in the sun, and dotted here and there with icebergs. The *Carpathia* ran close up, only 200 or 300 yards away, and steamed parallel to the floes, until towards night they saw to their infinite relief the last of the icebergs and the field fading away astern. Many of the rescued had no wish ever to see an iceberg again. They learnt afterwards that the field was nearly 70 miles long and 12 miles wide, and had lain between them and the *Birma* on her way to the rescue.

During the day, the bodies of four of the *Titanic's* crew were buried; three had been taken out of the lifeboats, and one had died during the day. The engines were stopped and all passengers on deck bared their heads while a short service was read; when it was over the ship steamed on again. The passengers on the *Carpathia* were by now hard at work finding clothing for the survivors. The barber's shop was raided for ties, collars, hair-pins, and combs; one good samaritan went round the ship with a box of toothbrushes offering them to everyone. In some cases, clothing could not be found for the women and they spent the rest of the time on board in the dressing-gowns and cloaks in which they had come away from the *Titanic*. They even slept in them, for, given the shortage of berths, women had to sleep each night on straw mattresses on the floors of the Saloons and in the Library, and it was not possible to undress properly. The men were given the Smoking Room floor and a supply of blankets, but there was little room, and some chose to sleep out on deck. Beesley found a pile of towels on the bathroom floor, and made up a comfortable bed. Later he was awoken in the middle of the night by a man offering him a berth in his cabin.

On Tuesday 16 April, a group of survivors from First Class met in the Saloon and formed a committee to collect subscriptions for a fund, out of which it was resolved to provide as far as possible for the destitute among the Third Class passengers, to present a gift to

Captain Rostron and medals to the officers and crew of the *Carpathia*, and to divide any surplus among the crew of the *Titanic*. The group included the lawyer Frederick J. Seward, Molly Brown, the prominent campaigner for women's rights, the military attaché Mauritz Björnström-Steffansson, the lawyer Isaac Frauenthal, the tennis player Karl Behr, Frederic Spedden, and the businessman George A. Harder.

To Beesley it seemed sensible, while he was on the *Carpathia*, to prepare an accurate account of the disaster and to have this ready for the press, in order to calm public opinion and to counter the incorrect and hysterical accounts which he felt some American reporters were in the habit of preparing on occasions of this kind. The first impression was often the most permanent, and in a disaster of this magnitude, where exact and accurate information was so necessary, the preparation of a report was essential. He wrote a letter to *The Times* in odd corners of the deck and Saloon, and he gave a longer account to the one reporter whom he thought could best deal with it, from the Associated Press. It was published in the *New York Times* on 19 April and syndicated all over the world; Beesley felt it had much of the effect that he had hoped for.

Edith and Elizabeth Brown, having been on the *Carpathia*'s deck for long periods of time in the hope of finding Thomas, felt cold again. They made for one of the lounges for some well-earned sleep, if sleep was possible. As the *Carpathia* steamed for New York, Edith and Elizabeth began to wonder what the future held for them. They agreed that they shouldn't give up hope until they arrived and a final check of survivors had been carried out. There were rumours that there was a possibility that other ships in the area had heard the distress calls and picked up survivors, but that their wireless equipment wasn't up to the job of reporting this news. Elizabeth knew that this was clutching at straws, but it was just possible, and it gave them hope until their arrival. During their voyage to New York, both women cried every time they spoke of Thomas not being rescued. But it was better not to think the worst.

The day before their arrival, Edith and Elizabeth were feeling improved after their experiences over the previous few days. As Thomas had said, it would all come out once they had arrived, and perhaps he would be there on the wharf, waiting for them. This thought made Edith feel better, and she was going to stick with it until she knew differently. Elizabeth, on the other hand, knew that it would take nothing short of a miracle to bring Thomas back. And she knew fairly soon she would have to prepare her daughter for the worst. Edith had idolized her father all her life, and he in turn had spoiled her since the death of her younger sister four years earlier.

Sitting in the lounge after lunch on the final day on board, Elizabeth explained to her daughter how their situation would be affected if Thomas had drowned. All their money to start up the new business in Seattle had been in Thomas's Gladstone Bag, locked away securely in the Purser's Office. Edith realized how much her mother was confiding in her. As a result, she was beginning to feel more grown-up and responsible. The stark realization of their predicament finally came home to Edith. She knew what Elizabeth was saying, but she didn't fully understand what it might mean for her future. The only thing that really mattered to her was whether she would ever see her father again. Edith asked her mother if she thought her father would have stayed in America after losing all that money. Sadly, her mother replied 'I wouldn't think so, my dear.'

The scene that greeted Edith and the other survivors on the dockside was overwhelming, one that she and her mother would never forget. It looked as though the whole of New York had braved the foul weather to come down to the wharves to witness their arrival. As the gangways were placed in position, there were shouts from the quayside to those leaning on the ship's rail. It was a never-ending barrage of questions. 'Did you see many dead bodies in the water?' 'Have you lost anyone?' 'Do you need any money?' And so it went on. The First Class survivors were the first off, amid a blaze of flash bulbs and dozens of reporters surging forward to the bottom of the gangway. They were soon protected by shore personnel and whisked away in taxis or their own transport. Edith and Elizabeth followed as the Second Class passengers were given instructions to go ashore. Once on the dockside, there was pushing and shoving, making it impossible to move forward at times, until several policemen cleared a path. When they slowly made their way into the cargo shed, they were led to a group of offices at one end. It had been decided that all single women would be under the care of the Junior League of New York. They would remain at a hostel until other suitable arrangements could be made and relatives contacted. The generosity shown by the Americans was something that Edith never forgot.

On arrival at the hostel, Edith and Elizabeth had a hot meal and bath, and finally retired for the night, exhausted by the day's events. The next day, they were taken shopping. They returned with more clothes than they would ever need. After the lengthy shopping spree, they were taken to several hospitals to check for survivors, but all to no avail. They knew in their hearts that they would never see Thomas again. During their stay at the Junior League, Elizabeth sent a telegram to her sister in Seattle, letting Josephine know they were safe, but that Thomas was feared drowned. She finished off by saying they would be taking an interstate train within a week.

Having left the *Californian* in charge of the search—even though it was hopeless—Arthur Rostron and the *Carpathia* had started on their return. They soon found their passage blocked by a tremendous ice field. They had seen the field before, but had no means of knowing how large it was. All they could see was that it stretched to the horizon—a remarkable sight with icebergs up to 200 feet in height standing out of the general field, which was itself 6 to 12 feet above the waterline. These little mountains were just catching the early sunshine. Minarets like cathedral towers turned to gold in the distance and, here and there, some seemed to shape themselves like great merchant ships under full sail. For nearly four hours Rostron sailed round this pack ice, 56 miles. Then they were clear and could set their course for New York.

The *Olympic*, which at the time of the disaster was some hundreds of miles to the West, having left New York on Saturday 13 April, had sent a message by wireless suggesting that she should take off the rescued. But Rostron was against any such move. Fortunately, J. Bruce Ismay, Chairman of the White Star Line, was among the survivors, and when Rostron suggested that it would be unwise to try to transfer the people who had just been saved from the lifeboats, Ismay immediately agreed and told Rostron to request the *Olympic* keep out of sight. So on they went, still passing other isolated icebergs from time to time. About noon, they passed the Russian steamer *Birma*, bound East, which tried to cut through the ice field but turned back again.

On Monday 15 April, the *Carpathia* sent to the *Olympic* the bare facts of the disaster, and a telegram to the Cunard Company, 'Deeply regret advise you Titanic sank this morning after collision with iceberg resulting in loss of life full particulars later Bruce Ismay', together with as many names of the survivors as they had. This offered the first chance they had of dispatching the news to shore. It was—owing to the short range of wireless—also the last opportunity they had of establishing communication until the Wednesday afternoon, and then they learnt how the world had waited in suspense for details and especially a correct and complete list of the survivors. After the ice, they ran into that other great enemy of ships at sea—fog. For hours it enshrouded them, and again on 17 April it came down thick, continuing more or less all the way to New York. The dismal nerve-racking noise of the foghorn every thirty seconds was particularly distressing to the survivors, and Rostron was sorry for their state of mind, having this after all their other experiences. They had taken three bodies from the lifeboats and one man died during Monday 15 April. All four were buried on the Monday afternoon.

During Wednesday 17 April, the *Carpathia* was in communication with the USS *Chester*—there was dense fog at the time—and through her they were able to send a more complete and corrected list of survivors. They picked up the Fire Island Lighthouse from its foghorn on Thursday 18 April and, about 6 p.m., stopped off the Ambrose Channel Lightship and took on their Pilot. It was now that they got some idea of the suspense everyone was in. Press boats literally surrounded them. Rostron decided that these journalists must not come on board. The comfort of the rescued had to be the first consideration. Rostron knew that to have them interviewed by dozens of alert young newspapermen, eager to get the most lurid details, and making them live it all over again, would cause endless distress. It was, of course, only in the nature of the reporters' jobs to get news, and when Rostron told them they would not be allowed on board they tried various tactics. These press boats carried huge placards announcing this was from such and such a paper and that from another. They badgered and pleaded to be allowed to interview Rostron and the passengers, but the Captain would not let them.

Two newspapermen adopted the ruse of coming in on the Pilot's boat. The Pilot was a friend of Rostron's, and it was not easy to give him a straight refusal. 'Can these fellows come aboard?' he yelled. Rostron cupped his hands and shouted 'I can't hear you.' 'They want to come aboard. They have friends on the ship.' 'I can't hear what you say,' Rostron shouted, and they knew he was prevaricating. When the Pilot had the ladder down, however, the Captain expected they would try to get on board after him. So Rostron had a rope attached to the bottom of the ladder and set two boys to haul it in as the Pilot came up. The moment the Pilot had lifted his foot from one rung to the next, the boys drew in the rope and the ladder was hoisted right under the man's heels. One of the two journalists in his boat jumped and tried to follow, but the ladder wasn't there and he fell backwards. Only one journalist got aboard. He made a jump that risked his life and landed on the deck. This was reported to Rostron and he had him brought to the Bridge. The Captain explained his reasons for not having anyone on board and said that he could not allow the passengers to be interviewed. Rostron made him promise not to leave the Bridge, and the journalist agreed. After they had docked and the passengers had left, he made a good story out of his exploit, being the only man to get aboard, and he was complimented. Rostron believed he deserved it for his resourcefulness.

But the weather changed again. It brought the most dramatic ending to the tragic episode. First it began to blow hard, then the rain tumbled down and, as a finale, as though the curtain had to come down under unusual surroundings, lightning started. Vivid flashes accompanied them all the way up the channel, and heavy thunderclaps rolled across the skies. This weather held until they were off the Cunard Dock. While on the Bridge in the pelting rain, a bundle of letters and telegrams were brought to Rostron. He couldn't examine them at the time and put them in his pocket. During a lull, later on, he went into his Chart Room, dipped a hand into his pocket and drew out only one item. It was a telegram from his wife.

It was a scene never to be forgotten. Press photographers on the dock set off their flashbulbs. All round the ship were dozens of tugboats and, before they could tie up, the *Titanic*'s lifeboats had to be lowered because they were in the way. Two of the rescued crew went in each of those boats, and to see them row into the dark night reminded Rostron of the last occasion when they had been lowered. After 9 p.m., the survivors left the *Carpathia*, and no one was more glad than Rostron to see them safely landed. Not that he wanted rid of them, but to think that they had been looked after and were safe. They had all been strained to the highest pitch of anxiety, and the extent of that concern was now the measure of their relief. The job was done.

The *Carpathia*'s journey back to New York encountered almost every kind of weather—icebergs, ice fields, and bitter cold to begin with; brilliant warm sun, thunder, and lightning in the middle of one night (and the peal followed the flash so closely that women in the Saloon leapt up in alarm, saying rockets were being sent up again); cold winds most of the time; fogs every morning and during most of one day, with the foghorn blowing constantly; and rain and choppy sea with the spray blowing overboard and coming in through the Saloon windows. The passengers said they had almost everything except hot weather and stormy seas. So when they were told on Thursday 18 April that the Nantucket Lightship had been sighted from the Bridge, a great sigh of relief went round to think New York and land would be reached before the following morning.

There was no doubt that many people found the waiting period of those four days very difficult. The ship was overcrowded, clothing and toiletries missing, and above all there was the anticipation of meeting relatives on the pier, with, in many cases, the knowledge that other friends had been left behind and would not return home again. A few people looked forward to meeting the friends to whom they had said goodbye on the *Titanic*'s deck, taken there by a faster boat, perhaps, or at any rate to hear that they were following on behind. It was only a few, for the thought of the icy water and the many hours' immersion made it unlikely. However Lawrence Beesley and his companions encouraged them to hope the *Californian* and the *Birma* had picked some up; stranger things had happened, and they had been through strange experiences.

But in the midst of this rather tense feeling, one fact stood out as remarkable—no one was ill. On Tuesday 16 April, Dr Frank McGee, the Surgeon, had reported a clean bill of health, except for frostbite and shaken nerves. There were none of the illnesses supposed to follow from exposure for hours in the cold night—many people had swum about for some time when the *Titanic* sank, and then either sat for hours in their wet clothes or lain flat on the upturned Engelhardt boat with the sea water washing over them until they were taken off in a lifeboat. There were no scenes of women weeping and brooding over their losses hour by hour until they were driven mad with grief. These women met their sorrow with the greatest courage, came on deck and talked with other men and women face to face, and in the midst of their loss did not forget to rejoice with those who had come with them in a lifeboat or rejoined their friends on the *Carpathia*'s deck. Eventually land was in sight, and it was very good to see it again—it was eight days since they had left Southampton, and it seemed more like eight weeks. So many dramatic incidents had been crowded into the previous few days that the first four peaceful, uneventful days, marked by nothing that seared the memory, had faded. It required an effort to return to Southampton, Cherbourg, and Queenstown, as though returning to an event of the previous year.

And so, with the rescue completed, the *Carpathia* returned to New York. Surrounded by tugs of every kind, from which (as well as from every available building near the Hudson River) there were flash guns from photographers, while reporters shouted for news of the disaster and photographs of passengers, the *Carpathia* drew slowly to her station at the Cunard pier. The gangways were pushed across, and Beesley and the other survivors set foot at last on American soil, very thankful, grateful people. There were some painful scenes of meeting between relatives of those who were lost, but once again the women showed their self-control and went through the ordeal in most cases with extraordinary calm. What was striking was the state of health of most of the rescued, their gratitude for their deliverance, and the thousand and one things that gave cause for rejoicing. Nothing had been a greater surprise than to find that people had for the most part remained calm.

It was in the dusk of evening that the *Carpathia* crept up the Hudson River into New York, where a crowd waited, hoping against hope that the messages that had been received had been false and that relatives might be among those on board. Long before they got near the dock, despairing enquiries were shouted across the intervening water. It was only then that they learnt that no other ship had found a soul. The horror of the tragedy was renewed all over again. Next day, with practical forethought, a group of people had collected clothing of every kind, which was brought down to the dock and spread out on tables, reminding Violet Jessop of a jumble sale. The clothes, though good, were second-hand, covering many seasons of fashion and some had obviously been stored for years. If it had happened when they were in a happier frame of mind, they might have derived much fun from the grotesque figures some of them cut when dressed. But this was not a time for humour. Violet and the other survivors looked like a lot of dismal wet hens. Of course, complete strangers in New York wanted to be kind to the survivors, to show them around or arrange lectures. However for Violet, publicity at that time seemed abhorrent, and all her thoughts were concentrated on getting home, though she secretly dreaded the voyage.

Eva Hart also found it was late on the evening of Thursday 18 April before the heavily laden *Carpathia* berthed at the New York dockside. Thousands of onlookers had waited many hours to see its arrival. Everybody was very kind to Eva and Esther when they disembarked and despite the loss of all their money, passports, and baggage there were no undue delays. Esther's first act was to send, on Saturday 20 April, a cable to her parents in England: 'Benjamin lost Eva and Esther safe will sail Celtic April 25 for Liverpool Esther.' The letter she had written on the Sunday afternoon on the *Titanic* had never been posted. After they were rescued, she found it in the pocket of Benjamin's coat.

Eva's aunt in New York had seen their names in the list of survivors radioed from the *Carpathia*, and was expecting them when they landed. They were fortunate that they were able to go straight to her home. Esther had not met her previously because her sister-in-law had left England when she was quite young, before Esther and Benjamin had met. She was very upset that after waiting all that time for her brother he should have died at sea in such tragic circumstances.

Although they were made very welcome in New York, Esther had already started looking to the future. When asked about her plans she quite calmly said, 'Well, I don't want to stay here and I don't want to go to Canada. Now I just want to get back to my own people.' She had no practical experience of the building trade and could see no point in continuing on. So Eva and Esther stayed in New York for a short time during which their main concern was obtaining berths on board a ship that could take them back to England. Somehow, Esther also managed to find the time and money to buy her daughter a doll to replace the one that had gone down with her teddy bear.

The first survivor list was sent from the *Carpathia* by wireless, which had a range of 200–300 miles. All transmissions were picked up by the wireless stations at Cape Race, Newfoundland, and Portland, Maine, and in turn were relayed to the station set up in Wanamaker's Department Store, New York. The *Carpathia*'s wireless station kept going for the entire time during the return trip to New York, sending out the names of survivors and messages of grief. The names of the First and Second Class passengers were sent immediately, and were published in the newspapers as soon as they were received. It was also predominantly the First Class passengers who sent or attempted to send messages. Elizabeth Shutes sent a message to her mother in New York, simply saying 'Safe Elizabeth'. Similarly Archibald Gracie prepared two messages, though they were never sent. The first, to his wife in Washington, said 'Safe on Carpathia', while the second said 'Meet me New York Bring clothes (Archibald Gracie)'.

A list of Third Class passengers and crew did not appear until Thursday 18 April, and contained only 135 names. This list was received by the Marconi station at Portland. Considering that 178 Third Class passengers and 212 crew were saved, this list was very incomplete. These spelling errors could have been a mistake by the *Carpathia*'s Purser, or changed through the various wireless relays. Another problem might have been the use of the Continental and American Morse codes. Many mistakes were made through the use of a code that was not entirely familiar to the operator. This was the first list on which Elin Hakkarainen's name was spelt 'Ellen', and her surname as 'Hakkarinen'. At that point Elin didn't care about their questions. In any case she spoke very little English.

The *Carpathia*'s list was compiled on the manifest of 'alien' passengers for the United States Immigration Service required under the 1907 Immigration Act. The register stated that 'saloon, cabin, and steerage aliens must be completely manifested'. Among the columns were family name, given name, age, whether married or single, calling or occupation, whether able to read and write, nationality, 'race or people', last permanent address, 'name and complete address of nearest relative or friend in country whence alien came', and final destination, state and city or town. There were around 174 First and Second Class passengers listed, and around 180 Third Class. Only the Third Class were listed alphabetically.

Elin found that the *Carpathia* did not go to Ellis Island, but directly to the White Star Line Pier to drop off the *Titanic* lifeboats, and then returned to Cunard's Pier 54. Thousands of people lined the pier and the streets beyond. The *Carpathia*'s regular passengers left the ship immediately upon docking. The First and Second Class survivors were next to leave. The Third Class survivors were held until about midnight while the immigration inspectors processed their entry papers. It was after midnight when Elin's group walked down the gangplank to the waiting buses. The large crowd had already left. The Women's Central Relief Association divided the survivors into groups according to nationality, listing Elin's name as 'Ellen Hakkarinen'. All those from Finland were taken to St Vincent's Hospital. Most did not require hospitalization, but the Sisters of Charity of St Vincent de Paul had volunteered to care for them until they could leave on their own. Elin never forgot the tender, loving care they received. It was the first, and most important, step in the recovery of their shattered lives.

On Sunday 21 April, Elin and other survivors each received a new outfit of clothes, hats, shoes, toilet articles, and a suitcase through the American Red Cross. As soon as it had heard of the disaster, the Red Cross had started to organize relief efforts and collect relief funds so that when the *Carpathia* arrived, it could begin to meet the needs of the survivors and make sure they received attention. Representatives of the Red Cross Committees were there when the *Carpathia* docked, and within two days, most of the *Titanic's* Third Class passengers were visited and interviewed, whether they were in a temporary shelter or in one of the local hospitals. Elin received $125 and a train ticket to Monessen from the Women's Central Relief Association, which had been charged with the responsibility of arranging temporary shelter, medical attention, clothing, and transportation for those who needed such assistance. There were a total of five survivors—four adults and a child—who travelled to Monessen. On Monday 22 April, Elin arrived in Monessen, on the 9.00 a.m. train from New York. Along with her were four other Finnish survivors, Helga Hirvonen, her daughter Hildur, Eiriik Jussila, and Eino Lindqvist. On arrival, they were met by friends and relatives.

The problems in spelling experienced by Elin were greater than those for the Touma family. The list from the *Carpathia*, dated 18 April 1912, listed the Touma family as 'Hanna, Mariana, and Georges Darwich, from Syria'. After arriving in New York, and having lost everything other than a few documents and mementos, Hanna and her children also received assistance from a women's group connected with the St Vincent's Hospital. They were photographed in a group of survivors by the *New York Evening Standard*, but named 'Louise, Mariana, and George Touna', and given two additional children. Meanwhile in Dowagiac, Michigan, Abraham was shocked at the news of the disaster and felt guilty because he believed he was the cause of his brother losing his family. How was he to tell him that they had been on the *Titanic* and now were gone? When he told Darwis, his brother went mad and chased him up and down the street; later the two cried in sadness and rage, both devastated. Five days later, on Saturday 20 April, they received a telegram from a priest who spoke Arabic. He had a message for someone in Dowagiac that his wife and children had been saved. Hanna and the children remained under the care of the relief group until they were put on a train on Thursday 25 April. Some fifty-six days after leaving her village, Hanna, Georges, and Maria arrived. The little piece of paper with 'Dowagiac, Michigan', had enabled her to find her husband. They arrived there the next day and were reunited with Darwis. On 3 May, Hanna received a cheque for $90, her share of the fund collected for the relief of destitute survivors.

'Mr Beesley's Simple Narrative'

The US Inquiry into the disaster (19 April–25 May 1912), by the Senate's Committee on Commerce and chaired by William Alden Smith, of Michigan, began immediately after the return of the *Carpathia* to New York. The first day's hearings began in the Waldorf Astoria Hotel, and on the following day, twenty-nine members of the *Titanic* crew were subpoenaed before they could leave for Plymouth on the Belgian Red Star Line's ship *Lapland*. After the *Lapland* left on Saturday 20 April, a tug went after it and brought a further five crew back. Other hearings took place in Washington. The American Inquiry heard evidence from eighty-two witnesses, fifty-three of them British, and twenty-nine American, including Harold Bride, Archibald Gracie, Herbert Lightoller, and Arthur Rostron.

Its report was published on 28 May. It found the *Titanic* had sailed with 2,223 people on board, of whom 1,517 were lost and 706 saved.

Overall, 60 per cent of the First Class passengers were saved; 42 per cent of the Second; 25 per cent of the Third; and 24 per cent of the crew. It found that many of the crew did not join the ship until a few hours before sailing, and the only drill at Southampton consisted of lowering two lifeboats on the starboard side into the water, with the boats being hoisted back up on to the deck within half an hour. No boat list designating the stations of the crew was posted up until several days after sailing from Southampton. While ice was reported, there was no discussion among the officers; the speed was not reduced; and the lookout was not increased. Moreover after the collision, no general alarm was sounded, no whistle blown, and no systematic warning given to the passengers. The Inquiry found that the *Californian* was nearer the *Titanic* than the 19 miles reported by its Captain, and that its officers and crew saw the distress signals of the *Titanic* and failed to respond to them. In terms of loading the lifeboats, there was no system; indecision about which deck they were to be loaded from; no direction as to the number of passengers to be carried by each; and no uniformity in loading them. On one side, only women and children were put into the lifeboats, while on the other an equal proportion of men and women were allowed in. The failure to use the full capacity of the lifeboats undoubtedly cost lives.

The American Inquiry made recommendations on lifeboats, radio-telegraphy, and the design of ships. Thus the Committee recommended that additional legislation was needed to secure safety at sea. Sufficient lifeboats were to be required to accommodate every passenger and member of the crew (the *Titanic* had a total lifeboat capacity of 1,176 people). Four members of the crew should be assigned to every lifeboat. There should be a radio operator on duty at all times, to ensure that all distress, warning, or other important calls were received immediately. All new ocean-going passenger steamships carrying 100 or more passengers were to have a watertight skin, either in the form of an inner bottom, or longitudinal watertight bulkheads. Moreover all ships carrying 100 or more passengers should have bulkheads spaced so that any two adjacent compartments of a ship could be flooded without destroying the floatability or stability of the ship. Watertight transverse bulkheads should extend from side to side of the ship.

The British Inquiry, held before Lord Mersey, Wreck Commissioner, opened in London on 2 May 1912 and ran until 3 July. John Bigham, a judge, was assisted by the Assessors Rear Admiral Sir Somerset Gough-Calthorpe, Captain A. W. Clarke, Commander F. C. A. Lyon, the naval architect Sir John Biles, and Mr E. C. Chaston. In all, there were thirty-seven public sittings, initially at the Scottish Hall, Buckingham Gate, Westminster, and latterly at the Caxton Hall, Caxton Street, Westminster, at which ninety-seven witnesses were examined, including Frederick Barrett, Harold Bride, Elizabeth Leather, Herbert Lightoller, and Arthur Rostron. The Board of Trade had formulated twenty-six questions. Its report was published on 30 July.

The British report had a much more detailed description of the ship, of its journey across the Atlantic including the warning messages received, the damage, the sinking, and the rescue. It found that when the *Titanic* left Queenstown on 11 April it had 885 crew and 1,316 passengers on board, or 2,201 in total, and that 712 of these were rescued by the *Carpathia*. Those saved represented 62.46 per cent of those in First Class; 41.40 per cent in Second; 37.94 per cent in Third; 23.95 per cent of the crew; and 32.30 per cent of all those on board. Much of the British Inquiry was taken up with the Board of Trade's administration. As with the American Inquiry, it found that there had been no proper boat drill or muster, but it also argued that the Third Class passengers had not been unfairly treated. Instead they were more reluctant to leave the ship; unwilling to part with their baggage; and it was difficult to get them up from their quarters. The *Californian* could have saved many of the lives that were lost. The report's main finding was that 'the loss of the said ship was due to collision with an iceberg, brought about by the excessive speed at which the ship was being navigated'. It provided an extensive investigation of the circumstances of the *Californian*, and concluded that the two vessels were 8 to 10 miles apart. It found that inadequate lookouts were kept on the *Titanic*; they had no binoculars; the speed was excessive; and that the disproportion between the numbers of passengers saved in the Classes had various causes, but was 'certainly not due to any discrimination by the officers or crew in assisting the passengers to the boats'.

The British Inquiry made recommendations on lifeboats, drills, and ice and speed. Its main recommendations were that a newly appointed Bulkhead Committee should inquire and report on the desirability and practicality of providing ships with a double skin carried up above the waterline; or with a longitudinal, watertight bulkhead on either side of the ship; or with a combination of the two. This was in addition to watertight transverse bulkheads. The provision of lifeboats and rafts on board 'foreign-going passenger and emigrant steamships' should be based on the number of people intended to be carried on the ship, and not on tonnage. The capacity of the lifeboats on the *Titanic* had been 1,178 people. The men manning the lifeboats should have more frequent drills than previously, and in all ships a boat drill, fire drill, and watertight door drill should be held as soon as possible after leaving the original port of departure, and at convenient intervals of not more than once a week during the voyage. These drills should be recorded in the official log. When ice was reported, ships should proceed at night at a moderate speed, or alter their course so as to be well clear of the danger zone.

The attention of Masters of vessels was to be drawn to the 1911 Maritime Conventions Act, that it was a misdemeanour not to go to the relief of a vessel in distress when it was possible to do so.

One effect of the disaster was that wireless was now perceived to be indispensable, and that it needed policies to regulate it, including the range of the apparatus, its power source, the hours a station could be operative, and the allocation of frequencies. In July 1912, an amendment to the 1910 Ship Wireless Act stated that vessels had to have two operators on duty, so that stations could function twenty-four hours a day, and an auxiliary power source. In December 1912, the Radio Act became law; all operators were to be licensed, and stations had to have a specific transmitted capacity and adhere to a particular wavelength. It also established new procedures for distress calls, with a distress frequency, and 'SOS' deemed to be the official distress call.

Nearly all of Archibald Gracie's male companions in First Class were drowned in the disaster, among them James Clinch Smith, John Jacob Astor, Archibald Butt, Clarence Moore, Francis D. Millet, Arthur Ryerson, John B. Thayer, and George D. Widener, along with Edith Evans. Ryerson's wife and children and the family's maid survived, as did Hugh Woolner. Of the crew members that Gracie encountered, Frederick Wright, the Racquet Court attendant, and Thomas McCawley, the Gymnasium steward, were both drowned, but Charles Cullen, the First Class steward, survived.

Gracie was met at the dock in New York by his daughter and son-in-law, and wrote an account of the tragedy, but he never finished correcting the proofs as he died in December 1912. He had never fully recovered from his injuries, and was the third survivor of the *Titanic* to die that year. The book was published after his death as *The Truth About the Titanic* in 1913. In 1942, Gracie Mansion, in Carl Schurz Park, built by one of his ancestors, became the official residence of the Mayor of New York City. Gracie was played in the 1958 film *A Night to Remember* by James Dyrenforth, and in the 1997 film *Titanic* by Bernard Fox. Interestingly, Fox had played Lookout Frederick Fleet in the 1958 film.

Arthur Rostron and the crew of the *Carpathia* at once thought of their own affairs. They had set out on 11 April for the Mediterranean, and had a fairly full complement of passengers. Rostron hastily replenished from a sister ship the linen, blankets, and other things used in the rescue, and on Friday 19 April—a week from the time of their previous sailing—they left the dock, with new stores, water, and coal.

For Rostron, the repercussions went on for some time. On 29 May, on his arrival from Naples, and first return to New York since the disaster, Rostron was awarded a silver 'loving cup' by the survivors. The presentation was made by Molly Brown, and Frederick Seward, Mauritz Björnström-Steffansson, Frederic Spedden, Karl Behr, Isaac Frauenthal, and George Harder were among those present. Another 300 officers and crew of the *Carpathia* who were onboard during the rescue voyage were presented with gold, silver, and bronze medals. The citation read: 'Presented to the Captain officers & crew of R. M. S. 'Carpathia' in recognition of gallant & heroic services from the survivors of the S. S. 'Titanic' April 15th 1912.' Rostron returned overland from Naples to England to attend the British Inquiry, and on 6 June, in Liverpool, he received the Liverpool Shipwreck and Humane Society's gold medal and certificate. It was in December that he left the *Carpathia*, leaving on board the testimonials with which he had been presented by the rescued. There followed a round of social functions. Rostron had to be in Washington in March 1913 to receive from President Taft the Congressional Medal of Honor. The British Ambassador, Lord Bryce, took Rostron and his wife to the White House to receive this, the highest honour the United States Government could bestow, and afterwards they returned to the British Embassy where Rostron was presented with the American Cross of Honor. Rostron also received a gold medal from the Shipwreck Society of New York.

After a year in command of the *Carpathia*, Rostron was transferred to the *Caronia*. He was on board the *Aulania* when the First World War broke out; it was hastily requisitioned as a troopship. He commanded various other ships during the War, including at Gallipoli. And it was during the War that the *Carpathia* was to end her days. She was torpedoed in May 1918, off the south of Ireland. Rostron remained with the *Mauretania* until July 1928. He received many honours, and was knighted in 1926; he was given the Freedom of New York. Rostron retired from the sea in 1931, and wrote his memoirs, *Home From the Sea*, published the following year. He lived in Southampton, dying in November 1940, and was played in the 1958 film by Anthony Bushell.

The two businessmen who helped Elizabeth Shutes, Howard Case and Washington Roebling, were both drowned in the disaster, as were the husbands of Elizabeth's Canadian companions in the lifeboat, Charles Hays and Thornton Davidson. Louis M. Hoffman also perished. But it gradually emerged that 'Louis M. Hoffman' was an assumed name; the boys' father was called Michel Navratil, the boys

'Loto' was really Michel (usually called Lolo), and 'Louis' was Edmond Roger (Momon). Michel Navratil had been born in Szered, Slovakia; he later moved to Hungary and then, in 1902, went to Nice, in France, where he worked as a tailor. He married Marcelle Caretto, who was originally from Italy, in London, in May 1907. However by 1912, the business was in trouble and Michel suspected Marcelle of having an affair. The couple separated, the two boys going with their mother. They went to stay with their father over the Easter weekend of 1912, but when Marcelle went to collect them, they had disappeared.

Michel had decided to take the two boys with him to America. After stopping in Monte Carlo, they sailed to England where they stayed at the Charing Cross Hotel in London. Michel bought Second Class tickets for £26, and boarded the *Titanic* at Southampton. Michel's assumed name was adopted from a friend who had helped them leave France. While on board, Michel wrote to his mother in Hungary, asking if his sister and her husband could care for the boys, perhaps anticipating that they might be unable to stay in America. On the night of the sinking, Michel dressed the boys and took them to the Boat Deck, and handed them through the ring of crew members guarding the Engelhardt C boat. Michel's body was later recovered. His effects included a loaded revolver, pocket book, gold watch and chain, silver sovereign purse containing £6, receipt from Thomas Cook & Co for notes exchanged, ticket, pipe in case, coins, keys, and bill for the Charing Cross Hotel. Because he had used a Jewish name, he was interred in the Baron de Hirsch Cemetery, Halifax, Nova Scotia, designated for Jewish victims.

Margaret Hays was from New York, and had boarded the *Titanic* at Cherbourg. She was travelling First Class with her friends Lily Potter and Olive Earnshaw, and had been rescued in Lifeboat 7. On the *Carpathia*, because she was a fluent French speaker, she volunteered to care for the two 'Hoffman' boys who had been unclaimed by any adult relative. Subsequently they stayed at her New York home, on West 83rd Street, under the auspices of the Children's Aid Society. The boys' mother Marcelle recognized her sons from the many newspaper accounts about them, and she was brought over to the United States by the White Star Line; she was reunited with her sons in May.

A 'Miss EW Shutes' was listed as dead in Marshall Everett's popular 'disaster book', *Wreck and Sinking of the Titanic: The Ocean's Greatest Disaster*, published in May, though it was noted that she was probably reported as saved as 'Miss Shutter'. The book's list of 914 dead was a revision based on reports from the *Carpathia*. An account by Elizabeth Shutes, 'When the Titanic Went Down', was incorporated in Archibald Gracie's *The Truth About the Titanic*. However Elizabeth did not remain as a governess in the Graham family's employment for long; Margaret viewed her as less than competent, and was not fond of her. Elizabeth died, unmarried, in Utica, New York, in October 1949. Margaret Graham married Eugene Moore, the senior executive of a law firm; she was active in the American Red Cross during the Second World War, and in local civic life throughout her life. She died in April 1976, leaving three children.

Most of the colleagues of Second Officer Herbert Lightoller were drowned, among them Chief Officer Henry Wilde, First Officer William Murdoch, and Sixth Officer James Moody. On the other hand, Third Officer Bert Pitman, Fourth Officer Joseph Boxhall, and Fifth Officer Harold Lowe survived. Samuel Hemming, the Lamp Trimmer, and Major Arthur Peuchen, the Canadian yachtsman, both survived, though Peuchen was later accused of cowardice.

Through the trip to New York, there were very many quiet acts of self-denial. Everybody's hope, as far as Lightoller and the rest of the *Titanic*'s crew were concerned, was that they might arrive in New York in time to catch the *Celtic* back to Liverpool and so escape the Inquiry that would otherwise be awaiting them. Their luck was out, and they were served with warrants immediately on arrival. After the Inquiry moved to take hearings in Washington, the crew were herded into a boarding house. Lightoller was called to testify at the American Inquiry; he was at pains to explain his actions, notably the loading of the lifeboats. On Thursday 2 May, Lightoller and other crew members departed from New York for Liverpool via Queens-town on the White Star liner *Adriatic*. They arrived back in Liverpool on Saturday 11 May. In 1913, following the American and British Inquiries, Lightoller returned to sea as First Officer of the *Oceanic*. With the outbreak of the First World War, the *Oceanic* became an armed merchant cruiser, and Lightoller a Lieutenant in the Royal Navy. The *Oceanic*'s job was to patrol the Shetland Islands, but in September 1914 she ran aground near the island of Foula. Lightoller was off watch and in his cabin, but once again he found himself supervising the loading and lowering of lifeboats. Three weeks later, the *Oceanic* broke up in a storm.

Lightoller's next assignment was to the *Campania*, a Cunard liner converted to a seaplane carrier. Just before Christmas 1915, he got his own command, the torpedo boat HMTB 117. He subsequently com-manded the torpedo-boat-destroyer *Falcon* and the destroyer *Garry*; he was awarded the Distinguished Service Cross. Lightoller left the Royal Navy as a Commander. With the return of peace, Lightoller was appointed Chief Officer on the *Celtic*, but he resigned from the White Star Line. The Lightollers opened a guesthouse, and purchased a discarded Admiralty steam launch, the *Sundowner*. Lightoller pub-lished an account of his experiences, 'Loss of the Titanic', in his book

Titanic and Other Ships (1935). In July 1939, the Lightollers were asked by the Royal Navy to carry out a survey of the German coastline; they did this under the guise of an elderly couple on vacation on their yacht. Then, in May 1940, the British Expeditionary Force was trapped at Dunkirk. At 5 p.m. on 31 May, Lightoller got a telephone call from the Admiralty asking him to take the *Sundowner* to Ramsgate, in Kent. On 1 June, the 66-year-old Lightoller, accompanied by his eldest son Roger and a Sea Scout, took the *Sundowner* and sailed for Dunkirk. Although the *Sundowner* had never carried more than 21 people, they succeeded in taking 130 men from the beaches. Despite bombing, they arrived safely back in Ramsgate twelve hours after they had departed. Lightoller then joined the Home Guard, but also worked with the Royal Navy. The couple's youngest son, Brian, was killed in a bombing raid on Wilhelmshaven on the first day of the War, and their eldest, Roger, during the final months of the War. Lightoller went on to run a boatyard, dying in December 1952. He was played in the 1958 film by Kenneth More, and his wife Sylvia by Jane Downs. Fourth Officer Boxhall, who later became a naval Commander, was the film's technical adviser. Lightoller was played in *Titanic* (1997) by Jonny Phillips.

On 17 April 1912, Harold Bride's father received at 58 Ravensbourne Avenue, Bromley, Kent, the telegram 'Officially advised by White Star Line Operator Bride saved from Titanic.' But his son had badly frozen and crushed feet, and contemporary photographs show him being carried off the *Carpathia*, his feet covered in bandages. An ambulance man was waiting with a stretcher, and Bride went with him. Reporter Jim Speers took down Bride's story, and it was published on the front page of the *New York Times* on 19 April. Bride

received $1,000 for the story. When Bride was called to testify at the American Inquiry, he was in a wheelchair, but was grilled by Senator Smith about his actions during the sinking. In honour of his bravery during the disaster, the Marconi Company presented him with a gold watch inscribed 'In recognition of having done his duty, and done it bravely.'

After a spell in St Vincent's Hospital, Bride returned to England. He arrived in Liverpool from New York on the *Baltic* on 18 May, and was met by his father. Finally he returned to work as a wireless operator. He was positive that marriage to Mabel Ludlow was not what he wanted, and he broke off the engagement in September after he met Lucy Downie. She had been born and brought up in Stranraer, and was 22 and had moved to London to take up a job as a teacher. They met by chance in the street when she recognized Bride from newspaper photographs. Bride was working as a telegrapher in a London Post Office at the time, then returned to sea in 1913 as a wireless operator aboard the *Medina*. In 1914, during the First World War, he was assigned to a relay station on the coast of Scotland (one of the first wireless interception stations), and leaving Marconi in 1916 served on the steamer *Mona's Isle*, a net layer, as a telegraphist in 1918 and 1919. His last sea-going appointment was on a Cross-Channel ferry, until 1922.

Bride married Lucy at Stranraer, in April 1920, and the couple had three children. However, he disliked discussing his experiences on the *Titanic*, particularly the loss of Jack Phillips. Partly because of this, the family moved to Scotland where Bride worked initially as a pharmacist in Stranraer, and later as a travelling salesman for a London pharmaceutical company. He lived out the rest of his days in comparative obscurity; he died in April 1956, aged 66. Bride was played in the 1958 film by David McCallum, and in the 1997 film by Craig Kelly. The family home at 58 Ravensbourne Avenue,

Shortlands, Bromley, Kent, now bears a blue plaque: 'Harold Bride, 1890–1956, Wireless Operator Aboard RMS Titanic, Lived Here 1903–1922'.

After the disaster, as we have seen, there were numerous errors with the spelling of survivors' names caused by the wireless transmissions. The fact that many names were incorrectly spelt caused problems with relatives who were trying to locate members of their family who were known to be passengers on the *Titanic*. Due to the various misspellings of Elin Hakkarainen's name, all her relatives presumed that she had perished. The American Senate investigation list (dated 10 April 1912) gave the names of all *Titanic* passengers, and was cabled to New York from London soon after the disaster. Elin and Pekka were listed as 'Elin and Pekko Hakkurainen'. 'Hakkurainen, Elin' and 'Hakkurainen, Pekka' appeared in the list of 914 dead in Marshall Everett's popular 'disaster book', *Wreck and Sinking of the Titanic*, and in Thomas H. Russell's edited collection *Sinking of the Titanic: World's Greatest Sea Disaster* (1912).

Elin managed to secure a job as a dressmaker/seamstress and lived in a Finnish boarding house in the United States for four years. In 1916, she moved to Weirton, West Virginia, a small town nestled in a valley along the Ohio River. She met and married Emil Nummi in April 1917. He was born in Turku, Finland, and was employed in the tin mill at the Weirton Steel Company. Elin and Emil had a son, Gerald. Other than memories, the only reminders salvaged from the tragedy included a small photograph of Elin and Pekka on their wedding day; a necklace that Elin wore; and a blanket from the *Carpathia*. Elin died at the age of 68, in January 1957. Earlier that evening she had been knitting and reading Walter Lord's *A Night to Remember*.

The book by her son Gerald E. Nummi and Janet A. White, '*I'm Going to See What has Happened*', was published in 1996.

Lawrence Beesley later found the small square of cardboard that was his receipt for the money that he had deposited in the Purser's safe: 'White Star Line, RMS Titanic, 208. This label must be given up when the article is returned. The property will be deposited in the Purser's safe. The Company will not be liable to passengers for the loss of money, jewels, or ornaments, by theft or otherwise, not so deposited.' Of his companions during the voyage, both the Reverend Ernest Carter and his wife Lily were drowned, as were the engineer from Leicester, Denzil Jarvis, and the American film-maker, William Harbeck, and his French mistress, Henriette Yvois. The Catholic priest from Leeds, Father Thomas Byles, and the Benedictine monk from Bavaria, Josef Peruschitz, were both drowned. After Harbeck's body had been recovered he was found to be clutching Henriette's purse. When his wife Catherine came from Toledo, Ohio, to claim the body in Halifax she was almost turned away as an imposter because officials told her that 'Mrs Harbeck' had drowned with her husband. Douglas Norman, the electrical engineer from Glasgow, died, and his body was also recovered; as with many of those whose bodies were recovered, he was buried in Halifax.

Of those who survived, Beesley's Irish piper, Eugene Daly, was rescued from the Englehardt B boat. Arthur West was drowned, but his wife Ada and daughters Constance and Barbara were rescued in Lifeboat 10. Olga Lundin, who had moved from Third Class to Second, survived, but her fiancée Nils Johnsson was drowned. Hilda Slayter, who had nursed Alden Caldwell in Beesley's lifeboat, lost all her luggage in the sinking including her wedding trousseau, but she went on to marry, in June 1912. Albert and Sylvia Caldwell were divorced in 1930; their son Alden died in 1992. Dr Washington Dodge was reunited with his wife and son aboard the *Carpathia*, but he suffered a breakdown and shot himself in June 1919.

Some five weeks after the survivors from the *Titanic* landed in New York, Beesley was the guest at a lunch given by Samuel J. Elder and Charles T. Gallagher, both well-known lawyers in Boston. After lunch, Beesley was asked to relate to those present the experiences of the survivors in leaving the *Titanic* and reaching the *Carpathia*. When he had done this, Robert Lincoln O'Brien, the editor of the *Boston Herald*, urged Beesley as a matter of public interest to write a history of the *Titanic* disaster, his reason being that he knew several publications were being prepared by people who had not been present, but who were piecing together a description of it from newspaper accounts. O'Brien said that these publications would be strewn with errors, full of highly coloured details, and generally misleading. He was supported in his request by many of those present, and under this general pressure Beesley went with him to the Houghton Mifflin Company, where they discussed the question of publication. The publisher took at that time the same view as Beesley, that it was probably not advisable to put on record the incidents connected with the *Titanic*'s sinking; it seemed better to forget about it as quickly as possible.

They decided to take a few days to think about it. At their next meeting, Beesley and the publisher found themselves in agreement again—but this time on the common ground that it would probably be wise to write a history of the *Titanic* disaster. Beesley was supported in this decision by the fact that the short account, which he had written at intervals on board the *Carpathia*, in the hope that it would calm public opinion by stating what had happened as nearly as he could recollect it, appeared in many newspapers. He was also aware of the duty that he, as a survivor of the disaster, owed to those who had gone down with the ship, to see that the reforms so urgently needed were not allowed to be forgotten. Beesley wrote the account in six weeks, and his book was published in June 1912, less than three months after the sinking, as *The Loss of the SS Titanic: Its Story and Lessons*. The reviewer in the *New York Times* commented that:

> The unconscious undertone of solemnity which one feels all through Mr Beesley's simple narrative gives it a peculiar fitness and impressiveness, and adds to its value as an exact chronicle a certain austere charm…the book is probably as authoritative and comprehensive an account of the greatest marine disaster of modern times as will ever be written, and as completely true and exact as it would be possible for anyone to write.

Beesley returned home on the *Laconia*. A widower, he married Mollie Greenwood in 1919, and the couple had three children. He continued teaching, and enjoyed crossword puzzles, detective novels, and golf; he played in the British Open several years running. Beesley's son Alec went on to marry the playwright and author Dodie Smith, author of numerous children's books, including *The Hundred and One Dalmatians*. But his daughter Dinah also recalled that one year the family went for a beach holiday and her father turned his deckchair round so that he had his back to the ocean; nothing could induce him to even look at his family splashing about in the water.

Beesley's account made him one of the best-known survivors of the disaster, and for fifty years, as the novelist Julian Barnes has suggested, he was regularly consulted by 'maritime historians, film researchers, journalists, souvenir hunters, bores, conspiracy theorists, and vexatious litigants'. Beesley was engaged as a consultant for the 1958 film, made at Pinewood Studios, and was keen to be included among the extras at the rail as the ship went down. The film's director, Roy Baker, was equally keen that Beesley should not appear in the film. But Beesley counterfeited the actors' union pass, dressed himself in period costume, and installed himself among the extras. Right at the last minute, as the cameras were due to roll, Baker spotted Beesley at the rail, picked up his megaphone, and told him to disembark. For the second time in his life, Beesley left the *Titanic* just before it was due to go down. In his later years he lived in Northwood, Middlesex. The underrated television film *S.O.S. Titanic* (1979) was based largely on Beesley's book. It depicts the disaster as seen through the eyes of three couples, one from each of the Classes on board. The part of Lawrence Beesley was played by David Warner; Harold Bride by Peter Bourke; Violet Jessop by Madge Ryan; Arthur Rostron by Philip Stone; and Herbert Lightoller by Malcolm Stoddard. Lawrence Beesley died at South Park, Lincoln, in February 1967, aged 89.

Many of Violet Jessop's fellow crew members were drowned, among them William O'Loughlin, the Surgeon; Hugh McElroy, the Purser; William Hughes, the steward; Thomas Kelland, the Library steward; and Jock Hume, the musician. After the passengers had departed from the *Carpathia*, the surviving crew were loaded on to the tender *George Starr* and taken to Pier 61 where they embarked on the *Lapland*. Subsequently, after an uneventful crossing, they arrived in Plymouth on Monday 29 April. The crew survivors were met there by White Star directors Harold Sanderson and E. C. Grenfell, Board of Trade representatives, custom officials, and others. The Board of Trade wished to immediately take down the crew's evidence, but were prevented by Thomas Lewis and Mr Cannon of the British Seafarers' Union, who refused permission to board the *Lapland*, hired a small boat, and spoke to *Titanic*'s crew through a megaphone.

On the tender *Sir Richard Grenville* the crew refused to speak to the Board of Trade, who were forced to invite Lewis and Cannon on board. The crew then gave their accounts, beginning with the stewardesses, and they finally landed at midday. All had to appear before the Receiver of Wrecks. To their surprise and annoyance they were detained in the dock's Third Class Waiting Room while their families, the press, and the general public remained outside a high iron fence while depositions (sworn witness statements) continued. All of the crew had to stay overnight; bedding, tables, and food were provided, and they talked to their friends and families through the windows when they got the chance. Finally released after 1.30 p.m. when the press swooped, some eighty-five seamen and firemen left for Southampton on the 6 p.m. train. Travel plans for the stewards and stewardesses (including Violet Jessop and Elizabeth Leather), cooks, and other kitchen staff were cancelled, and they returned to Southampton the next day. On both days, there was a large and emotional reception for the returning survivors at Southampton West Station.

Violet later discovered through hints and sometimes tactlessly expressed comments that some people thought that the survivors among the crew had done well out of the tragedy. This was incorrect. Violet, for instance, knew from her own experience that they received no other gifts, apart from £25 generously given by the *Daily Telegraph*, and the full trip's wages given by the White Star Line. Violet also received her fare home. When they eventually reached home, they received a letter from the Mayor of Southampton, inviting them to his office. They received his congratulations and a gift of £10, for which they were grateful, as they had to replace their lost uniforms. They were shocked, however, when later they received a request from the Mayor, who had heard of the *Daily Telegraph*'s gift, that they should return the £10. They did this with bitter feelings.

Elizabeth Leather gave evidence at the British Inquiry, on 20 May 1912, and finally retired from the White Star Line in 1928. The *Olympic* had entered Harland & Wolff for a refit, and Violet Jessop rejoined it from June 1912. During the First World War, she enlisted as a junior nurse in a Voluntary Aid Detachment (VAD), a nursing organization set up in 1908 by the British Red Cross Society at the invitation of the War Office; it formed a hospital arm for the newly-established Territorial Army. Violet was well-suited to nursing, but she was aboard the *Britannic* when it was sunk in the Aegean in November 1916. Violet was repatriated in January 1917, and worked in a bank until she signed on again with the White Star Line, and went back to sea in June 1920. Later she resumed her life as a stewardess on the *Olympic*, and then on the *Majestic*. In the Spring of 1926, she signed on with the Red Star Line, on the *Belgenland*, and sailed on five world cruises.

Violet had married briefly in the late 1920s, a fellow crewmember, but all her life she cherished her independence. In July 1935, she returned to the Royal Mail Line, and served on the *Alcantara* until the outbreak of the Second World War. During the War, she worked in a censorship office in Holborn, London. With peace, she worked in a government office in Acton, and in factory work at Sanderson's, the wallpaper manufacturer, in Ealing. She again returned to the Royal Mail Line, from September 1948, on the *Andes*, until she signed off just before Christmas 1950. Now 63, she had followed her career as a stewardess since 1908, and had spent 42 years at sea. She was interviewed for *Woman* magazine when the 1958 film was released. She retired to Suffolk, and died in May 1971.

Violet had either evaded, or was ignored by, the army of journalists when the *Carpathia* docked in New York, but she completed an unpublished memoir, written under the pseudonym 'Constance Ransom', in 1934. After she died in 1971, her sisters passed it on to a publisher, who passed it on to Walter Lord. Lord mentioned that

John Maxtone-Graham was interested in her story; he had met and interviewed her in the summer of 1970 while he was researching his book *The North Atlantic Run: 'The Only Way to Cross'* (1972). Her story was published in John Maxtone-Graham's edited collection, *Titanic Survivor: The Memoirs of Violet Jessop Stewardess* (1997).

The American Inquiry listed the Touma family as Third Class passengers embarked at Cherbourg, as 'Hanne, Marian, and Georges Youssef', while Marshall Everett's popular 'disaster book', *Wreck and Sinking of the Titanic*, recorded among the dead 'Hane, Youssef, and two children'. After settling in Dowagiac with her husband Darwis, Hanna gave birth to three more sons: Samual, Francis, and Joseph. The family lived in Michigan City, Indiana, for three years, before settling permanently in Burton, Michigan. Hanna lived with her grandson Joseph and his wife Phyllis from 1961, when she was 76. The family later anglicized their name to 'Thomas'. Hanna died in June 1976, at the age of 91. Hanna had outlived her daughter Maria (Mary Thomas) and her son Francis. Her oldest son Georges (George) had gone into the grocery and real estate business, and served as the first mayor of Burton. During his retirement, he often spoke about his experiences on the *Titanic*. Although confined to a wheelchair, he attended a reunion of survivors in 1982, in Philadelphia. He died in December 1991, at the age of 87. Hanna's story was published by her grandson Joseph L. Thomas as *Grandma Survived the Titanic*, in 2002.

As well as Frank Goldsmith's father, whose body was never found, Tom Theobald and Alfred Rush were both drowned in the disaster.

Frank and Emily received money from the American Titanic Relief Committee. In Strood, in England, Tom Theobald's widow received financial assistance every month of her life until she died in 1961. But all Emily got from the White Star Line was $15, and two rail tickets to Detroit via Niagara Falls. Frank and Emily settled there, where he grew up near the Tiger Stadium; when the Tigers played, the roar of the crowd reminded him of the sound of the *Titanic* sinking, and so he never took his children to baseball games.

Frank started work at 14, but then he went back to school part-time for two years. As a young man, he found employment as a milk cart driver, a job he held for many years. He met his future wife Victoria in Detroit when he was 18, and she 15. He had just returned from a two-month trip to Strood. Frank and Victoria married in 1926, and they had three sons. After that, Frank was employed in advertising until the 1929 Depression. Frank and Victoria had to move in with Frank's mother for three and a half years. Frank lost his advertising job but found another with the Detroit Creamery Co, for the next 13 years. In 1936, Frank and Victoria bought their first house with money from the Women's Central Relief Association of New York, from which his mother had received $2,400. They lived there until 1942, when Frank went to work for the United States Air Force as a civilian employee, in the Photographic Unit. The family had moved to Wilmington, Ohio, and in 1943 Frank was sent to Denver, Colorado. In 1945, the couple started a photographic and art supply store in Mansfield, Ohio. Emily remarried and died in 1955; Frank only began to talk about the *Titanic* in the 1960s. He died in January 1982, and his story, *Echoes in the Night: Memories of a Titanic Survivor*, was published in 1991 by the Titanic Historical Society.

Benjamin Hart's body was never recovered. Eva's friend Nina Harper survived the disaster, as did Jessie Leitch, but John Harper was drowned. As Esther Hart could see no future for them in the United States without her husband, she booked them on the White Star liner *Celtic* which was due to sail on 25 April. Eva was very surprised to see that Esther slept soundly every night on that return journey. Eva was the one who was frightened. Even when they were back on dry land, Eva had recurrent nightmares for years. She was terribly upset at the loss of her father, as was Esther. Eva's mother was never quite the same again, mainly because she felt that that short period of pleasure in her life was all she was to have. Eva was also miserable because she could see Esther's unhappiness as she tried to start her life all over again without him.

Esther and Eva arrived in Liverpool on the *Celtic* on Saturday 4 May. They had no home of their own to go to so they had to stay with Esther's parents who were living in Chadwell Heath, about seven miles from Seven Kings, in Greater London. There was no question of returning to their own home. Not only had the house been sold, but it would have been too large for just the two of them. However, they could not stay with relatives indefinitely so had to find another home of their own. Fortunately, two doors away from Eva's grandparents' house was one which her father had built and had sold to a friend as an investment. This house became empty at just about the time they came back to England, and the owner said to Esther he would sell it to her and she could pay him back later. So Eva and Esther were able to move into this house, in Whalebone Grove, Chadwell Heath. Their standard of living dropped considerably. Although it was never necessary for Esther to go out to work, there were some very difficult times. It was not until nine months after the *Titanic* sank that Esther was told she would receive from the Titanic Disaster Fund one guinea per week for herself, and 3s

6d per week for Eva. She had also persuaded the fund administrators to pay a small amount to cover part of the cost of Eva's education until she was 18.

Before the Titanic Disaster Fund started to assist with the cost of Eva's education, she attended a small village school in Chadwell Heath. Later, she was able to attend St Mary's Convent School in Western Road, Romford, although it meant a journey of several miles there and back. Eva stayed at that school until the age of 16. She loved music, and when she left school, started to teach it to young children. She was also interested in politics, and helped form, and became Secretary of, the Junior Imperial and Constitutional League (forerunner of the Young Conservatives). As Eva grew up, and during the whole of her adolescence, she tried to draw a curtain over her memory of the disaster. Because it was so painful and horrifying she had no wish to recall it. Esther later remarried. Eva was plagued by nightmares and on the death of her mother in 1928, when she was 23, returned to sea and locked herself in a cabin for four days until the nightmares went away. Eva visited relatives in Singapore and Australia, and on returning to England worked in the wholesale department of a motor dealer's in Goodmayes, near Chadwell Heath.

During the Second World War, Eva offered her services to Air Raid Precautions (ARP), and later also worked for the Women's Voluntary Service (WVS), and the Housewives Service. Subsequently, she became a Welfare Officer at the Sterling Engineering Company, which had developed and manufactured the Sterling submachine gun, and it was the field of welfare that became her major interest. Eva maintained her singing career, and became a magistrate in 1956. She was active in voluntary work, notably the Family Planning Association, and was awarded an MBE for her political and public services in 1974. Eva could not watch the filming of the 1958 film, but she attended its première, at the Odeon in Leicester Square, London, and later she gave regular newspaper, radio, and television interviews about the *Titanic*. She was one of the most outspoken critics of the lack of lifeboats and of salvage attempts after 1985. Her biography by Ronald C. Denney, *Shadow of the Titanic: A Survivor's Story*, was published in 1994. Eva Hart died in February 1996, aged 91. A Wetherspoon's pub in Chadwell Heath is named 'The Eva Hart'.

The New York newspapers were full of the disaster, and Elizabeth and Edith Brown scanned them daily in the hope they might find details of Thomas. It was beginning to look pointless, and so Elizabeth decided to make arrangements for their journey to Seattle. She told her daughter that whenever they travelled, they always had gold sovereigns with them. These were carried in a money belt around her father's waist or were sewn into the seams of some of his waistcoats. Edith asked if this was all the money that they had left in the world. Her mother said that her father had left some shares in the wine and brandy companies back in South Africa, but she didn't know how much they were worth. During their stay in New York, the press hounded them everywhere they went, stopping them in the street, and forever asking the same questions. Both women became expert with ready answers. Elizabeth knew only too well it was because of the press that so many people came forward to help them, and for that, they would be forever grateful. At other times, they would duck into a ladies' lavatory to get away from the throng and collect their thoughts.

The body of Thomas Brown was never recovered. Edith and her mother decided they would travel by train to Seattle at the end of the week. They had no idea how far it was, but had been advised that the journey could take up to five days. Their last day in New York was one of sadness, feeling in a strange sort of way that they were finally laying Thomas to rest. There was also sadness at leaving behind the many kind people who had, in such a short time, become their friends. On arrival at Grand Central Station, several well-wishers and the inevitable press greeted Elizabeth and her daughter. They were to journey through ten states, a journey totalling some 2,000 miles. Neither looked forward to it, but there was no alternative. There were shouts of 'good luck' from those left behind on the platform as they started on their great journey west. As the train cleared the station and gathered speed, they settled back in their seats for the first leg of their journey.

On arrival in Seattle, reporters once again confronted them. The newspapers were still full of stories about the *Titanic*, and both women were inundated with a barrage of questions. Esther's sister Josephine and her husband, Ed Acton, arrived on the scene and helped them get away from the surging crowds. Once away from the station, Elizabeth broke down. The long train journey had been a distraction from their tragedy, allowing them to take in the scenery as it swept past their carriage windows day after day. To be confronted by all those reporters on their arrival had just been too much after such a long journey. Josephine and her husband did their best, organizing a room for them, making life as comfortable as possible, and giving both women some peace and quiet for several days. Once they were feeling up to it, they were able to give some lengthy interviews. After several weeks of living with Edward and Josephine, it became clear that, with Thomas gone, there wasn't any future for Elizabeth and her daughter in Seattle. There was the matter of tying up Thomas's estate back in South Africa. Besides, Elizabeth and her daughter were virtually penniless after using up what sovereigns they had left. The time had come for them to start planning their return trip to Cape Town. Although both women were dreading the long journey back across America and then the North Atlantic, there was no alternative.

Edward had been busy organizing their journey by rail and sea with the help of his colleagues at the bank. Once back in New York, they would stay for a few days before sailing for Liverpool. They said their tearful goodbyes at the train station in Seattle and once again settled down for the long journey ahead of them. After a short stay in New York, Edith Brown and her mother boarded their ship. This was to be a nervous time for both of them, knowing they would be travelling over the same course as that taken by the *Titanic*. On disembarkation in Liverpool, they caught the train for Southampton, where they stayed for a few days before sailing for Cape Town. Some weeks later, Thomas's estate was settled. Once the settlement had been reached, Elizabeth thought it was time to move on again. Edith, like her mother, had never really known her father's children from his first marriage, and she was glad to get away. Elizabeth and Edith moved to Johannesburg in 1914, and Edith's mother remarried shortly after her daughter's 18th birthday. Edith herself married Frederick Haisman, in June 1917. Born in London, Frederick had lived in Southampton before moving to Johannesburg with his parents. In 1920, the couple moved back to Southampton, where Frederick pursued his career as an engineer. Elizabeth died in Salisbury, Rhodesia, in June 1926.

Edith and Frederick were to have ten children in all, experiencing heavy air raids in Southampton during the Second World War. At this stage, Frederick was working for the Admiralty, in Portsmouth, and in 1943 he was posted to Simonstown, South Africa; the family joined him there in 1944. In May 1947, an article was published in Simonstown's weekly magazine on Edith's experiences on the *Titanic*. However the family were soon on the move again, and returned to

Southampton in 1948. Arriving at a time of a national housing short-age, they lived initially in a prefab, and for two years in a Nissen hut, before moving to the suburb of Bitterne. Edith attended the South-ampton premiere of *A Night to Remember*. In 1965, Frederick and Edith retired to Australia, but by 1969 they were back in England. Edith visited the site of the wreck of the *Titanic*, in 1995. Frederick had died in 1977, and Edith was to outlive both her husband and four of her own children before she herself died, at the age of 100, in January 1997. Until that point she had been the world's oldest living survivor of the *Titanic* disaster. The book by her son David Haisman, *Titanic: The Edith Brown Story*, was published in 2009.

Conclusion

Walter Lord's book *A Night to Remember* (1955) is still the benchmark against which all subsequent books about the disaster have to be measured. Lord was born on 8 October 1917 in Baltimore in the United States, the only son of a prominent lawyer. As a boy he had enjoyed a transatlantic cruise on the *Olympic*, during which he had fantasized about what it must have been like to have been aboard the *Titanic*. He attended private schools in Baltimore and then read history at Princeton, graduating in 1939. Shortly after going to work for the J. Walter Thompson advertising agency in New York, Lord published *The Freemantle Diary*, edited and annotated from the journals of a British officer and Confederate sympathiser who had toured the American South for three months in 1863. It was reasonably successful on its publication in 1954. But it was the success of his book *A Night to Remember* (1955) which enabled Lord to leave advertising and write full time. Published in November 1955, the book had sold 60,000 copies by January of the following year, and it stayed on the best-seller list for six months. Condensed versions appeared in the November 1955 *Ladies Home Journal* and the January 1956 *Reader's Digest*, and it was the first of Lord's several 'Book of the Month Club' selections, in June 1956.

A successful television adaptation, directed by George Roy Hill and narrated by Claude Rains, was broadcast in the United States on

28 March 1956; it attracted 28 million viewers. The British-made film of the same name, directed by Roy Baker, and starring Kenneth More, Honor Blackman, and David McCallum, was released on 3 July 1958. Made by the Rank Organisation, the producer was William Mac-Quitty, and the screenplay was by Eric Ambler. MacQuitty had been born in Bangor in May 1905, and his father took him to see the launch of the Titanic on 30 May 1911; on 2 April 1912 he saw the fitted-out *Titanic* as she sailed away to begin her maiden voyage.

Bantam issued a paperback edition of *A Night to Remember* in October 1956, and the book has never been out of print. Holt published a fiftieth-anniversary edition in 2005. On its first publication, the book was well-received. In fact, no books on the *Titanic* had been published since 1913. The *New York Times* said that the book was 'stunning…one of the most exciting books of this or any other year', while the *Atlantic Monthly* declared of it 'a magnificent job of re-creative chronicling, enthralling from the first word to the last'. The reviewer for the magazine *USA Today* wrote that the book was 'the most riveting narrative of the disaster', and *Entertainment Weekly* declared it 'seamless and skilful…it's clear why this is many a researcher's Titanic bible'. In the *New York Herald Tribune*, reviewer Stanley Walker drew attention to Lord's technique as being 'a kind of literary pointillism, the arrangement of contrasting bits of fact and emotion in such a fashion that a vividly real impression of an event is conveyed to the reader'. He argued that Lord had clearly succeeded in depicting the human side to the story. Unlike the earlier narratives which described heroism and cowardice in terms of class, gender, and ethnicity, Lord's book showed a range of behaviour among people of all kinds.

Cultural historian Steven Biel has noted that the book was well marketed, but also explains the resonance of the narrative through the visual images and sounds it summoned up and evoked. Lord opens the book with Lookout Frederick Fleet peering into a dazzling night, thus immediately plunging the reader into the moment. He blurred history into news and drama, collapsing 'historical duration into intense moments of lived experience'. Biel notes similarly how the book takes an imaginative approach to time and space, in which the ship seems infinitely complex, and the disaster assumes unity and order only from far away. Lord 'constructs a modernist narrative around a modernist event', manipulating and violating a simple chronology, juggling an enormous cast of characters. Every moment is split into multiple perspectives. Lord resists easy closure by suggesting that the multiple perspectives could be multiplied several times over, so that the narrative is fragmented, uncertain, and open-ended. He managed to move at a slow pace while dramatizing the full duration of the disaster.

It has been argued that Lord chose to foreground memory because he thought of his book as a collage of memories. His book is constructed from a network of incidents taking place in different but related locations. Lord shows how the ship has been constructed to keep the First, Second, and Third Class passengers apart. The social space of the ship is 'a microcosm of an earlier, highly stratified society, suddenly evident in its failure'. The technique is a modernist one of montage and fragmentation, characterized by rapid cuts from point to point across the field of the action.

Writing in the Introduction to the fiftieth-anniversary edition, the writer Nathaniel Philbrick noted that *A Night to Remember* was the first significant book about the disaster. There had been more than sixty survivors alive for Lord to interview. Philbrick argued that what distinguished the book was the restraint and compression of the storytelling. With the brevity of the book, its readable style, and its mundane title, Lord worked against the inherent extravagance of the material. He built suspense, making the reader care about the characters, and forcing them to take part in the scramble for the lifeboats. Again, Philbrick made the point that the book was about the people who inhabited the *Titanic*. Lord lived in Manhattan in New York, and died in May 2002.

The main development since the publication of Lord's *A Night to Remember* has been the discovery of the wreck by Robert Ballard in 1985. Apart from passengers such as Hanna Touma, closer in Third Class to the actual point of impact, the collision was not felt by most passengers, and those that did feel it described it as a 'slight shock'. Immediately after the disaster, most people thought that the *Titanic* sank because of a 300-foot gash along the starboard side. But the main question has been, was the steel cut open, or did the seams that were riveted let go? Underwater evidence from Robert Ballard's 1985 expedition has proved that, contrary to most eye-witness accounts, the *Titanic* broke in two. Moreover it has dispelled the 300-foot gash theory, revealing instead a series of tiny openings, as well as providing evidence of steel plates that were missing rivets, and rivets whose heads were missing. Attention thus turned away from the 'brittle steel theory', that the steel plates of the hull shattered, towards the rivets that held the ship together.

The collision with the iceberg caused damage to the bottom of the starboard side of the ship, about 10 feet above the level of the keel. There was damage in the Fore Peak, No. 1 Hold, No. 2 Hold, No. 3 Hold, No. 6 Boiler Room, and No. 5 Boiler Room. This damage extended over 300 feet. It was estimated that as the ship was travelling at over 20 knots, it would have covered 300 feet in about ten seconds.

In the first ten minutes, there was seven feet of water in No. 1 Hold, and in No. 2 Hold water was seen rushing in at the bottom of the firemen's passage. Meanwhile in No. 3 Hold, the Mail Room, the floor of which was 24 feet above the keel, was filled soon after the collision. In No. 6 Boiler Room, as Frederick Barrett testified, water poured in about two feet above the plates in the stokehold, and some of the firemen immediately went through the watertight door opening to No. 5 Boiler Room. The watertight doors in the engine rooms were shut from the Bridge almost immediately after the collision. After ten minutes, there was 8 feet of water in No. 6 Boiler Room. No. 5 Boiler Room was also damaged, and water poured in, 2 feet above the stokehold plates, in the words of Barrett 'as it would from an ordinary fire hose'. In No. 4 Boiler Room, in the early stages, there was no sign of damage.

Therefore all six compartments forward of No. 4 Boiler Room were open to the sea by damage which existed 10 feet above the keel. Ten minutes after the collision, the water had risen 14 feet above the keel in all these compartments except No. 5 Boiler Room. This was a rate with which the ship's pumps could not cope. After the first ten minutes, the water rose steadily in all these six compartments.

As it had been constructed, the *Titanic* could not have remained afloat long after sustaining this damage. The bulkheads were spaced so that she could remain afloat with any two compartments flooded. Even with four compartments flooded, the ship would have remained afloat. But it could not remain afloat with the four forward compartments and the forward Boiler Room (No. 6) also flooded. This caused the water to flow over the bulkhead in the forward Boiler Room (No. 6), then into the next Boiler Room (No. 5), then into No. 4 Boiler Room, and so on until the ship ultimately filled and sank.

As recent research has shown, the *Titanic* was triple-riveted over three-fifths of its length, while doubly riveted seams, formed from wrought iron rivets, were used in the bow and the stern. From testimony, it is clear that the impact with the iceberg occurred in a part of the ship constructed from doubly riveted seams, formed from hand-installed, wrought iron rivets. Metallographic analysis of rivets salvaged from the *Titanic* has revealed that they contained larger than expected amounts of slag, the solid scum on melted metal, an average of over four times the normal slag content. The evidence suggested that the *Titanic*'s wrought iron stock was not worked for a sufficient puddling time (not enough time to mix it well) and at too low a temperature (not enough heat to squeeze out the excess slag easily) to refine the slag particles. The higher slag content led to low ductility (how far it could be drawn out without breaking) and lower tensile strength (the strength of a material when it is being stretched, or the greatest stress it can resist before breaking). Moreover, hammering the heads of the rivets during installation produced weaknesses near the junction of the head and the shaft.

Computer recreations of the collision have showed the non-uniform way in which it impacted on the outside of the hull plates; the stress pulled on the heads of the rivets instead of shearing the shafts. Research showed that steel rivets required five times higher load than wrought iron rivets in order to fail. The higher yield strength, tensile strength, and ductility of the steel allowed it to withstand large residual stresses on cooling, but made it more suitable for bearing higher loads and stretching further before failure.

Harland & Wolff often made use of small, relatively unknown foundries. Using wrought iron rivets made in various foundries speeded up manufacturing, but sidestepped the prolonged testing period and additional charges required for steel rivets. While this solved problems of mass production, it was not a model for consistent quality. Steel rivets would have become brittle when heated too much during installation, but iron rivets could still be riveted without any sign of a problem. The *Titanic* sustained only a limited amount of damage—a series of six slits across the hull in areas where it was held together by hand-riveted, wrought iron rivets.

Tests on rivets showed that heads popped off the shafts and left a fracture profile that was very similar to those recovered from the *Titanic* on the 1985 expedition. Overall, then, these experiments have served to destroy the brittle steel theory. All the evidence points in the direction of the rivets. Jennifer Hooper McCarty and Tim Foecke, who carried out this research, conclude that:

> The quality of the wrought iron rivets installed in the bow is the most quantifiable factor in the iceberg damage to, and the loss of, the *Titanic*. Regardless of all the unsinkable features on *Titanic*, the ship had her own structural Achilles' heel. Just like every other riveted ship in history, the *Titanic* was only as strong as its weakest riveted seam.

The brittle steel theory is therefore wrong. Tests have shown that the steel plates of the hull had adequate fracture toughness at ice-water temperatures. On the other hand, a significant amount of the wrought iron provided to Harland & Wolff was fabricated incorrectly, worked too little, or at the wrong temperature, or both. When the *Titanic* set sail, some of the rivets were already near their material's ultimate tensile strength, creating riveted joints with insufficient strength to withstand any additional load. With the rivets made of wrought iron, the inspection methods used in 1911 would have made it almost impossible to detect a rivet that had become brittle through installation at too high a temperature, or one weakened by the presence of too much slag. In the collision, the drawn-out bumping produced non-uniform, poking, prodding blows that served to disperse the force of the impact along the riveted seams of the ship, the weakest links. The rivets failed and the seams opened, rather than the steel fracturing mid-plate. However the collision occurred, the *Titanic* suffered additional strain on the riveted joints in the outer-fifths length of the starboard bow where the wrought iron riveted seams were located. As each rivet failed, the load it was carrying was transferred to the neighbouring rivets. These rivets, whether of suitable quality or not, were not designed to see an increase in load that could be as high as 20 per cent. The seams steadily bulged open as the rivets failed.

The impact between the iceberg and the hull of the *Titanic* was a long, scraping, glancing blow that strained the steel plates discontinuously. Had the rivet quality been higher, the ship would not have suffered as much damage. The last seams that broke might have held, and the ship would have taken more time to flood and sink. It is the case that any quality of rivets would have failed the strain of the initial impact and opened a number of compartments to the sea. However, while a better quality of the raw material that went into the rivets would not have prevented the ship from sinking, it would have changed the length of time of the sinking. Hooper McCarty and Foecke have therefore concluded that 'if it sank just a little slower, the word "Titanic" would not have had its meaning permanently changed in the English language'.

Neither the American nor British Inquiry made any mention of the rivets, hardly surprising given that the evidence that became available following the Ballard underwater expedition was not available to them. Walter Lord's later reflections on the *Titanic* were published as *The Night Lives On* (1986). Nevertheless while *A Night to Remember* has been extremely successful, and has huge strengths, other aspects of the book are less successful. It is only in Chapter 7 that Lord interrupts his narrative for pieces of historical analysis, characterized by what Biel calls 'a kind of genteel liberalism'. In the hands of Lord, modernism becomes nostalgia. Biel argues that the compatibility between modernism and nostalgia perhaps helps explain the success of the book in 1950s America. But irony is absent. Lord is nostalgic for chivalry, but he also appealed to nostalgia for an older kind of disaster. In this respect, the success of *A Night to Remember* revealed as much about 1950s America, alive to the threat of nuclear attack, as it did about the *Titanic* itself. Lord offers a historical assessment, but one that includes claims that are 'historically unfounded'. For Lord's own treatment of historical issues is much less assured than his minute-by-minute description of events. As Arthur Calder-Marshall noted in his review in the *Times Literary Supplement*, published in June 1956, 'Mr Lord was clearly correct in adhering closely to the facts. When he tries to generalise he grows wild.'

As we have seen, social class, nationality, and language still determined the course of people's lives after the arrival of the *Titanic* survivors in New York. Elin Hakkarainen found that it was the Third Class passengers who were the last to leave the *Carpathia*. Moreover, once they disembarked, those in First and Second Class in many cases had friends and relatives living nearby, or had other resources, notably money. But as we have noted, the city's charities played an important role for Third Class passengers, many of whom were effectively destitute. Key organizations which provided help in the form of clothing, temporary accommodation, medical attention, and train tickets, were the Junior League, the Women's Central Relief Association, the Salvation Army, and the American Red Cross, along with St Vincent's Hospital and the Sisters of Charity of St Vincent de Paul. Overall, the involvement of these charities with *Titanic* survivors was short-lived, but it was the Third Class passengers, particularly migrants, along with some members of the crew, who required their assistance.

In *A Night to Remember*, Walter Lord makes several assertions about social class. He suggests that if the experiences of Third Class passengers were neglected, 'never again would First Class have it so good...One of the more trying legacies left by those on the *Titanic* has been a new standard of conduct for measuring the behaviour of prominent people under stress.' He argues that never again did established wealth occupy people's minds so thoroughly, and never again was wealth so spectacular: 'it never was the same again. First the War, then the income tax, made sure of that.' Similarly nobler instincts were lost, with Lord claiming that 'men would go on being brave, but never again would they be brave in quite the same way...today nobody could carry off these little gestures of chivalry, but they did that night.' Perhaps most importantly, Lord argues that the *Titanic* marked the end of a general feeling of confidence, and never again would people be so sure of themselves. The *Titanic* was the first step in a process of disillusionment: 'before the *Titanic*, all was quiet. Afterward, all was tumult.' Lord argues that 'the *Titanic* more than any other single event marks the end of the old days, and the beginning of a new, uneasy era'.

However the wealthier sections of societies continued to have it pretty good, in both the United States and Britain. Wealth and poverty would continue to coexist through the rest of the twentieth century, on the liners, as more generally in society. The spacious First Class cabins on the *Queen Mary* (1936–1967) were in contrast to the cramped accommodation in Third Class, while the Art Deco interiors were one of the most remarked-upon features of the *Ile de France* (1927–1959). On the *Normandie*, which entered service in 1935, the majority of accommodation was First Class, reflecting the decline of migration to the United States. Moreover while it was suggested that the advent of mass air travel in the 1960s coincided with an assault on class and privilege, cruise ships are more popular today than ever before. If anything there is much evidence to show that the 'very rich' have got richer. Perhaps there was a decline in chivalry, bravery, and in ideals of noble behaviour. But it is much easier to assert that there was a decline in such attitudes and perceptions than to prove the existence of such an alleged decline beyond doubt. Similar points are often made about the First World War as marking some kind of watershed, but identifying turning points, while tempting, is difficult. Overall, the historian is often more inclined through the evidence, or on occasions the lack of evidence, to stress continuity rather than change.

As historian Stephanie Barczewski has shown, the *Titanic* was closely associated with Ireland. Not only was it built in Belfast, but it called at Queenstown on the morning of 11 April 1912 to collect passengers, many of them Irish migrants. As we have seen, Thomas Andrews, designer of the *Titanic* and Managing Director of Harland & Wolff, was on the ship. But the *Titanic* also came to have a more complex place in Irish history. During November 1909, the House of Lords had rejected the Liberal Government's budget, prompting a constitutional crisis. Herbert Asquith as Prime Minister assured the Irish Nationalists of Liberal commitment to Home Rule. Although the Liberals won the election, the Irish Nationalists held the balance of power. Ulster Unionists, alarmed at the prospect of Home Rule, regrouped under Sir Edward Carson. During the early weeks of 1912, the political atmosphere in Ulster had become increasingly tense. The third Home Rule Bill was introduced into the House of Commons on 11 April 1912, the day after the *Titanic* sailed, for a first reading. It later passed through Parliament in September 1914 on the understanding that it would not become law until the War was over.

Apart from Thomas Andrews, seven other Harland & Wolff workers died in the disaster: William Parr, Assistant Manager of the electrical department; Roderick Chisholm, Ships' Draughtsman; Anthony Frost, Foreman Engineer; Robert Knight, Leading Hand Engineer; William Campbell, Apprentice Joiner; Frank Parkes, Apprentice Plumber; and Ennis Watson, Apprentice Electrician. After the disaster, Andrews was quickly elevated to the status of a hero. A telegram sent from New York on 21 April 1912 stated that 'when last seen, officers say, he [Andrews] was throwing overboard deck chairs and other objects to people in the water, his chief concern the safety of everyone but himself'. A very uncritical biography, *Thomas Andrews: Shipbuilder*, was commissioned from the Irish writer Shan Bullock and published in 1912, and the Thomas Andrews Junior Memorial Hall was opened in Comber, County Down, in February 1915.

However with the sinking, pride in the *Titanic* became a challenge for Protestants, as much a problem as there was to be pride in the achievements of the 36th Ulster Division on the first day of the Battle of the Somme, 1 July 1916. The sinking could be represented as the result of faulty engineering; negligence on the part of the crew; and the result of divine intervention. But none of these gave much comfort to Ulster Protestants. After the disaster, newspapers stressed the heroism of the twenty-two men from Belfast who had died. But the *Titanic* memorial in Belfast was erected only in 1920. Irish emigration notwithstanding, the Republic of Ireland also showed little interest in the *Titanic* story; a memorial was erected in Queenstown, renamed Cobh in 1920, only in 1998. It is thus only much more recently that the *Titanic* has managed to shed its earlier links with Ulster Unionism, and become instead the symbol of a city. Novelist Mary Costello's memoir of her Belfast childhood was called *Titanic Town* (1992), and the Ulster Titanic Society was formed the same year.

The *Titanic Guide: Belfast & Greater Belfast* (2009) suggested that 'Belfast is Titanic Town. Nowhere else in the world can claim a greater or prouder association with the most famous ship ever constructed.' Despite the sinking, the ship 'remains a source of enduring pride in the city where she was built—Belfast'. Similarly Alan Clarke, Chief Executive of the Northern Ireland Tourist Board, said that 'nowhere else has the ability to tell the story of the most famous ship in the world'. The annual 'Titanic: Made in Belfast' festival began in 2002. The Programme for 2010 stated that the proposed Titanic Signature Building would 'firmly establish Belfast as the home of the Titanic. It will position the Titanic at the heart of the proud industrial heritage that has helped shape Belfast into the vibrant and inspirational city that it is today.' At the time of writing, there are plans for a £7 billion Titanic Quarter, with a new £97m Titanic Signature Building housing a museum of both the ship and the city in the former Harland & Wolff shipyard, due to open in March 2012. However the restoration of the Cherbourg tender *Nomadic* has proceeded very slowly, and with public spending cuts it seems doubtful if much of Titanic Quarter will ever be built. Having left Northern Ireland in 1979, I return frequently to visit my parents; on flying into George Best Airport, in Belfast, the yellow cranes of Harland & Wolff are still the first structures on the ground that I look for. For Ireland, as for the rest of the world, the last night of the small town that was the *Titanic* continues to have an enduring fascination.

NOTE ON SOURCES

As the account in the Introduction by novelist Julian Barnes of the elderly Lawrence Beesley reminds us, each of the twelve narratives drawn upon here presents different challenges to the author who attempts to use them. Whereas the account by Harold Bride was originally published in the *New York Times* on 19 April 1912, that by Violet Jessop is only part of a full-length autobiography. Some of the accounts were written and published as autobiographical accounts soon after the disaster (Beesley and Bride in 1912; and Gracie and Shutes in 1913); some around twenty or thirty years later (Rostron in 1931; Jessop in 1934; and Lightoller in 1935); and others as memoirs much later, including with the help of friends or relations (Goldsmith in 1991; Hart in 1994; Hakkarainen in 1996; Touma in 2002; and Brown in 2009). There are a range of issues here. They include attempts made to defend actions taken at the time; punctuation; language, such as the use of 'ladies' that is clearly of its time, or 'dagos' now regarded as offensive; contradictions between accounts and factual details that are clearly incorrect; the fallibility of 'memories'; people claiming to have predicted the disaster; and stories that have been reconstructed as memoirs, drawing on evidence given at the Inquiries and earlier accounts.

Some accounts are clearly motivated by the need to defend actions taken at the time of the disaster, and this is perhaps most obviously true of the account of Herbert Lightoller, the most senior crew member to survive, and whose behaviour came under particular scrutiny during the Inquiries. Drawing on the evidence that he gave, Lightoller is at pains to explain why many lifeboats left the ship only partially filled. Lightoller is the main character in the 1958 film *A Night to Remember*, and it presents a largely sympathetic portrait of both him and his actions.

Bride's account is particularly challenging, though for different reasons. For one thing, given that it was prepared originally as a story for the *New York Times*, it is extremely short. Moreover while it is a vivid account, it is also a very subjective one. Among the areas of uncertainty are: Bride's account of how he and Jack Phillips repaired the equipment the day before the disaster; the incident involving the stoker whom he knocked on the head; and his account of Jack Phillips on the Engelhardt boat. Particularly dubious is the claim that, on the *Carpathia*, Bride and Harold Cottam restricted themselves, in telegraphing messages after the disaster, to the lists of survivors and private messages. We know that Bride was already negotiating to sell his story to the *New York Times*, and that the USS *Chester*'s operators in fact did know Continental Morse. Bride could not have been unaware that the radio operator Jack Binns had made a significant amount of money following the sinking of the *Republic*, in 1909. Bride's and Cottam's stonewalling was certainly at best unorthodox, and it is clear that they acted as operators, deciding when and what news should be dispatched. Bride was cross-examined at the American Inquiry about his behaviour. There remain important contradictions between Bride's story as it appeared in the *New York Times*; what he said at the American Inquiry; and a private account that he prepared later on.

One of the key problems with Violet Jessop's account is that she uses pseudonyms. When she wrote up her experiences in the 1930s, she was still employed as a stewardess. Thus while her account does feature real people, among them Thomas Andrews, Dr William O'Loughlin, the Surgeon, and John 'Jock' Hume, the musician, there are a large number of other characters whose names we know to be false. These include her friends 'Ann Turnbull', 'Jim', 'Stanley' the steward, 'Matthews' the Chief Pantryman, and 'Jack Stevens'; and the passengers that she calls 'Miss Marcia Spatz', 'Miss Townsend', and 'Mrs Klapton'. It seems likely that these are composite characters of all the passengers that Violet came across during her employment. As John Maxtone-Graham has suggested, here 'Ann Turnbull' has been identified as Elizabeth Leather.

The later accounts, by which I mean those by Goldsmith, Hart, Hakkarainen, Touma, and Brown, are in some ways more accessible, simply because their writing style and punctuation is more recognizably modern. Nevertheless arguably here 'memory' is less reliable, and has been augmented by letters, diaries, and photographs. Several of these accounts have been produced by family members or friends. There is no doubt that many of these have been clearly influenced by the earlier narratives, perhaps most notably those of Beesley, Gracie, and Lightoller, and by other sources, such as the evidence given at the American and British Inquiries, by Lord's *A Night to Remember*, and by the 1958 film. The account by Beesley, in particular, can best be viewed as a kind of master narrative. Edith Brown's story, by her son David Haisman, is an imaginative reconstruction, drawing in part on Haisman's extensive experience in the shipping industry, but it is a reconstruction. A further problem, particularly evident in the account of Eva Hart, is the tendency to overstate the role of superstition, in the sense of characters (in this case her mother) anticipating the disaster. Overall, however, while the sources present many and varied problems to the historian, they do offer a unique and vivid perspective.

NOTES

Preface

On the *Princess Victoria*, see Stephen Cameron's excellent *Death in the North Channel: The Loss of the Princess Victoria January 1953* (Belfast: Universities Press, 2002).

Introduction

On Walter Lord, see *A Night to Remember* (New York: Henry Holt, 1995 and 2005); and Walter Lord, *The Night Lives On* (New York: Harper Collins, 1986; New York: William Morrow, 1998; London: Penguin, 1998). For the *Titanic* and literature, see John Wilson Foster, *The Titanic Complex: A Cultural Manifest* (Vancouver, BC: Belcouver Press, 1997); and John Wilson Foster (ed.), *Titanic* (Harmondsworth: Penguin Books, 1999). Stephanie Barczewski's claim is in her *Titanic: A Night Remembered* (London: Hambledon Continuum, 2004). Julian Barnes mentions Lawrence Beesley in his *A History of the World in 10½ Chapters* (London: Jonathan Cape, 1989; London: Vintage, 2009), pp. 171–5.

1. 'The Biggest Anchor in the World'

For biographical information on passengers and crew, all scholars are indebted to John P. Eaton and Charles A Haas, *Titanic: Triumph and Tragedy* (Wellingborough: Patrick Stephens, 1986); and <http://www.encyclopedia-titanica.org> accessed 21 March 2011. Edith Brown's story is taken from David Haisman, *Titanic: The Edith Brown Story* (Milton Keynes: Authorwise,

2009). On women and children, see also Judith B. Geller, *Titanic: Women and Children First* (Sparkford: Patrick Stephens, 1998).

For Eva Hart's story, see Ronald C. Denney and Eva Hart, *Shadow of the Titanic: A Survivor's Story* (Dartford: Greenwich University Press, 1994). Eva Hart featured in a BBC Radio 4 'Today' programme, 'Eva Hart, Titanic Survivor', first broadcast on 22 December 1983, and in another BBC radio broadcast 'The Way It Was', first broadcast on 11 April 1987. Both are available at <http://www.bbc.co.uk/archive/titanic/5047.shtml> accessed 29 June 2010. Frank Goldsmith's account is taken from Frank J. W. Goldsmith, *Echoes in the Night: Memories of a Titanic Survivor* (Indian Orchard, MA: Titanic Historical Society, 1991).

For details of the construction of the *Titanic* see 'Electric Lifts on the Olympic and Titanic', *Engineer* (24 June 1910), p. 640; 'The White Star Liner "Titanic"', *Engineering*, 91 (26 May 1911), pp. 678–81; 'Launch of the White Star Liner "Titanic"', *Engineering*, 91 (2 June 1911), p. 734; and 'The White Star Triple-Screw Atlantic Liners "Olympic" and "Titanic", 45,000 Tons: The Largest Steamships in the World', *Shipbuilder*, vol. VI, no. 21, Midsummer 1911, Souvenir Number. See also Michael Moss and John R. Hume, *Shipbuilders to the World: 125 Years of Harland and Wolff, Belfast, 1861–1986* (Belfast: Blackstaff Press, 1986); Michael McCaughan, *The Birth of the Titanic* (Belfast: Blackstaff Press, 1999); and Barczewski, *Titanic: A Night Remembered*. Details of the *Titanic*'s anchors can be found in Derek Whale, 'Titanic's Anchors Then and Now', *Titanic Commutator*, 36, 193 (2011), pp. 46–9; and its Black Country connections at <http://blackcountryhistory.org/collections> accessed 14 December 2010. There are entries on 'Sir Thomas Andrews', 'J. Bruce Ismay', and 'William Pirrie, Viscount Pirrie' in the *Oxford Dictionary of National Biography* (Oxford: Oxford University Press, 2004). On the liners more generally, see John Maxtone-Graham, *The North Atlantic Run: 'The Only Way to Cross'* (London: Cassell, 1972).

The account by Herbert Lightoller comes from Comdr Lightoller, 'Loss of the Titanic', in Comdr Lightoller, *Titanic and Other Ships* (London: Ivor Nicholson and Watson Limited, 1935). It is reproduced in Jack Winocour (ed.), *The Story of the Titanic as Told by its Survivors* (New York: Dover Publications 1960), pp. 271–308. A BBC radio programme 'I Was There' featuring Lightoller was first broadcast on 1 November 1936. It is available at <http://www.bbc.co.uk/archive/titanic/5047.shtml> accessed 29 June 2010. See also Patrick Stenson, *Titanic Voyager: The Odyssey of C. H. Lightoller* (New York: W.W. Norton, 1984; second revised edition, Tiverton: Halsgrove, 1998), and Wilson Foster, *Titanic*, pp. 97–100. There is an entry on 'Edward John Smith' in the *Oxford Dictionary of National Biography* (Oxford: Oxford University Press, 2004). Violet Jessop's story comes from John Maxtone-Graham (ed.), *Titanic Survivor: The Memoirs of Violet Jessop Stewardess* (Dobbs Ferry, NY: Sheridan House, 1997; UK: Sutton Publishing, 2007). Harold Bride and Herbert Lightoller feature in Alan Scarth, *Titanic and Liverpool* (Liverpool: Liverpool University Press/National Museums Liverpool, 2009).

2. 'Like a Big Expectant Family'

The original *Titanic* passenger lists for Southampton, 10 April 1912, and for Queenstown, 11 April 1912, are available at the National Archives, Kew, London, file BT 27/780B for those embarking at Southampton and BT 27/776/2 for those embarking at Queenstown. These are now available through <http://www.findmypast.co.uk> accessed 16 December 2010. On the Southampton perspective, see Donald Hyslop, Alastair Forsyth, and Sheila Jemima (eds), *Titanic Voices: Memories from the Fateful Voyage* (Southampton: Southampton City Council, 1994; Thrupp: Sutton Publishing/Southampton City Council, 1997).

Lawrence Beesley's article 'The Passing Away of Human Theories' was published in the *Christian Science Journal* (1909), pp. 163–7. For Beesley's story, see the *New York Times*, 19 April 1912, and Lawrence Beesley, *The Loss of the SS Titanic: Its Story and Its Lessons* (Boston and New York: Houghton Mifflin Co., 1912; World Library edition, 2005). It is reproduced in Winocour (ed.), *Story of the Titanic as Told by its Survivors*, pp. 1–109. See also Wilson Foster, *Titanic*, pp. 85–8.

Elin Hakkarainen's account is contained in Gerald E. Nummi and Janet A. White, *'I'm Going to See What Has Happened': The Personal Experience of Third Class Finnish Titanic Survivor, Mrs Elin Hakkarainen, Including the Stories of Miss Laina*

Heikkinen and Miss Anna Sofia Turja (Janet White, 1996). On Elizabeth Leather, see Scarth, *Titanic and Liverpool*.

On migration, see Alan M. Kraut, *Silent Travelers: Germs, Genes, and the 'Immigrant Menace'* (New York: BasicBooks, 1994); Senan Moloney, *The Irish Aboard Titanic* (Dublin: Wolfhound Press, 2000); Amy L. Fairchild, *Science at the Borders: Immigrant Medical Inspection and the Shaping of the Modern Industrial Labor Force* (Baltimore: Johns Hopkins University Press, 2003); and Alison Bashford (ed.), *Medicine at the Border: Disease, Globalization and Security, 1850 to the Present* (Basingstoke: Palgrave Macmillan, 2006).

For photographs of the Boat Train at Waterloo; Thomas McCawley; Harold Bride; and others including the near collision with the *New York*, see E. E. O'Donnell, *Father Browne's Titanic Album: A Passenger's Photographs and Personal Memoir* (Dublin: Wolfhound Press, 1997), pp. 47, 62, and 70.

3. 'A Wonderful Passage Up To Now'

Hanna Touma's account is taken from Anna Thomas and Joseph L. Thomas, *Grandma Survived the Titanic* (Victoria, BC: Trafford Publishing, 2002). On Queenstown, including the photograph of the *Titanic* with the stoker at the top of the funnel, see O'Donnell, *Father Browne's Titanic Album*, p. 73.

Archibald Gracie's story comes from Colonel Archibald Gracie, *The Truth About the Titanic* (New York: Mitchell Kennerley, 1913), and reproduced in Winocour (ed.), *Story of the Titanic as Told by its Survivors*, pp. 111–269. It has also been published as Colonel Archibald Gracie, *Titanic: A Survivor's Story* (first published as *The Truth About the Titanic*) (New York: Mitchell Kennerley, 1913; Stroud: The History Press, 2008). See also Wilson Foster, *Titanic*, pp. 101–7.

There is an entry on 'Guglielmo Marconi' in the *Oxford Dictionary of National Biography* (Oxford: Oxford University Press, 2004). On radio, see also W. J. Baker, *A History of the Marconi Company* (London: Methuen, 1970); Hugh G. J. Aitken, *Syntony and Spark: The Origins of Radio* (New York: Wiley, 1976); Hugh G. J. Aitken, *The Continuous Wave: Technology and American Radio, 1900–1932* (Princeton, NJ: Princeton University Press, 1985); and Gavin Weightman, *Signor Marconi's Magic Box: How an Amateur Inventor Defied Scientists and Began the Radio Revolution* (London: HarperCollins, 2003). Material on Jack Binns and the sinking of the *Republic* is available at <http://www.en.wikipedia.org> accessed 8 October 2010. The article by Harold Bride, 'Thrilling Tale by Titanic's Surviving Wireless Man', originally appeared in the *New York Times*, 19 April 1912, and was reprinted on 28 April 1912. It is reproduced in Winocour (ed.), *Story of the Titanic as Told by its Survivors*, pp. 313–20. See also Wilson Foster, *Titanic*, pp. 127–33.

4. 'Ice, Flat Like a Pocket Watch'

For the evidence of Frederick Fleet and Frederick Barrett, see the official reports, PP 1912–13 (Cd 6352), *Shipping Casualties (Loss of the Steamship 'Titanic'): Report of a Formal Investigation into the Circumstances Attending the Foundering on 15th April, 1912, of the British Steamship Titanic, of Liverpool, After Striking Ice on or Near Latitude 41° 46' N, Longitude 50° 14' W, North Atlantic Ocean, Whereby Loss of Life Ensued*; and the US Senate Report No 806, 62nd Congress, 2nd Session, *'Titanic' Disaster. Report of the Committee on Commerce US Senate Pursuant to S. Res. 283 Directing the Committee on Commerce to Investigate the Causes Leading to the Wreck of the White Star Liner Titanic* (1912). The transcripts of the Inquiries are available at <http://www.titanicinquiry.org/> last accessed 1 April 2011.

The story by Elizabeth Shutes, 'When the Titanic Went Down', was incorporated in Gracie, *Titanic: A Survivor's Story*, and is reproduced in Winocour (ed.), *Story of the Titanic as Told by its Survivors*, pp. 235–40. See also Wilson Foster, *Titanic*, pp. 81–4.

There is a photograph of a *Titanic* life jacket at <http://www.bbc.co.uk/ahistoryoftheworld/objects> accessed 27 January 2010. The article about the patents for the Mae West inflatable life jacket was published in the *New York Times* on 16 May 2005. On maritime history more generally, see Maxtone-Graham, *North Atlantic Run*; and Christopher Harvie, *A Floating Commonwealth: Politics, Culture and Technology on Britain's Atlantic Coast, 1860–1930* (Oxford: Oxford University Press, 2008). On ice, see Francis Spufford, *I May Be Some Time: Ice and the English Imagination* (London: Faber, 1996; paperback edition, 1997); and on metaphor, Hans Blumenberg, *Shipwreck with Spectator: Paradigm of a Metaphor for Existence* (Cambridge, MA: MIT Press, 1997).

5. 'We Have Collision with Iceberg'

The article from *Engineering*, 1 July 1910, on the Welin Quadrant Davit, is reproduced at <http://titanic-model.com> accessed 27 January 2010. An article by Robert Hahn, 'The Engelhardt Collapsible' (which includes some interesting photographs) is reproduced at <http://titanic-model.com> accessed 27 January 2010. For the history of the Welin Davit Company see <http://welin.mymediaroom.com> accessed 14 December 2010. An article by Bob Read, 'The Titanic 30 ft. Main Lifeboats' is reproduced at <http://titanic-model.com> accessed 27 January 2010.

6. 'Latitude 41° 46' N, Longitude 50° 14' W'

Arthur Rostron's story is taken from Sir Arthur H. Rostron, *Home From the Sea* (London: Cassell, 1931), pp. 55–84. On Rostron, see Scarth, *Titanic and Liverpool*. There is an entry on 'Archibald Joyce' in the *Oxford Dictionary of National Biography* (Oxford: Oxford University Press, 2004).

On the sinking and mystery, see L. M. Collins, *The Sinking of the Titanic: The Mystery Solved* (St Johns, Newfoundland: Bleakwater Books-Souvenir Press, 2003); and Paul Lee, *The Titanic and the Indifferent Stranger: The Complete Story of the Titanic and the Californian* (Paul Lee, 2009). More generally, see Simon Martin, *The Other Titanic* (Newton Abbot: David & Charles, 1980); John P. Eaton and Charles A. Haas, *Titanic: A Journey Through Time* (Sparkford: Patrick Stephens, 1999); and Tim Coates (ed.), *Tragic Journeys* (London: The Stationery Office, 2001).

7. 'She's Gone, Lads; Row Like Hell'

On lifeboats, see Yann Martel, *Life of Pi: A Novel* (Edinburgh: Canongate Books 2002, 2003), and Anthony Cunningham, *The Titanic Diaries: Dramatic Accounts of Shipwreck Survival* (Great Addington, Kettering: Silver Link Publishing, 2005). An obituary of Bess Cummings, survivor of the *City of Benares*, sunk September 1940, was published in the *Daily Telegraph*, 19 August 2010. Norman Gibson's account, 'Indian Ocean Rescue: 16 Days on a Lifeboat', is available at <http://www.bbc.co.uk/ww2peopleswar/> accessed 23 September

2010. For details of the film *Lifeboat* (1944), see <http://www.imdb.com/title/tt0037017/> accessed 23 March 2011.

8. 'A Dark Speck on the Horizon'

On the media, see Paul Heyer, *Titanic Legacy: Disaster as Media Event and Myth* (Westport, CT: Praeger, 1995). On Harold Bride, see also John Booth and Sean Coughlan, *Titanic: Signals of Disaster* (Westbury: White Star Publications, 1993).

9. 'Arranged for Your Exclusive Story'

The Maritime Archives & Library, Merseyside Maritime Museum, Liverpool, has the Esther Hart telegram (DX/1549/R). The photograph of the Touma family in New York is in Eaton and Haas, *Titanic: Triumph and Tragedy*, p. 196. On the media, see Heyer, *Titanic Legacy*.

10. 'Mr Beesley's Simple Narrative'

There are entries on 'John Charles Bigham, Viscount Mersey'; 'Sir John Biles'; 'Sir Somerset Arthur Gough Calthorpe'; and 'Robert Finlay, Viscount Finlay' in the *Oxford Dictionary of National Biography* (Oxford: Oxford University Press, 2004). On the aftermath, see J. H. Biles, 'The Loss of the Titanic', *Engineer* (19 April 1912), pp. 409–10. For official reports, see PP 1912–13 (Cd 6352), *Shipping Casualties (Loss of the Steamship 'Titanic')*; and the US Senate, *'Titanic' Disaster*.

For contemporary accounts, see Marshall Everett, *Wreck and Sinking of the Titanic: The Ocean's Greatest Disaster* (London: Homewood Press, 1912), republished as Martin Breese (ed.), *The Titanic Story: The Ocean's Greatest Disaster* (London: Breese Books, 1998). On the medals awarded to the crew of the *Carpathia*, see Mike Litherland, 'A Titanic Tale', *Lancashire Magazine* (April, 2011), p. 116.

On the Navratils, see the fictionalized account, Elisabeth Navratil, *Survivors: A True-Life Titanic Story* (Dublin: O'Brien Press, 1999). The telegram received by Harold Bride's father is mentioned in Eaton and Haas, *Titanic: Triumph and Tragedy*, p. 212. On Beesley, see Barnes, *A History of the World in 10½ Chapters*, pp. 171–5, and for his daughter Dinah's recollections see Cunningham, *Titanic Diaries*, p. 26. On the television film *S.O.S. Titanic* (1979), see <http://www.imdb.com/title/tt0079836/> accessed 29 March 2011.

On film, see David M. Lubin, *Titanic* (London: British Film Institute, 1999); Kevin S. Sandler and Gaylyn Sudlar (eds), *Titanic: Anatomy of a Blockbuster* (New Brunswick, NJ: Rutgers University Press, 1999); and Jeffrey Richards, *A Night to Remember: The Definitive Titanic Film* (London: I. B.Tauris, 2003). The film *A Night to Remember* (1958) is well worth watching, as is the documentary *The Making of A Night to Remember* (1993), which features interviews with William MacQuitty and Walter Lord. The DVD is distributed by Carlton Home Entertainment. Details of the cast list and other information are available at <http://www.imdb.com/title/tt0051994/fullcredits> accessed 21 March 2011. For the responses of Beesley and Hart to the filming, see William MacQuitty, *Titanic Memories: The Making of A Night to Remember* (London: National Maritime Museum, 2000), pp. 19–22.

On myth, see Richard Howells, *The Myth of the Titanic* (Basingstoke: Macmillan, 1999), and Bergfelder and Street, *The Titanic in Myth and Memory*.

Conclusion

For obituaries of Walter Lord, see the *New York Times*, 20 May 2002; and the *Independent*, 22 May 2002. On the reception of Lord's book see Steven Biel, *Down with the Old Canoe: A Cultural History of the Titanic Disaster* (New York: W.W. Norton & Company, 1996); and especially Peter Middleton and Tim Woods, 'Textual Memory: The Making of the Titanic's Archive', in Tim Bergfelder and Sarah Street (eds), *The Titanic in Myth and Memory: Representations in Visual and Literary Culture* (London: I. B.Tauris, 2004), pp. 63–72. The critical review was Arthur Calder-Marshall, 'Tragic Muddle', *Times Literary Supplement*, 8 June 1956, p. 343. On William MacQuitty's memories, see MacQuitty, *Titanic Memories*, p. 8.

On Robert Ballard's discovery of the wreck, see Robert D. Ballard, *The Discovery of the Titanic* (London: Hodder & Stoughton, 1987); and Robert

Ballard, 'Why is Titanic Vanishing?', *National Geographic* (December 2004), pp. 96–113. On forensic work, see Jennifer Hooper McCarty and Tim Foecke, *What Really Sank the Titanic: New Forensic Discoveries* (New York: Citadel Press, 2008). On new theories about the sinking, see Robert Dex, 'Titanic Survivor's Granddaughter "Reveals Truth"', *Independent*, 22 September 2010, and Ian Jack, 'A Titanic Mistake That We Can All Learn From', *Guardian*, 25 September 2010, p. 27.

Walter Lord's assertions about the *Titanic* and social history more generally are in his *A Night to Remember*. See also Wilson Foster, *The Titanic*, pp. 23, 44–6, 49. On the *Queen Mary*, see <http://www.ocean-liners.com/ships/qm.asp> accessed 21 March 2011; on the *Ile de France* see <http://www.ocean-liners.com/ships/ile.asp> accessed 21 March 2011; and on the *Normandie* see <http://www.ocean-liners.com/ships/normandie.asp> accessed 21 March 2011. On the BBC documentary 'The Last Days of the Liners', presented by Paul Atterbury and shown on 17 February 2011, see <http://www.bbc.co.uk/programmes/b00nrtj6> accessed 23 March 2011.

On the 'submerged tenth', see William Booth, *In Darkest England And The Way Out* (London: Salvation Army, 1890); Gareth Stedman Jones, *Outcast London: A Study in the Relationship Between Classes in Victorian Society* (Oxford: Oxford University Press, 1971); Wilson Foster, *The Titanic*, pp. 52–3, 58; Wilson Foster, *Titanic*, p. xiv. There are entries on 'William Booth' and 'William (Bramwell) Booth' in the *Oxford Dictionary of National Biography* (Oxford: Oxford University Press, 2004). On the Salvation Army, see Diane Winston, *Red-Hot and Righteous: The Urban Religion of the Salvation Army* (Cambridge, MA: Harvard University Press, 1999); and Pamela J. Walker, *Pulling the Devil's Kingdom Down: The Salvation Army in Victorian Britain* (Berkeley and Los Angeles: University of California Press, 2001). On the Red Cross, see Roger Mayou, *International Red Cross and Red Crescent Museum* (Geneva: International Red Cross and Red Crescent Museum, 2000), and subsequent editions. The museum in Geneva is very well worth visiting.

On Ireland and the aftermath of the disaster, see Shan F. Bullock, *Thomas Andrews: Shipbuilder* (Dublin and London: Maunsel & Company, 1912; Belfast: The Blackstaff Press, 1999); John Wilson Foster, 'Imagining the Titanic', in Eve Patten (ed.), *Returning to Ourselves: Second Volume of Papers From the John*

Hewitt International Summer School (1995), pp. 325–43; Fran Brearton, 'Dancing Unto Death: Perceptions of the Somme, the Titanic and Ulster Protestantism', *Irish Review*, 20 (1997), pp. 89–103; Wilson Foster, *The Titanic*, pp. 69–89; Stephen Cameron, *Titanic: Belfast's Own* (Dublin: Wolfhound Press, 1998); and Barczewski, *Titanic: A Night Remembered*. There is an entry on 'Shan Bullock' in the *Oxford Dictionary of National Biography* (Oxford: Oxford University Press, 2004). On plans for Titanic Quarter see <http://www.titanic-quarter.com/> accessed 3 March 2011, and the *Belfast Telegraph*, 12 April 2011, p. 8.

FURTHER READING

Barczewski, Stephanie, *Titanic: A Night Remembered* (London: Hambledon and London, 2004).

Biel, Steven, *Down with the Old Canoe: A Cultural History of the Titanic Disaster* (New York: W.W. Norton & Company, 1996).

Booth, John and Coughlan, Sean, *Titanic: Signals of Disaster* (Westbury: White Star Publications, 1993).

Eaton, John P. and Haas, Charles A., *Titanic: Triumph and Tragedy* (Wellingborough: Patrick Stephens, 1986).

Heyer, Paul, *Titanic Legacy: Disaster as Media Event and Myth* (Westport, CT: Praeger, 1995).

Hooper McCarty, Jennifer and Foecke, Tim, *What Really Sank the Titanic: New Forensic Discoveries* (New York: Citadel Press, 2008).

Howells, Richard, *The Myth of the Titanic* (Basingstoke: Macmillan, 1999).

Lord, Walter, *A Night to Remember* (New York: Henry Holt 1955, 2005).

Middleton, Peter and Woods, Tim, 'Textual Memory: The Making of the Titanic's Archive', in Tim Bergfelder and Sarah Street (eds), *The Titanic in Myth and Memory: Representations in Visual and Literary Culture* (London: I.B.Tauris, 2004), pp. 63–72.

O'Donnell, E. E., *Father Browne's Titanic Album: A Passenger's Photographs and Personal Memoir* (Dublin: Wolfhound Press, 1997).

Richards, Jeffrey, *A Night to Remember: The Definitive Titanic Film* (London: I.B.Tauris, 2003).

Scarth, Alan, *Titanic and Liverpool* (Liverpool: Liverpool University Press/ National Museums Liverpool, 2009).

Wilson Foster, John (ed.), *Titanic* (Harmondsworth: Penguin Books, 1999).

INDEX